Freeing Yourself from Anxiety

Freeing Yourself from Anxiety

*Four Simple Steps to Overcome Worry
and Create the Life You Want*

TAMAR E. CHANSKY, PHD

Illustrations by Phillip Stern

Da Capo

LIFE
LONG

A MEMBER OF THE PERSEUS BOOKS GROUP

Set in 11 point Warnock Pro by the Perseus Books Group

Cataloging-in-Publication data for this book is available from the Library of
Congress.

First Da Capo Press edition 2012
ISBN 978-0-7382-1483-2
ISBN 978-0-7382-1541-9 (e-book)

Published by Da Capo Press
A Member of the Perseus Books Group
www.dacapopress.com

Portion of "Give Me Back My Name" by David Byrne reprinted with
permission from Warner-Chappell

Note: The information in this book is true and complete to the best of our
knowledge. This book is intended only as an informative guide for those
wishing to know more about health issues. In no way is this book intended
to replace, countermand, or conflict with the advice given to you by your
own physician. The ultimate decision concerning care should be made
between you and your doctor. We strongly recommend you follow his or her
advice. Information in this book is general and is offered with no guarantees
on the part of the authors or Da Capo Press. The authors and publisher
disclaim all liability in connection with the use of this book. The names and
identifying details of people associated with events described in this book
have been changed. Any similarity to actual persons is coincidental.

Da Capo Press books are available at special discounts for bulk purchases in
the U.S. by corporations, institutions, and other organizations. For more
information, please contact the Special Markets Department at the Perseus
Books Group, 44 Farnsworth Street, 3rd Floor, Boston, MA, 02210, or call
(800) 810–4145, ext. 5000, or e-mail special.markets@perseusbooks.com.

LSC-H

10 9 8 7

For Phil, Meredith, and Raia

Your mind, this globe of awareness, is a starry universe. When you push off with your foot, a thousand new roads become clear.

—RUMI

CONTENTS

THE STORY IS IN THE TELLING AND YOU CAN IMPROVE THE STORY

The art of being wise is the art of knowing what to overlook.

—WILLIAM JAMES

Justin is losing sleep over his job. Although the job is going well, he can't turn off his whirring head. Finishing things provides no relief, because there's always the next thing, another day, another disaster he fears he has to avert.

Lucia has a knot in her stomach that won't let up. She worries about her children, even though they're grown. With grandchildren now, she worries even more because something is always unsettled: Will they get bullied, will they get hurt, will they do well in school?

Gabby is facing chemotherapy. Her doctor describes her prognosis as very good, but when Gabby thinks about her cancer, she can't stop worrying. She knows it's not good for her health, but she just feels like she can't cope.

Manny wants to start dating, but whenever he tries to talk to a woman, he thinks of everything he's doing wrong. Feeling completely inadequate, Manny has started to doubt why anyone would even be interested in him.

Whether you are in the midst of a difficult time in your life, or you simply want to live more optimally with everyday hurdles, you are not alone. All of us are looking for happy endings. But the way our anxious mind tells the story, even day-to-day transactions can feel risky—even harrowing. Out of scant details, mere hints of threat can create a frightening scenario that debilitates you. You react physically and emotionally to every hairpin turn, gearing up *as if* the story your mind is showing you is really happening. You are a captive audience.

What is anxiety? It is the first-reaction of a sensitive system that is wired to keep us alert to danger and protected from harm. In our more primitive days, anxiety worked beautifully in a fight or flight reaction to help us escape hungry tigers, woolly mammoths, and other dangerous threats. But today, with our best interests in mind, anxiety sometimes makes mistakes, overshooting and overpreparing. Especially when we are facing challenges, we need to be at our best. But anxiety can put any of us at a disadvantage. You don't need worry running through disastrous plot lines and consequently wearing you out and gearing you up unnecessarily for the wrong things. You just want to take good care of yourself and be well-prepared for life. Your life.

Fortunately, your survival-oriented brain is not the only one running the show. You have a choice. Rather than stay glued to your seat, white-knuckling your way through a life that in reality is supremely better than your anxiety would have you think, you can walk out and trade in your tickets for a different show. You are the protagonist of your life story. You are the hero who comes through for yourself every time. *And* you get to decide who narrates.

Whether you're one of the millions of people trying to reduce stress and improve the quality of your life, or perhaps one of the 17 million people suffering from depression or one of the 40 million adults with an anxiety disorder in a given year, the news is good—very good. Not only are anxiety and depression the most treatable mental health conditions, they can be effectively prevented. The strategies here will show you how. So pull out your director's chair—you are now running the show.

As a psychologist who specializes in the treatment of anxiety, I have been immersed in the world of worry for more than two decades. Most of my working hours are spent listening closely to the experiences of thousands of patients who bravely come into treatment for one simple reason. They want to do something in their life and fear is getting in the way. From my youngest patients who want to ride the bus, go on a sleepover, or raise their hand in class to the adults who want to go out on a date, leave a relationship, ask for a raise, or simply live life without being derailed by electric jolts of fear throughout their day, it is the nature of the human spirit to want to grow. And that's a good thing. You want more for yourself, and you don't want to be on the sidelines of life. But how do you know how all those new experiences will turn out? That's just it. You don't. Putting your toes in those uncertain waters is just where anxiety comes in. As it waits at the ready to show you remote possibilities, it is adamant that you treat them as probabilities. That protection can lead you astray, grabbing your attention from what you need to focus on and insisting that you instead grapple with worst-case scenarios.

Everyone's worry story has a similar plot line, and it doesn't end well. *What if something goes wrong? What if I mess up? What if I make a fool of myself?* These thoughts flood your attention, threaten your sense of security, throw you into a tailspin, and discourage you from pursuing important plans. You feel like you are falling off a cliff, when in reality you are stepping off the curb. Or if you push through your fear, often you do so at a great cost, shaking in your boots, freaking out in your mind, and feeling like you have enough nervous energy to power a small city. Fortunately, no one knows. Although it may seem to others around you that you are gliding along the surface of your life, you know that you are paddling like mad underneath, and that secret adds to your stress. Worry makes you scared and muddles your thinking. It gives you things to worry about that aren't helpful or necessary, and these things take on a life of their own.

DON'T STOP THE THOUGHTS, JUST CHANGE THE REACTION TO THE THOUGHTS

When I was a psychology graduate student back in the 1980s, we were trained in a then popular technique for handling unpleasant thoughts called "thought-stopping." We taught patients that every time they experienced an unpleasant, depressive thought like *My life is worthless* or an anxious thought like *What if I mess up? I'll get fired*, they should snap a rubber band on their wrist to remind themselves not to have the thought. Ouch! We've come a long way in our understanding of how thoughts work. Rather than swatting away a bad thought like a bee at a picnic, you need to take a close look at the bad thought, consider the source, realize it is of no use—or no *good* use to you—and swap it out for something better. Something truer. Your bad thoughts are negative exaggerations of the story of your life. You're not worthless or going to get fired. You're just having a bad thought. Better thoughts tell it like it really is.

Not all thoughts are created equal. If a thought sounds *too* bad to be true it probably is. Just because the first words out of your mouth or mind are *I'm going to ruin this, everyone will think badly of me, what a disaster*, that doesn't mean it will come true. This is exactly how "first thoughts" operate. It's a story, but a story that will be disproven each and every time, hours or days later by intervening events. You didn't get fired, the party was a hit, and the kids came home safely. Those facts don't help you in the moment for one simple reason—they haven't arrived yet. If you stop at your first thoughts, you plummet in a downward spiral of doubt or an escalating chain of catastrophes; meanwhile, other more healthy and accurate interpretations are right there waiting to be discovered. You have to look for the other thoughts, and when you do, you'll find them in abundance.

A PREVIEW OF THE FOUR STEPS: FROM CATASTROPHE TO CLARITY

Most of us are familiar with the telltale sounds of anxious and negative thinking. It's fast, it's first, it's worst, but most important—it's wrong. When the brain says, *Think this!* you know that these first thoughts are irrational and not healthy, much as you know that reaching for the apple is going to serve you far better than gorging on donuts. But once the anxious or negative story line starts, it's hard to know where the *Think that!* is. You're stressed, and you don't know how to get from the disastrous story playing out in your head to the quite manageable reality that is your life.

Being less stressed is one important reason to learn how to reframe and downgrade the importance of these anxious thoughts. But there's something bigger. In the very moment of confusion in which you need to pay careful attention to incoming data about whatever challenge you face, anxiety completely distracts you. Like being buzzed by a low-flying plane, suddenly you are attending to your worry instead of your life. That's a problem.

So how do you get from catastrophe to clarity? The first step is to *relabel*. When you think, *I'm a total screw up! The board is going to have me fired,* relabel that thought. Relabeling means recognizing that those catastrophes are *first thoughts*, coming from an unreliable source in the mind, you tag them as such and demote their significance: It's just Disaster Man grabbing the microphone again. This prevents you from wasting your time rehearsing and imagining what would happen if you really were going to be fired—something that deep down you probably don't believe will happen. The second step is to *get specific* and narrow down the problem from *I made a fool of myself at the board meeting* to a realistic assessment of what actually occurred, such as *I am having trouble with my PowerPoint presentations and need to ask for help.* Rather than distracting yourself with the least reliable data, getting specific hones in on the trustworthy data that are actually there.

Once you've narrowed the problem, you need to broaden the solutions, or *optimize*—looking beyond your own perspectives to call in lifelines—real or imagined—from other trusted voices. Finally, once you've turned the problem and solutions around, you can *mobilize* and decide how to address the situation or move on: You're going to rehearse your presentations with a colleague first, or observe colleagues' presentations to see what is most effective. You've gone from being convinced you're going to lose your job to finding ways to improve your performance in just four simple steps. Not only will you feel better by following these steps, but chances are you're going to *do* better, too.

The good news is that once you learn these steps, they become second nature. You no longer have to approach challenges with dread, suffer sleepless nights, or nurse the knots out of an unhappy digestive tract. You have more energy, you feel happier and more like yourself, and you're not going from one imagined overwhelming situation to the next—just barely catching your breath in between. You are writing the story. You are living your life the way you want.

ANXIETY MANAGEMENT WITH A HUMOROUS TWIST

If you've flipped ahead through the pages of the book, you've probably noticed that this book has pictures. In the three books that I've written for parents of anxious children, time after time, as much as they appreciate the words, they remember the pictures. They photocopy them, hang them on the fridge, and use them to explain concepts not just to their kids, but to adults like the teachers, nurses, coaches, and doctors who work with their children.

Pictures get more of your brain working on learning, and faster. As Daniel Pink, author of *A Whole New Mind*, offers, the left brain is for details, the right brain is about the big picture. When we are giving directions, do we say—drive exactly 2.34 miles and turn right, then another .47 miles and go left? No, we offer easily visible landmarks—turn right at the McDonald's and left at the post office. Pictures also provide shortcuts to get the brain working on releasing us from those first anxious reactions to life, quickly revealing the hidden escape hatch to the predicament we are in. When we are upset, seeing ourselves as spinning on the Ferris wheel of worry, it suddenly clicks: We don't need to keep spinning, we can step off that ride.

There is an additional and unique benefit to using pictures: They throw in some levity. When you're already anxious, feeling like you have to learn something new and serious can be daunting. It can feel like more of what you're already experiencing. Lightening things up can help you learn more calmly and quickly.

Improving your well-being can be approached with levity, and you can do it from the comfort of your own living room. For example, seeing your anxious predictions as worthy of the *National Enquirer* but not the *New York Times* flips a switch in your mind. You can then spend far less time on the unnecessary worry missions and damaging nosedives in self-confidence and far more time tackling and mastering the very challenges that set off anxious thinking in the first place.

Anxiety and depression are serious mental health concerns, costing $46 billion a year in treatment and lost time at work, but they are preventable and treatable. The most effective approach is cognitive behavioral therapy (CBT), which is based on the idea that changing how you handle your thoughts changes how you think and feel and what you do. Decades of research and hundreds of studies have proven that CBT is a highly effective, empirically supported treatment for anxiety-related conditions. But there is no requirement that these techniques be dry or tedious. They will be far more successful when they are natural, accessible, and even entertaining. That helps us have a positive association with the strategy, and most important, helps us remember it.

WHO WILL BENEFIT FROM READING THIS BOOK?

Whether you are in college, in midlife, or approaching retirement, this book is for you. All of us experience moments dominated by worry or pessimism. Whether you are struggling to climb out of anxiety or depression, stave them off, or simply optimize your effectiveness in life by minimizing the impact and fallout of uncertainties and fears, you want to feel better. This book is for you, if you:

- Have an anxiety disorder
- Feel stressed with day-to-day situations
- Want to avoid treating your anxiety with medication
- Are on medication for anxiety or depression, but want to get more relief
- Get disappointed easily and can't shake it
- Are at a transition point in your life
- Have worry that feels uncontrollable
- Want to learn how to not get so upset by the ups and downs of life

Whether you are tackling the things you want or managing the unexpected things in life that you didn't sign up for—worry just gets in the way.

This book will give you clear steps to make better use of your time and better decisions in your life, and enjoy the results more.

Remembering that catastrophe is usually a no-show, you can instead refocus your energies on learning the right things from the challenges you encounter. You will find here the precise steps you can use to successfully overcome automatic anxious and negative thoughts and put them in their proper place. Rather than simply thinking positively, you will learn to relabel and devalue the significance of your undermining thoughts as unreliable; then you'll identify solutions and mobilize resources to remedy them.

ENLISTING THE MIND
TO CHANGE THE BRAIN

Some of you may be thinking—*This sounds great, but it's not for me, I've been like this for too long, I can't change.* The fact is that neuroscience, and specifically the burgeoning field of neuroplasticity, is documenting the great capacity of the brain to change or rewire connections, even those that are long-standing. This offers hard evidence that each one of us is entirely capable of learning new connections and changing the paths that our minds take. In time, perspective will come without having to actively seek it out. And it's never too late. As a Chinese proverb suggests, "The best time to plant a tree was twenty years ago, the next best time is now."

When did you last say, "Thank goodness I wasted, I mean, *spent* the last three hours freaking out about that job interview. The worry was so helpful and I feel much better now"? Anxious and negative thinking is not how you solve problems. That is the obstacle that you need to navigate around so that you can think clearly to solve problems. Although we'd all like to dump our worries and speed away fast, we may have moments in which we believe we *need* to worry and think that a situation warrants it. Think again. Serious situations warrant clear thinking, not spinning around with worry. The more you remember ahead of time the harried, frantic, desperate place that worry takes you, the more you will choose to save yourself an unpleasant and unnecessary trip. Why not arrive refreshed before an important meeting, doctor's appointment, or blind date rather than completely flattened?

YOU AND BEYOND:
INTERACTIONAL OPTIMISM

Throughout each chapter you'll find quick exercises entitled "Try This" that summarize the main points of the chapter for you. At the end of each chapter comes a suggestion called "You and Beyond." An interesting thing starts to happen when you work on freeing yourself from anxiety and negative thinking. It spills over in positive ways to the people around you. You respond more patiently and compassionately to others' anxious and negative moments because you understand them from the inside out. You start to bring out the best in others, by not latching on to the negative. As you see unexpected possibilities popping up in the corner of your mind's eye, you feel lighter and discover those untapped resources in others around you. If you intentionally apply these strategies to yourself and to the people around you, and they begin to feel less stressed, there will be less worry and more happiness all around. Think of this as a community clean-up effort—for your family, your co-workers, your classmates, the planet.

HOW THIS BOOK IS ORGANIZED

Part I, "Getting to Know Your Mind and How to Change It," explains the backstory on anxious and negative thinking, why the brain seems wired against you, how to handle doubt and uncertainty, and what choices we have *besides* anxious thoughts.

Part II, "The Four Steps: The Master Plan for Overcoming Anxious Thinking to Create the Life You Want," explains four steps for overcoming the hurdles created by distorted thoughts. It presents a powerful, practical plan for shrinking the worry moment back to its appropriate size, honing in on the real problem, and what we need to expand the universe of solutions and take action. This section ends with a quick look at the anxiety disorders and guidelines for knowing when you may benefit from professional help.

Part III, "Additional Tools to Free Yourself," examines the nuts and bolts of how negative emotions work, how to identify your strengths and how to rein in your expectations to save yourself from unnecessary disappointment later. It also outlines the power of getting outside yourself to tap into empathy and gratitude.

Part IV, "Shortcuts: How to Find Your Way Through the Detours of Life," test-drives the steps in the context of the real-life bumps in the road and the natural reactions you build in response, such as jealousy, anger, hurt, disappointment, and shame. Although these feelings are natural first reactions, they are the gateway to anxiety and negative thinking, boxing you in or controlling you with fears. We also look at the cages you may create for yourself—procrastination, perfectionism, difficulty with criticism—and see how to work your way out of patterns that have become automatic.

SMALL THINGS, OFTEN

Rather than feeling like you have to dodge and hide from life's inevitable obstacles, you can use this book to equip yourself to face them head on. You will find simple, everyday exercises that you can do with much less effort than it takes to be dragged around by an anxious or negative spin. As you work with the strategies in this book, you'll find that detours will be temporary and your recovery time faster. You can work hard at this, but this book is about how to work on it easily. With small changes that you incorporate often, you'll soon find that the new pathways become second nature to you, as natural as worrying used to be. So, come as you are, whether you are deep in these patterns or only an occasional visitor, and find the skills to create a better life—the life you want to lead.

PART I

Getting to Know Your Mind and How to Change It

While it is usually a good idea to follow your instincts or feelings, this is the wrong approach when you're anxious. You have to do the opposite of your instincts. That's because anxiety is paradoxical. The more you try to defend yourself, the more frightened you become.

—AARON T. BECK AND GARY EMERY,
ANXIETY DISORDERS AND PHOBIAS

What are typically the first two words out of a well-meaning friend or loved one's mouth when you are upset? "Don't worry." If only it were so simple. With catastrophic pictures racing through your mind, you're not exactly going to turn out the lights, go to bed, and think, *Right, this can wait till tomorrow.* On the contrary, you may get caught up worrying that there's something wrong with you simply because you're worrying, that if you were more competent you wouldn't be worrying about this or the twenty other things on your list. It takes very little for worry to spiral out of control, taking your confidence and rationality with it.

In these first few chapters you'll learn how your mind works, exactly why the brain works you up over things, and how you can retrain it to only warn you about the things that really matter. In Chapter 1, we'll learn that though the brain is wired to detect threat first and safety much later, there are important things that you can do to shorten the gap between the two. So, as much as it is an instinct to worry, you'll learn that you have another instinct as well, maybe one you didn't know you were allowed to have: an instinct to buffer yourself from unnecessary worry. That is the instinct that you will strengthen by reading this book.

Worry rushes in where there is uncertainty. And whether it's *Will my child be okay at school today, will my mother's surgery go well,* or *will my boss like my proposal,* uncertainty is part of life. But the way anxiety tells the story, the uncertainty always leads to what can go wrong. We approach most things in life with what we could call calculated uncertainty. It's not that we have *no idea* what's going to happen, we just don't know *exactly* what will happen. Worry tempts us because we don't like to be caught off guard. We are afraid to let go of rehearsing for all the catastrophes that could occur. It's a discipline to resist getting roped into worry, but in Chapter 2 we'll learn how to shrink back the risk that we perceive to its appropriate size, which will allow us to be better prepared for the actual situations we face.

Thinking positively is another standard antidote that we may try when we are anxious. We'll see in Chapter 3 that although positive experiences are to be cherished, positive thinking is not the exit route out of worry, and forcing ourselves in that direction may backfire. When we are stuck with negative thinking, we feel out of options, so to exit out of that we need to be reminded of all the options we do have. Rather than telling yourself to "think positive," you can remind yourself to "think possible."

Chapter 1

YOUR MIND UNDER NEW MANAGEMENT

*Our genetic preparation to learn about ances-
tral dangers can get us into trouble, as when it
causes us to develop fears of things that are not
particularly dangerous in our world.*
—JOSEPH LEDOUX, *THE EMOTIONAL BRAIN*

❧ *Poised to pitch your new idea for a reality television program,
you go into the team meeting stoked and ready. A few minutes into
the presentation one of the executives picks up his cell phone and
returns a text, another mumbles something to the person next to her.
Suddenly you're panicked and experiencing high-voltage anxiety.
You can't help thinking: They're bored. They hate it—they hate me—
what if I blew this whole thing? I've been working on it for months,
and now—wait! I can't even remember what I was supposed to be
saying. Now I've messed up for real.* ❧

DON'T LET YOUR BRAIN RUIN YOUR DAY

Going about the business of everyday life, we hit snags. They
come in small forms like a snub or an offhand remark, or big
ones like an illness or the threat of job layoffs. These events in

and of themselves are not insurmountable. In fact, the small ones you recover from quickly and hardly remember, but the bigger ones often evolve into the hidden stepping stones to growth. But that's not how they feel at the time. In the blink of an eye, the mere hint of a threat, rejection, or disappointment launches us into a high-speed preview of a chain of unstoppable catastrophes. Our bodies amp up in response to that show, readying us as if those possibilities are not only imminent, but actually upon us. Why is it that at the very moment when we need to think straight, our internal program makes us spin in spirals of worry?

Here's why: At the other end of the line when you perceive that initial reaction of distress is the *amygdala,* the brain's emotional response center. The amygdala is your round-the-clock surveillance system, overseeing your safety and in charge of the brain's 100 billion neurons and more. For early man, who lived with such threats to survival as stealthy hungry leopards and venomous pythons, the anxious brain erred on the side of caution. With the slightest crunch in the grass, we were out of there.

But how well does that serve us today in the concrete jungle of modern life? Now the danger that lurks may be that someone will cut you off in traffic, that your child might not get accepted to college, that your neighbor won't keep his dog on his side of the fence, or that you'll choke giving your acceptance speech for your community award. With the amygdala, it's not the moment of truth. It's the moment of survival. Truth is a luxury that gets sorted out once you are safely back in your cave (or two-bedroom apartment) and you can review whether that really was a snake slithering toward you, or just a harmless twig that moved when you accidentally kicked it. Because it doesn't take chances and won't distinguish between real or imagined threats, when the amygdala speaks, your entire body listens.

The amygdala dictates where your attention goes, and at the least sign of danger it instantly mobilizes your body to fight or run for your life. Every ounce of energy you have becomes immediately available to defend your survival. That leaves very few ounces to do something rational like take a closer look at the situation to evaluate whether there really is a threat or just a temporary uncomfortable moment. With a one-size-fits-all "catastrophe phone," it doesn't have a separate ringtone for small, medium, or large dangers. The alert is always the same: fight or flee. Well-intentioned but overprotective, this is how the brain, and more specifically, the amygdala can ruin our day. We are living our lives with what neuropsychologist David J. Linden refers to as "yesterday's parts."

In trying to do its job, your amygdala can actually prevent you from doing the very smart things that would be functional in a situation, like ignoring the rude colleagues in the meeting or making a joke about taking a BlackBerry break. It picks you up out of your senses and plunks you down in a place where you are ready to explode, cry, run, or simply spin, unable to get a grip. It leaves you reeling from the adrenaline jolt that occurred in response to a possibility, a hint, a shadow of a doubt. Knowing that the brain can make mistakes is the beginning of learning how you can take back control over your life.

Some of us are genetically more susceptible to these anxious reactions. There is no one genetic cause for them, but rather an interplay of multiple genes regulating our biochemistry, memory, and the reactive thresholds of different parts of the brain. Others of us have lived through stressful events or endured stressful conditions that have primed the emergency response to stay in the "on" position. But whether you are especially prone to these thoughts or simply encounter them in response to day-to-day stresses, you can reroute the initial survival-oriented thoughts and not be detoured by the big threats these thoughts invent from small events.

You can outsmart the overprotective brain. Our Stone Age defensive systems have become troublemakers in modern times, albeit well-meaning ones. You need to understand that the amygdala is the default navigator and resist the urge to jump at every false alarm or dress rehearsal for

WORRY DETOUR
AHEAD
KEEP IT
SHORT

doom or despair. The key to taking back control of the wheel is to put your voice of reason in the driver's seat.

That's where the cortex comes in, the "take a closer look" part of the brain. It is supremely prepared to help us sort out the real dangers from the false alarms, to make good decisions and not be deterred by our overprotective brain. Whether you're working or watching television, the cortex seeks out facts, and analyses, synthesizes, and reaches a well-thought-out assessment of a situation and arrives at an appropriate response. If you can quickly recognize the amygdala's interruptions as unnecessary detours from the solid course you are on, you can reduce the time wasted on anxiety and worry. This allows you to stay focused on important things and get back on track with your life's path. It's an issue, but one that you can overcome. Let's see how.

REPROGRAMMING YOUR INTERNAL GPS

While driving through the Italian countryside a few years back, our language skills limited to *gelato*, my husband and I had our first experience using a global positioning system (GPS). One day, trying to make our way to the sleepy town of Arezzo, we made a wrong turn. Nicole, the voice of our GPS, ever vigilant to our route, alerted us immediately. "Turn around as soon as possible, turn around as soon as possible," she urged. My husband, insisting that he could figure it out, pulled the plug on Nicole. What should have been a pleasant thirty-minute excursion through the gentle Tuscan landscape became a neck-breaking two-hour detour high on mountain roads full of stomach-turning switchbacks. Our younger daughter updated us every few minutes on her degree of car sickness. Although we did eventually reach our destination, tired, hungry, and frustrated, we just wanted to go home.

Getting lost in the Italian countryside is no real hardship. But when the easily misconstrued, innocuous gesture of a co-worker—a simple roll of the eyes—causes you to think *She hates me, she's going to backstab me and sabotage my project*, you sud-

---

TRY THIS

Choose the voice of your internal GPS. It could be someone you know, like a trusted friend or adviser, or someone
you don't know, like a celebrity or character from a film
or novel. Picture in your mind that person calmly or
comically letting you know that you can "turn around as
soon as possible," reminding you that it's okay to get back
on your track and not get detoured farther by that emotional wrong turn. Write it on a sign to stick over your
workstation or desk. The more you remember that turning around is an option, and a good one, the sooner you'll
take advantage of it.

---

denly find yourself on treacherous terrain. All the confidence that
you had walking into that lunch has gone out the window. You're
disoriented and no longer have your wits about you. What an
unfortunate way to conduct a business meeting.

What if, instead of going farther on the mental detour and
looking for all the ways that your fears could be true, you recognize that your interpretations took a wrong turn? Rather than
get run off your route, put yourself back in the driver's seat of
your life, invoke your internal GPS, and make the choice to turn
around as soon as possible. You decide whether that side trip
through a landscape of disasters is really worth your time and attention. You'll be able to do this when you realize that just because worry took over the wheel, that doesn't mean it knows the
way. In fact, it's in the way.

THE TOP-DOWN ORGANIZATION
OF THE MIND: THOUGHTS LEAD TO
FEELINGS LEAD TO ACTIONS

A fundamental premise of cognitive behavioral therapy is that
what you think in a situation dictates how you feel and behave.
When you perceive a threat, the brain sends a message to the

body to defend against the threat by running or hiding. Something so wrong—"My husband is late, what if he got into a car accident? What if he is so hurt that he can't even call me?"—feels so true because once you think it, your body immediately responds frantically. We think that because we feel scared, very scared, there actually is a danger. You see yourself acting nervous and this compounds the feeling that something bad is about to happen, so you start acting *as if* it is imminent. When you go to *second* thoughts—accurate appraisals of the situation—they send a different signal: "That's unlikely, he is often late, I just got really frightened by the idea." With that approach, we feel calmer, no longer braced for the worst. The brain started on the worry track, but you can decide whether to stay on that track or go with your reasoned track.

Looking at the brain train on page 9, we see that one situation can lead to two very different outcomes, depending on your thoughts about the situation. When you are facing a new job, in one scenario you are a wreck the night before, but in the other, you are excited and confident. What changed? It wasn't the job, it was the thinking. Cultivating the habit of the two-track mind will help you switch over to a more realistic track.

Just as overprotective parents have the best intentions in mind, anxiety and negative thinking can become too much of a good thing. With anxiety, the brain errs on the side of caution, making you afraid of dangers that aren't real risks to you. With negative thinking, the brain tries to protect you from *feeling* like a failure, by going overboard with warnings so that you'll quit rather than fail. It's the brain's version of "You can't fire me, I already quit." But if you aren't really in danger, and you aren't really going to fail, this approach presents a problem. What your brain deemed a possibility was an extremely remote one. Yet that very remote possibility has now become the focus. The problem that you are now mentally prepared for is worse than the situation you are actually in. You need to prevent normal fears and doubts from turning into an emotional detour. Eventually, when you do

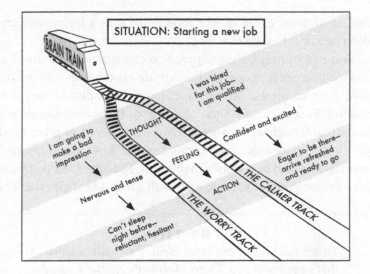

SITUATION: Starting a new job

BRAIN TRAIN

I was hired for this job— I am qualified

I am going to make a bad impression

THOUGHT

Confident and excited

FEELING

Nervous and tense

Eager to be there— arrive refreshed and ready to go

ACTION

THE CALMER TRACK

Can't sleep night before— reluctant, hesitant

THE WORRY TRACK

get back on your path, having dodged an imaginary danger, you get nothing good from all that time spent worrying. And you might have missed something that is actually important. When you find yourself veering on those detours you need a traffic report: Significant delays on that route. Great distress, much ventured, nothing gained.

Take Sandra. She is an extremely competent, diligent, talented worker in the field of health care. Her supervisor wishes all her employees were like Sandra, and yet every single day Sandra dreaded going to work because she thought she was going to do something wrong, let someone down, or forget something. She couldn't eat or sleep as a result. Sandra and I talked about how her brain was warning the wrong person. The signal got crossed with someone else who really *should* be worrying about her job, but that's not her. When I asked Sandra if she needed the alarms to be motivated every day or whether they were overkill, she said, "They make me crazy. I'm so stressed out I can't think." By understanding that the alarms were automatic but out of sync with her real life, Sandra could give them less authority and was able to enjoy more of what she was doing. When that electric-shock feeling of panic came in, she thought of it as a faulty wire and didn't allow it to take over.

Some of us may be more prone to categorizing situations as risky, either because of genetics, our life experiences, or our current circumstances. But all of us have the ability to turn this around. Recognize when the brain sends the wrong signals and know that though we are wired to survive, some wires get crossed, give us faulty feedback, and create trouble. After all, you weren't actually attacked by a woolly mammoth. Did your boss really just give the assignment to your archrival? Or is it that you think he

---

TRY THIS

To get the idea of the brain train, start with a situation that's not about you. Think of something that a friend or spouse is afraid of, but you are not. Skiing? Highway driving? Dogs? Write down what the other person's thoughts, feelings, and actions are on the worry track. Next write down your information on the calm track. See how the same situation can lead to two entirely different results, all depending on the story you are telling yourself. Now, take a situation that you are anxious about. The party you are planning? The test you have to take for your law license? The repairs that need to be done on your roof? Start with your worry track and fill in the boxes. What are your worry thoughts about it? How does that make you feel inside? What do your feet want to do as a result—approach, or run? Always start with the worry track because that is what's there first in your mind. Now ask yourself, how would you think of that same situation if worry were quiet. What would the answers look like if you were actually trying to write the *right* answers rather than the most dramatic or upsetting answers. Next time you are feeling anxious, remind yourself of which track you are on, and run the story down the other track. Chances are that you will arrive at the destination you really wanted to reach before worry switched the signal.

---

might, or he possibly *could*, even though he probably won't? The time you spend treating these intrusions like a life-threatening emergency that requires all of your attention is time wasted. What's the alternative? Know the flaws of the system. Pick up your car Fred Flintstone style, turn yourself around, your mood around, and get back on the track you were on before your overprotective brain interrupted.

AVOIDING DETOURS

In order to effectively stay on your route, you need to become familiar with the nature of these intrusions that cause you so much grief, on the spot or in the middle of the night. We all know

---

TRY THIS:
Down, Dog, Down

Another way to understand worry is to see it as a barking dog. Some dogs bark at anything that moves—safe things like the mailman or your mother-in-law, and unsafe things like an intruder. The stimuli are all treated equally. Like the dog that barks at everything that *could* be a threat, the amygdala can sound the alarm when there is no danger.

Next time you begin a "what-if" worry marathon or feel a surge of panic, imagine the barking dog. If there is no danger, you can confidently quiet the dog. If there is something worrying you that warrants your attention, talk to your amygdala. Tell it respectfully but firmly to sit, and stay. You'll work with it, if it will work with you. You get to choose whether to rattle your nerves for fifteen minutes listening to a barking dog, or to quiet the worry and benefit from fifteen minutes of clear thinking. The more frequently you give yourself this choice, the more your brain will remember to *bark* only at the real dangers.

YOU AND BEYOND:
Helping Each Other Turn Around

How can we help each other slow down and see how worry has run us off the road? When a friend gets overrun by anxiousness and draws dramatic and hasty conclusions, suggest that she retrace her steps. Ask her, "What were you thinking before you had that argument with your husband—were you thinking that you were totally incompatible? Or, before you got that bill in the mail, were you thinking that you were in danger financially? As much as she may have the dire words in her head, *This changes everything,* you can help her settle down by asking: "What has really changed? What has stayed the same?" Help her see that being anxious doesn't change events, it just changes how we feel. Disappointing and uncertain news, or less than cheery interactions, may temporarily throw people off the path, but we can help each other shorten the detours.

---

when we are engaging in that first-track, fast-track thinking that invariably makes us feel bad. What we don't know is that these thoughts don't warrant the authority they appear to have. Originally installed in your brain to protect you from danger, they are an emotional reflex. (With friends like these, who needs the nightly news?) You need to know that it's okay to turn around and sidestep those holes of doubt and despair.

So, you've learned how to reinterpret and quiet the primitive, faulty alarms that the overprotective brain offers in response to uncertainty. But what do you do with the reasonable fear and doubt that remain? You aren't frantic about it, but it still doesn't feel good. Now the real work can begin.

Chapter 2

GETTING BETTER AT RISK AND UNCERTAINTY

My life has been a series of tragedies, none of which actually happened.

—MARK TWAIN

❧ *I've never picked the right things to worry about; I've spent my whole life worrying about the wrong things. Every single thing that I've spent all my time worrying over and trying to prevent has never happened. Three kids, all these years. No. I've been wrong every time. The things that did happen, well, those I never would have predicted. And in the end those things turned out fine. Why do I do this to myself?* ❧

THE WORST-CASE SCENARIO IS JUST THE *FIRST*-CASE SCENARIO

While visiting the Baltimore Aquarium, I overheard a mother talking to her young daughter. The mother was excitedly describing how the girl was going to get to see a *real* shark! At which point

the little girl burst into tears. She was old enough to know that sharks were dangerous, but not old enough to understand that she would be able to look at them safely from outside the tank. The equation "high risk + low protection = panic" was operating perfectly in her young mind.

Fueled by imagination and not enough facts, how often do we react like the young girl? When unknowns appear we may often picture ourselves right there in the shark tank. Hearing about a friend's heart attack, a house fire, a tragic item on the news launches us into worry mode. Part of it we can't help. It's the instantaneous work of the survival brain, the amygdala, overriding our good common sense. It's what psychologist Daniel Goleman calls the "amygdala hijack," and it has us reacting before we can think. But we can prevent much of it by thinking again.

You can't be certain that those things won't ever happen. But because something is *possible* doesn't make it *probable*. Keeping this distinction firmly in mind can help you better handle risk and uncertainty. What you do next with that uncertainty is up to you. Fortunately, we are caught in the clutches of the *picture*, not the *shark*. We can change the picture, because it is in our minds; the shark, not so much. But remember, we encounter very few sharks in our daily life. So when worry strikes, remind yourself it's not the job, the relationship, or the argument that's the problem, it's what you are picturing in your mind about those things that's getting in the way. And that's something you can change.

THE ANSWERS ARE NOT AS BAD AS YOU THINK

Attention-grabbing worst-case scenarios travel fast and get there first. They instantly fill in the blanks that uncertainty creates for us. We may not necessarily believe them, but harboring those fears contributes to the problem and keeps us at a disadvantage. Whether in negative situations like getting an illness, or positive opportunities like starting a job, getting pulled into worst-case scenarios prevents us from evaluating risks accurately.

The future hasn't happened yet. What's stopping you from pursuing your dreams or getting the help you need is an anxious thought. To minimize the damage caused by things that haven't happened, and most likely won't, look fear or the "what if's" squarely in the eye to see if a kernel of a concern requires your attention. Then look beyond the fear to "what is" or the story of what you really believe will happen. Tragedy, as Mr. Twain suggests, is usually a no-show.

OPEN THE DOOR TO FOCUS ON THE RIGHT THINGS

🍂 *"I am so nervous every Sunday night," says Betta. "Thinking about going back to my job the next day, my stomach is in knots and I can't sleep. What am I afraid of? I don't know—work! What am I afraid of at work? I don't know—everything! I'm just so nervous!"* 🍂

Anxiety management can be summed up in two words: shrink and approach. Like Betta, we see things as daunting because we

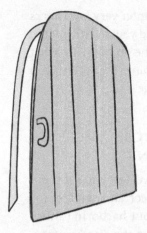

haven't investigated closely to see whether they might be safe or manageable, so we assume then that we need to avoid or hide from those things. Rather than take worry's word for it, you can shrink the actual risk down to size by determining if your fears are warranted. Dismiss the worries that on closer inspection you deem unlikely to happen and focus instead on the aspects of a new or uncertain situation that would truly benefit from your attention. But to do this, you need to be willing to open the door and see what's really there. When you open the door, it's okay if you don't know some of the answers to worthwhile questions that you find there. However, with a

TRY THIS
First-Case Scenario
Ask yourself: What am I *most afraid* will happen?

What if _____ were to actually happen to me? What would I do? How would I ever handle that?

Second-Case Scenario
Ask yourself: What do I *really believe* will happen?

Wait! Is this what I really need to worry about? I need more information. What is more likely to happen in this situation?

Notice the differences between those two scenarios and most important, notice how differently you feel when you are thinking one versus the other. Fortunately, and not surprisingly, we feel calmer and clearer when we are thinking about what is actually true. Always ask yourself *both* questions. You get to choose what to think. Choose well.

JUST OPEN THE DOOR AND
THE LIGHT GOES ON

Worry is the commentary that happens with eyes closed, outside the door. Your internal voice of reason gets automatically turned on—like a refrigerator light—when you open the door to see what's really inside.

---

more accurate picture in mind, looking with your smarts rather than your fearful imagination, you'll be able to see that you are not putting yourself in harm's way. The shark, in effect, will be safely back in the tank so you won't have to brace yourself to take a look; you'll be ready and even curious to see what's there. You'll be much more willing to stretch your comfort zone and approach the situation that you want to learn about. Maybe you'll call that friend you thought was mad at you, knowing that she won't bite, or tell your boss about a mistake because you realize he'll want to help, or even call that person about the blind date. What do you really have to lose? Imagine all you have to gain.

In between shrinking the risk and being willing to approach the situation, you might need to do a few things to calm your body down. First, don't let your fear of the unknown keep you from doing the essential work of exploring and evaluating the things you do know. If you can keep the door open and keep looking at the probabilities and the facts, chances are you'll find that the news is better than you think. In any case, you want to be sure that if there's something you need to plan for, get more information about, or problem solve, worry won't deprive you of that opportunity.

Many of us have moments where we spin with anxiety, but when pressed to pinpoint what we are afraid of, we don't know. Sometimes it doesn't even occur to us to figure it out, to think that there could be another way of responding to that situation besides worrying. This is the closed door of anxiety.

SIDE-BY-SIDE COMPARISONS

We are very good consumers. We research online, aren't easily taken in by sales pitches, we do the side-by-side comparisons of prices and products. Put your worry through the same consumer test. Take a situation that you are feeling uneasy about, list your worst fears on one side of the page. Now draw a vertical line down the middle of the page, and on the other side write what you truly believe will happen. Seeing is believing.

HOW TO MANAGE WORRY: COGNITION, PHYSIOLOGICAL RESPONSES, AND TAKING ACTION

Correcting Your Cognition

The opposite of uncertainty and risk is not certainty, but simply information. In this section we look at the special effects that worry uses to magnify your fears. Once you better understand the mechanisms behind these tricks, you can recognize them and avoid falling under their spell.

Strategy #1: Separate Facts from Feelings

I'm afraid to get on that plane, what if it crashes? I can't take that driver's test, what if I don't pass? The more upset you get, the more convinced you feel that it makes sense to be afraid. When we think of something tragic or stressful, we're going to feel upset. But don't take that feeling as a sign of the increased likelihood of that tragic event happening. Both facts and feelings are important, but you want to base your decisions and assessments on the facts, which are stable, rather than on emotions, which are variable.

It helps to have a place to express those intense feelings, but also to see them as distinct from what even you yourself believe

Worst Case: What If?	Most Likely Outcome: What Is?	Additional Ideas: What Else
I lose my job?	No one is talking about layoffs now.	We are in a good position to ride this out.
We have to relocate?	My projects are going well.	They will probably avoid layoffs at all costs.
I can't find a job?	I do have seniority; I bring a lot of business to the firm.	Our industry has been relatively unaffected by the poor economy.

Notice how your stress level changes depending on which scenario you are reading. Thoughts manipulate feelings. Just because you *can* think of bad things happening doesn't mean that they will occur. Stick with the facts—don't commit time to the fiction.

to be true. No matter how strong the feelings are, they don't change the facts. As you begin to act on the facts, notice how the feelings quickly dissolve. Remember, there are two distinct versions of the story. Don't confuse them.

Strategy #2: Recognize the Power of Suggestion

When I explain this phenomenon to patients in my home office, which has a high vaulted ceiling, I say, "Imagine that I was afraid that the ceiling was going to fall in." Patients always look up. I

BRING THE REAL PICTURE IN FOCUS

Ask yourself:
- What am I most afraid of about this?
- How much do I really believe that will happen?
- What do I think is the most likely thing to happen?
- What is the most unlikely thing to occur?
- What could I do if that happened?

Tell yourself:
- Ideas can sound frightening, but that doesn't make them true.
- Just because I'm afraid and can picture something doesn't make it more likely.
- The degree of how afraid I feel isn't a good measurement of the actual risk in the situation. My anxious thoughts are manipulating my feelings.
- If I stick with what I really believe is most likely to happen, then I can effectively plan how to handle the likely scenario.

point out that until I had mentioned the ceiling, no one was worrying about it, and nobody will be thinking about it a few minutes from now, because it is a non-issue. But in assessing risk, if we focused on just that split second of fear as a barometer, we would have assessed it as high. Calculating absolute risk based on our emotional reactions is volatile and unreliable.

The power of suggestion is the temporary manipulation of your fears, in reaction to a mention of something frightening. If, for example, someone mentions cancer, heart attacks, or accidents, we imagine that happening to us and we may even react physically, by feeling light-headed or having our heart rate speed up. Or consider what happens when someone mentions a stomach bug and we feel suddenly queasy or mentions the dreaded lice and we feel an unbearable itching all over our scalp. But when you learn to expect the temporary reaction, you won't overthink it and you

TRY THIS

Take a situation that you are worried about. Ask yourself:

- How *nervous* am I that I will completely mess up the presentation?
- How much of me truly *believes* that I will mess up the presentation?
- What do I really believe will happen?
- You might feel 100 percent frightened about something, but only 5 percent of you believes that it will truly happen. Base your "take away message" on the facts and not the feelings.

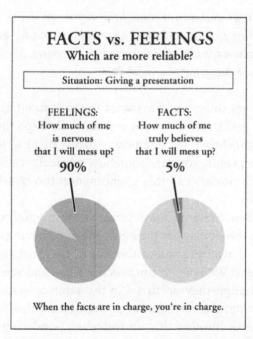

FACTS vs. FEELINGS
Which are more reliable?

Situation: Giving a presentation

FEELINGS:
How much of me
is nervous
that I will mess up?
90%

FACTS:
How much of me
truly believes
that I will mess up?
5%

When the facts are in charge, you're in charge.

won't overvalue it. You'll come to realize that it's a natural reaction to the mention of something scary, just like you get scared watching a horror movie. If you stamp it as the power of suggestion, the fear will more quickly loosen its grip.

Strategy #3: Bring the Wisdom of Your Experience to the Front

When you worry about a situation, rather than getting stuck with all the what if's, fast-forward to the end. Ask yourself how you think it will really end, then cut and paste that more realistic scenario into your plan and thinking. Let the belief that it will be okay appear at the very beginning of your exploration so that if you can't save yourself the worry trip, at least you can shorten it.

Strategy #4: Thinking Something Bad Doesn't Make It Come True

🐟 *I saw an ambulance. I thought of my mom dying. Does that mean it's going to happen? Am I a terrible person for having that thought? I saw a plane crash reported on the news. My husband is flying today. Is he going to crash?* 🐟

Often the very things we don't want to think about are the very things that find their way in. So you suffer through the fear that those thoughts bring, but often you also fear that just in thinking about these events, you may somehow magically cause them to occur. Psychologists call this phenomenon thought-likelihood fusion (TLF).

A coincidence of time doesn't create a meaningful connection. If that were the case, every time you imagined having a beautiful cooked meal awaiting you at the end of the workday, *voilà*! It would appear! We need to uncross the wires and see that these events, although they occurred in the same *sentence*, have no other meaningful connection or power beyond that.

The intense emotion that we feel when pondering these distressing scenarios results from simply having the thought. As convincing as it feels, it offers a poor gauge of the likelihood of the event. Rather than dwell on the frightening picture, identify it and say, "That's just TLF." Then, swap out the worry that we are magically responsible for making bad things happen and pinpoint whether anything remains to warrant your concern.

Strategy #5: The Word "Some" Can Offer Perspective

When things don't look great, that doesn't mean they're terrible. You and your spouse had a tiff this morning and didn't say goodbye. You think: *We didn't kiss good-bye. That's it, we can't agree on anything, he doesn't understand me at all, we can't communicate, how can we raise children together if we can't even agree on when to pay the bills, he'll never listen to me, nothing's working, we're not compatible. It's a disaster. What if it really is the end? What if we're through? What if I end up alone?*

Notice how just that one small thought or observation: *We didn't kiss good-bye* has served as a starting gun to get you running a worry marathon in your mind. To get rid of the absolutes of "everything" and "nothing," we need to summon the notion of "some." *We can't agree on some things, but some things we can. We don't listen to each other sometimes, but sometimes (often!) we do. Some things are working very well in our relationship, some things are not. I know how some things will work out, but some things I don't.* Picture a salt shaker—you are shaking perspective on the situation and making it palatable. Next time you hear the "all or nothings" in your mind, reach for the power of some and watch your stress level come down. Create a "Some Shaker" for your home or office and keep it well within reach—it's an emotional staple for life.

Strategy #6: Stay in Your Time Zone, the Present

Quick! What are you going to be doing ten years from now? Ten months? We can't control the future, but we are the ones who create the stepping stones that take us there, maneuvering each moment along the way. If you find yourself worrying too much, you may have stretched too far out into the future. Like a measuring tape, snap yourself back! Just thinking about the future can put

Some people...
Some of the time...
Some things went well...

Shake "SOME" today on your ALL-OR-NONE thoughts!

us in an anxious state because we don't have enough data yet to predict it. Instead of projecting, let life unfold. Even if the future does take us by surprise—how does worrying buy anything in the way of security?

Remind yourself to stay on a shorter time line. Just because anxiety and worry are flipping ahead to future chapters in the book of life doesn't mean *you* have to. By the time you get to those chapters, so much will have changed. Why skip ahead trying to solve problems that may never materialize? It's like forcing yourself to decide today which cell phone model you will need to buy three years from now. The choices will change, you will change, so don't invest time now in committing to something that will surely become obsolete at some point. So it is with worry.

Managing Your Physiological Responses: Getting the Body on Board

Notice as soon as we think that something might be wrong, we feel a tightening in our chest or our heart beating faster. Fear isn't just in the mind; it's in the body, too.

Thank goodness for the body's early warning system. When we're stopped at a red light and getting ready to turn and a car

---

TRY THIS

Visualize a calendar. Rather than flip forward, flip back the pages to this month, to this week. Don't worry about the future, because things may well have changed by the time you get there. If you need to, make an appointment with yourself for a future date when it would make sense to start thinking about an issue: *I'll think about how we'll deal with being empty nesters exactly two years from now; I'll think about what I'm going to do for a summer job in March (not September).*

---

suddenly darts out of nowhere into our lane, we don't have to manually input the data—*car coming, certain disaster, swerve!*—it all happens in a flash. The body instantly mobilizes to slam on the brakes and get out of harm's way. The downside of that ever-ready system, however, as you learned in Chapter 1, is that it doesn't distinguish the oncoming car from the thought that we're going to bomb our interview tomorrow. A perception of threat, real or imagined, sets off the survival program in our body to defend itself. In fight-or-flight mode, our heart races to pump blood faster to the extremities so that we *could* run or fight, our arms and legs tingle in response, our breathing gets shallow and faster to give our lungs more power, our stomach may be in knots, and finally, we may sweat to prevent overheating (or even to make our skin slippery to escape the clutch of a predator). This physiological fight-or-flight reaction has a quick start and a gradual taper, which is why it may take several blocks before we breathe easily again when we do avoid that accident at the light. Calming the body takes some time.

Fortunately, there are things that you can do to help that happen faster. For those of you who overthink and suffer from frequent headaches, low energy, fatigue, or digestive problems as a result, chances are that the repeated mobilizing of the primary defense system has taken its toll. It will be helpful to learn how to quiet the body even before it responds to worry.

The body and mind are in constant conversation, so you want to help both sides tell the same story. Telling yourself that the coast is clear will simultaneously send a physical message that helps the body to calm down as well. At the same time, intentionally calming the body down lets the mind know that there is no emergency.

Strategy #1: Lower Your Baseline Level of Stress

"How the heck are we going to get out of this parking garage!" I grumbled to my older daughter on a recent outing after going around in circles in the lot. "Calmly," she replied. What an interesting thought. Getting worked up about it really doesn't make things work better.

If you can lower your daily stress level, then only on special occasions when you are faced with an extreme challenge—an approaching deadline, an unexpected medical issue or family obligation—will you feel the stress. If your baseline stress level is high, it takes less to tip the scales to make you feel agitated or plagued by physical symptoms even in minor situations.

Lowering baseline stress is best accomplished through simple daily practices that take about as much time as brushing your teeth. And like brushing your teeth, it helps to have set times of day when you are sure to practice, such as before bed or before each meal. In addition to specific moments where you intentionally calm yourself, you can imagine adopting a state of mind that prioritizes calm. Start by becoming more aware of your baseline. When you notice yourself clenching and stressing at any point in your day, take the opportunity to remind yourself that you have a choice and opportunity to set out on solid footing and handle it calmly. Chances are, not only will you *feel* better, but with less static on the line, you'll likely *do* better, too.

Strategy #2: Intentional Breathing

> *With each breath, you begin again and all things*
> *are possible.*
>
> —SUSAN PIVER

What is your breathing saying about your state of mind? Is it saying: My life is a completely stressed, out-of-control mess? You don't want to breathe any more of that message in than you have to. Decide that for the next five minutes—even just two minutes—you are going to put down whatever it is that you are carrying. Give yourself a moment where there's nothing else on your to-do list but *breathing.* Unplug and refresh, so that when operations start up again, they will start anew. Just as a computer runs better when it is shut off daily, we do better when we can reset to baseline at least once a day. Once you get into this habit, you may even find that you are naturally taking a breathing break many times a day because of how good it feels and how much better you can function when you do.

There are other things you can do to relieve stress—exercise, take a long bath, or watch a movie, but there's so much that can happen simply from paying attention to your breathing. In fact, the act of breathing calmly and intentionally can have an immediate effect on your blood pressure, the release of stress hormones in the body, and the pH level in your bloodstream, which is the ultimate measure of balance in your system. The more you practice calm breathing, the more it will be there for you when you need it. Fast, shallow breathing triggers the sympathetic nervous system (SNS)—the accelerator in your body. It mobilizes the fight-or-flight reaction and results in stress and agitation. In contrast, the parasympathetic nervous system (PNS) helps the body reset to baseline after a surge in adrenaline. When we breathe calmly and deeply, it signals to the PNS to engage the brakes.

My experience teaching deep breathing for over twenty years has shown me that even three or four focused deep breaths can

TRY THIS

Choose a time of day to focus on your breathing for a few minutes. It could be as soon as you wake up in the morning, while you are eating lunch at your desk, when you arrive a few minutes early for your next appointment, or when you get in bed at night. Make it convenient so that you do it daily. It generally takes approximately three weeks to establish a habit, so be patient. Find a place to simply close your eyes; then choose a visualization and follow the path of your breath as it unfurls up from your abdomen and out through your mouth. You might picture lying on a serene beach with the sun warming your skin or being in a cozy bed; it could be a place you've been, or it could be in your imagination. The brain thrives on pattern, so if you choose a place to go to consistently for a couple of days or weeks, as soon as you decide that you are going to do your breathing, your brain will bring up the image for you, and the relaxation can begin that much sooner.

I use soap bubbles to teach children how to deep breathe, but even adults are allowed to have fun. Why not try it? Breathe in slowly and then breathe out slowly through the wand—you'll know you are exhaling fully when you're surrounded by bubbles.

---

bring a person into deep relaxation. Just as brushing your teeth at night is a signal to your body that you're getting ready to go to sleep, practicing your breathing for five breaths can transport you to a different state of mind by truly changing what is going on in your body. Anxiety triggers the body's alarm system even when there's no emergency, but breathing calmly and deeply from the abdomen, the way that we do when we are relaxed or sleeping, is like punching in the security code to shut off the alarm.

Your breath is the equipment that you never leave home without. Literally your lifeline, you can call on it at any time. Getting

---

TRY THIS

Stretch your arms overhead and then let them drop slowly, stretching them out slowly to the side and slightly behind you. Picture a bird spreading its wings behind it. Feel your back crack slightly. Repeat. Now take another deep breath and notice how much more deeply you can breathe just by opening and relaxing the chest.

---

into the regular practice of intentional breathing, even if it is brief, is enough to help your body remember where the brakes are and to use them even in a stressful situation. With less adrenaline racing through your body, you'll be able to think more clearly, even in a stressful situation.

Like creating a strong muscle memory, the more you practice and know how to locate that all-clear message, the faster and more automatically your system will be able to downshift. And then when you really need it in a pinch, calm will be within your grasp.

Strategy #3: A Quick Stretch and Release

We store tension in many different places in our body, but most of us know the feeling of tension in our chest. Your chest houses the most vital organs, the heart and lungs, so you are programmed to guard that area above all else. Opening up the chest muscles offers the fastest way to send a feeling of relaxation through your body. You can practice an easy chest-opening exercise at home, and then it can be done discreetly in a bathroom stall, at your desk, or even right out there in public. (Notice how many other people, taking your cue, realize they need the release and start to stretch, too!)

Strategy #4: Dissolve Stress with Visualization

There are times when we know we are stressed because of the tight feeling in our throat or the tight feeling in our chest or stomach. One way to dispel stress is to visualize the shape of the stress in your body. What are its outlines? What color is it? As you engage in your breathing exercise, imagine that as you breathe in, you are sending healing light to that part of your body, and as you exhale, the tension is breaking up, becoming granular like sand. As you exhale, you blow the stress away to reveal that part of your body with a healthy, calm shape and color. Repeat a few times. You can also imagine that you are shining a healing silvery-blue light onto the area to break up and release the tension, leaving your body feeling lighter and calmer.

Taking Action One Small Step at a Time

Earlier in this chapter you learned how to change the messages that you tell yourself so that you don't feel so daunted. Then you learned strategies to calm your body down. Now you're in a better position to approach whatever situation you've been avoiding. *Not so fast,* you may be thinking. *I said I'm considering going back to school, I'm not ready to actually sign up for classes.* Or, *I do want to work at a museum, but I'm not ready to actually call my friend who works there.* As eager to move on as we may be, we still may feel stymied by the final step in overcoming anxiety— taking action.

But there's a reason for that reluctance, and it's not just fear. It's thinking that we need to bite off more than we can chew, go faster than we need to. We scare ourselves off with unrealistic expectations. For example, you might think about transitioning to a retirement community, but then you look around at your three-story house filled with a lifetime of memorabilia, and think—*I could never pack all this stuff up.* Then you retreat. Right, you can't pack this up tomorrow, or even in a month. It's a process: One box at a time. And that's not even the first step— just looking at retirement communities could take several years. So, it's not the goal that presents the problem, it's that we picture ourselves needing to meet it immediately.

You might not have heard of "systematic desensitization," but chances are you're familiar with the strategy. If someone is afraid of dogs, to conquer that fear, first they look at pictures of dogs, then they watch them sleep behind a glass door or in a cage, then they look at them across the street, then pet them on a leash . . . you get the idea. They don't have to start by sitting in the middle of Puppy World with a slew of hounds slobbering all over them to get the job done! Feared situations are overcome one small step at a time. Ask children about how they got over their fears, or think back to your own childhood—the bugs, the dogs, the diving board—and they'll say, "I just got used to it." Getting Used To It is how everyone grows. This may seem like child's play, but imagine if you are working with a new piece of computer equipment, learning a sport, building a business plan, or even starting to date after a relationship breaks up. The best way for you to master the goal is by breaking it down into small, manageable steps. If the steps are too big—or if there are none—break it down. Once you start, you are on your way.

Strategy #1: Trust That You Will Adjust

When we're trying to get used to things, it's important to recognize that even good things, even the *right* things, can feel uncomfortable at first. Think of the swimming pool. You jump or inch your way in and how does it feel? Cold! Very uncomfortable, *at first*. A few minutes later you feel fine. Did something change? No, *you* changed. You adjusted. If you jumped out as soon as you got in, you would never know that just on the other side of that discomfort, a pleasant experience awaited. Knowing that we have this ability to adapt is what gets us in the pool. So, when embarking on a new project and anticipating the discomfort, remember that this is just what happens first, until you adjust.

Strategy #2: Practice Brings Confidence and Mastery

First time driving somewhere new, first time giving a presentation in front of a group, first time starting to write a book. No one knows how to do things on their first try. And that's okay. Learning is all about practice.

Let's say you are planning a trip to Spain, and you want to have some phrases under your belt. You wouldn't expect to just be able to say them on demand—you would get out the materials and practice. As children, we all learned the humbling lesson that riding a bike, playing the violin, and running track all improve with experience. When it comes to emotional management skills, perhaps *because* no equipment is required, people often assume that they don't need to practice. Then, not surprisingly, when they pick up the phone to start making cold calls, they freeze up. Try to dispense with the belief that you just *should* know how to do something. Instead, think how you would teach someone else to do it, then sketch out a practice routine for yourself. Create a script, practice in the mirror, practice with a friend. All of these steps will reduce your anxiety and increase your competency.

FREEING YOURSELF: IN ACTION

Richard's family insisted that he go to therapy. Working in the financial sector, he was not alone in feeling anxiety about work. But Richard's anxiety had a fierce grip on him. He was on edge all the time, always thinking ahead to the next problem, and he no longer enjoyed his work. Glued to his BlackBerry, it was the first thing he checked each morning and the last thing at night before bed, because he didn't want to risk missing a thing. Richard experienced free-floating anxiety, a vague feeling that something bad was about to happen that he needed to prevent, and it drove him to spend more hours at work. That made him more available to clients, but it was also leaving him running on fumes. His charisma with clients had been a big piece of his success, but he didn't feel up to it anymore.

When I asked Richard what he was most afraid of happening, he looked at me like I had two heads. "It's such a bad time, the recession, people are losing their jobs left and right," he said.

"Yes," I said, "it is a recession, but what are *you* really afraid of? Are you afraid of losing your job?" Richard knew that his firm

YOU AND BEYOND

When people near you hit that intense worry zone, resist the urge to just say everything will be okay. It won't be convincing. Instead, offer to be their memory bank. It's a kinder and more constructive alternative to "I told you so." Help them remember how similar situations turned out by posing questions. Gently ask, "The last time you were in this situation, do you remember what happened?" If they say they don't, then remind them of something similar that happened to you that turned out okay. This isn't to diminish their concern but rather, through your empathy, to get them to focus on the finish line, where things turn out okay. It will help them to hear you say, "I am always preparing for the worst, and later wish I hadn't wasted my time on that." Rather than digging deeper into fear, they will be able to switch to a different vantage point and save themselves the trip.

---

was very secure and he was secure in it. The picture he had created in his mind warned him that he had to run to keep up because things were so unstable in his profession. Yet this running and being prepared for everything had worn him out. When he slowed down to see the real risks and what he brought to the table to address them, he started to see that he was quite overprepared. For Richard, the solution was to acknowledge that just because the climate was stressed in his office and profession, giving in to fear would hurt him the most. If situations cropped up where he needed to be flexible, being burned out would not help. He had to live with some unknowns, but he also needed to acknowledge the positive indicators, such as his consistent success in his current position, and he couldn't let the climate hijack the things he knew how to do well.

Anyone who has watched a movie with a companion under the age of ten or so expects to be interrupted every few minutes

TRY THIS
Take a Worry Vacation

Whether it's the day-to-day stresses that keep ticking through your mind, or matters of great gravity, it does no good to be on round-the-clock worry duty. When you find yourself thinking about something all the time, even feeling guilty about it, it is important to remember that no matter how serious the matter is, you still need to function. Especially when you have actual problems to solve, you need to pace yourself, make sure that you can get perspective, and get sleep and nourishment.

In a stressful situation, if you aren't constantly thinking about what's wrong, you may feel that you are unprepared or acting irresponsibly. Actually, you are a much more effective problem solver when you have perspective. You can accomplish this in one of two ways. The first way is to take a vacation from worry by setting aside time each day to do things that you would do if you weren't in the crisis. Make a nice meal, go for a walk, listen to music. It is important to schedule this time, or you will likely "skip" your vacation. Think of it as closing the worry door and putting a "Do Not Disturb" sign on it. You'll return refreshed and ready for what's next.

Set Up a Worry Time

A second way to maximize your problem-solving potential is to not let worry have twenty-four-hour access to you, but rather to make it wait by establishing a set "worry time" each day—ten minutes when you write down the concerns on your mind on one side of a page, and on the other side rephrase the concern in a more rational, accurate format. Then when worry tries to slip in at other times of the day, tell it: "No, it's not worry time." When worry time arrives, if you find you no longer feel the need to think through those thoughts, all the better.

When Worry Hits at Bedtime

Sometimes we're able to get through our days without much trouble, but as soon as the business of the day is done and our heads hit the pillow, there are no distractions and worry rushes in to fill the void. You can keep a pad of paper by your bed to do your side-by-side comparisons of "What If?" and "What Is," but if nighttime worry is a frequent occurrence for you, it will be better if you make an appointment with yourself an hour or so before bedtime to work on this while you are awake enough to have your wits about you. After you complete your two lists, fold the paper in half so that only your "What Is" list is showing. If you start to worry at bedtime, you can read through the wise conclusions you reached about your life a little bit ago, before waves of fatigue made you feel that everything was impossible.

If your worry is actually about falling asleep, *What if I can't sleep, I'll be a wreck tomorrow, the day will be shot*, notice how just saying that makes you feel more anxious. The more anxious you feel, the more the amygdala beeps, and the less you're going be able to sleep. Save yourself the trip. While you're busy winding up, waking up your brain by doing the exact calculation of how disastrous *not* sleeping will be, you could be (and really want to be) using your time readying yourself for sleep. How do you turn the amygdala alarm off? It's a paradox. If you can let go of the urgency of sleep, then actually sleep will come to you faster. Use the relaxation techniques earlier in this chapter to tense and release your muscles, starting with your feet and working your way up to your face and head. Create new thoughts that turn off the alarms: *My body knows how to fall asleep; sleep will come to me when I'm ready. I am going to let my body sink into the softness of my bed and let the process happen. There's nothing I need to do; my body will find its way to sleep.* If you want to add a visualization to this process, you can track the gentle flight of snowflakes or leaves slowly falling, or visualize a winding staircase that you are walking down into a beautiful garden.

with one simple question: How does it end? Young children—pulled into the drama and having only a limited amount of worldly experience—are actually scared and not sure. They haven't learned yet that pretty much any movie they would be admitted to see is going to end well. We would be wise to remember this, too. When faced with a new or uncertain situation, anxious and negative thoughts rush in. We don't have to swim in that stream. Before we panic, pause and consider. If it is all going to end well enough, is panic the response that makes the most sense? What are the other options? Is there something else besides disaster that would be helpful to consider and plan for? Open the door, don't let your worry be a black box, let the answers in, and start to get your feet wet. Trust that you'll adjust.

Chapter 3

POSITIVE THINKING? NEGATIVE THINKING? ACCURATE THINKING

There's nothing either good or bad, but thinking makes it so.

—WILLIAM SHAKESPEARE

🦐 *Now that I'm doing better with my panic attacks, I never want to feel that way again. I keep telling myself that it won't ever happen again, that this is in the past, that my life is good now and I'm totally safe, but I don't feel reassured and I don't know why.* 🦐

YOU DON'T HAVE TO MAKE PROMISES YOU CAN'T KEEP: TAKING THE PRESSURE OFF THE POSITIVE VALVE

You've come to see that worry is not the detour to take, but what's the alternative? What is the normal sound of a mind at work? What *should* we be thinking? In *My Big Fat Greek Wedding*, the father, Gus Portokalos, believes that Windex is the panacea for everything from a blemish to a swollen toe. Many of us have grown up believing that if there's a problem, positive thinking is the cure-all. Just think positively and you'll feel better.

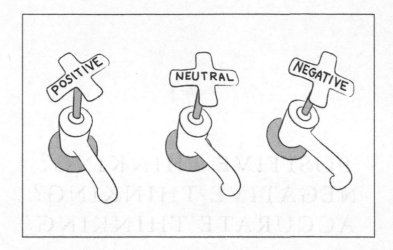

In fact, many of us believe that thinking positively is normal to do always. With that theory, when you don't feel great, you immediately think, *What's wrong with me?* Rather than reading this as a temporary fluctuation in mood, you can dig yourself into a hole. When you don't feel *great*, anxiety ensues. Doubt sneaks in: "Am I really happy? Am I happy enough? Will I stay happy? Am I as happy as that guy?" Suddenly you can't enjoy the very life that you are worried about, because you're not really living it. You're too busy monitoring your level of happiness from the sidelines.

It's time to take the pressure off the positive valve. Rather than trying to think "positive" (how things need to be great) when you are feeling stuck, think "possible" (the multitude of options and directions you could take to resolve the situation). Emotional resilience is about being able to bounce back from the disappointments, hurdles, and obstacles that life presents us along with the gifts, triumphs, and joys. Having the flexibility to see the bumps in the road as normal occurrences helps you more easily access alternate routes and move forward rather than get stuck anguishing over the fact that these challenges have happened in the first place.

The Perils of Positive Thinking

What's wrong with positive thinking? The short answer is: nothing. There is nothing wrong with feeling genuinely positive or even thinking positively when it's real. When you are wowed by the beauty you see, the kindness of another, gearing up for a challenge and you envision your success—it is authentic and based in reality. The problems begin when you disregard reality and apply positive thinking like a disinfectant to kill the negative of what is going on. When you're down and you pretend you're up, there's a problem with credibility. Not only do you not buy it, but the backbreaking stretch causes psychological pain.

So, the bad news is that just trying to be positive when you don't really feel that way won't work and may cause you to feel worse. The important news is that you can cut those stretches out of your daily routine and discard the painful, false grin, and you'll be better off.

It can seem baffling and at times impossible to distinguish "right" and "wrong" ways to think, but we could narrow it down to one simple rule. Think what is real or true, whether happy or sad, and don't tamper with the truth by making the story either more positive or negative than it actually is. Don't say things that would require you to cross your fingers behind your back. In other words, don't lie to yourself. Going too far in either direction, by catastrophizing or by sugar coating, creates an internal conflict and causes the amygdala to start "beeping."

A friend once told me that when she was a child, her mom had two jars in the kitchen—one marked "positive thoughts" and the other marked "negative thoughts." Her mother was instructed to put a penny in the jar whenever she had a certain type of thought. The negative jar was always overflowing, but there was not one single penny that went into that positive thought jar, *ever.*

She may have believed, as we all can in a moment of dejection, that unhappiness is the opposite of happiness, that they are mutually exclusive. But research has documented that in the normal course of life, happiness and sadness, or *positive affect* and *negative affect*, are independent of each other. That is, they are not opposite states like an on-off switch. In happy times, there can be sadness and even loss, and in dark times, you can often find inspiration and connection. You are not locked into feeling one thing or another. Things can change. It's not true that "normal" people feel good all the time. Nor can positive thoughts be forced. That is like repairing a warp in a piece of wood by simply bending it the other way. It will snap. Yikes. Research has also found that when you are down and you force yourself to say "positive" things to yourself, you end up feeling worse. Think about it. When you are feeling great, singing "I Feel Pretty" like Maria in *West Side Story* will pump up your mood. But when you're having a bad day, if you could even muster the pluck to sing it, you would probably want to break something while you sang it. And you're a peaceful person. In the same way that anxiety stretches reality in a negative direction, if you think you should navigate toward constant happiness, you will be forced to tell yourself stories that aren't true. And just like putting fancy paint on a poorly prepared surface, it just won't stick. There's a better way.

Make Possible Thinking the Default Thinking

When you're having a bad day, your inner dialogue may go something like this: *My life is a total disaster, I'm a total failure, I can't do anything right. Nobody cares and why should they?* The negative faucet seems to have a leak—drip, drip, drip—this is wrong, that's wrong, what if this happens? Meanwhile, you could do the far reach for the positive faucet, but as we've just seen, forcing it on won't make you feel better, and given the mismatch with the moment, could likely make you feel worse. What's the other option? I'd like to introduce you to your new best friend. It's what I call "middle faucet." Middle faucet doesn't put a positive or negative spin on life—it's your source of unbiased information. Neutral, non-negative thoughts are the stepping stones to new possibilities.

Take Anna, for example. For years, her discouragement would creep in every morning when her husband would sit down and wait for her to bring breakfast, never thinking to reciprocate. Instead of the negative track—*I'm trapped, my husband is totally unaware of my needs, this marriage isn't working*—turning on the neutral faucet meant thinking: *My husband is used to me getting breakfast for him, that has been our pattern throughout our marriage. He is not trying to ignore me, he is just doing what we are used to. I'd like it to be different. I have options. I can talk to him about my needs.*

The value of these thoughts is not that they are memorable or even noticeable, they are merely factual. They are objective observations. But the facts shift your perspective out of the impossible to the possible. They hand you what's right there in front of you, discreetly making life easier. It's like getting the information without the excessive question marks and exclamation points, and that's a story that we can work with much better. Instead of: *My boss wants to see me??!!!* It's simply: *My boss wants to see me.* It still may not be great news, but it encourages you to wait and see rather than sprint to disaster. The more you learn to reach for these neutral thoughts, the more clearly you'll be able to think about a situation, and the better off you'll feel. You'll no longer have jolts of dread coursing through your veins. When you start to tip too much in the direction of fear or in the direction of clutching onto promises and guarantees, the neutral faucet puts you back in balance, offering you just the information at hand without the instantaneous negative commentary.

You don't need to feel fantastic when you're having a bad day, you just need to know that there are other options and that you're not stuck or trapped in the picture you've painted for yourself. Possible thinking sounds like this: "Right now I'm feeling like things aren't working for me. This project has a glitch in it, and that's making me feel like a failure, but it's just a glitch I haven't figured out yet, and most likely I will be able to solve it like every other glitch I've encountered. So this uncomfortable feeling is temporary. I'll probably work it out and when I do I won't feel this way any more."

Remember, you don't have to be jumping up and down for joy in life all of the time. You don't need a day at the spa to recover from a day jinxed by Murphy's Law, just a day where you can get from Point A to Point B without event. So, whether you are preparing for a wedding, a meeting, your two-year-old's birthday party, or simply a regular day of work, whenever your mind starts commenting unhelpfully—*What if you're late? What if people don't like what you're doing? What if it rains? Why can't you be less anxious? What's wrong with you?*—you can summon your neutral thinking, which reminds you to not get ahead of yourself, just focus on what you are doing now, and trust that if a challenge should arise, you have options about how to handle it once you are actually faced with the situation. The opposite of negative thinking isn't positive thinking; it's simply possible thinking. You will no longer be wedged in a corner—and the difference between being stuck and being free is enormous.

The Power of Non-Negative Thinking

In 1981, psychologists Philip Kendall and Steve Hollon were studying the automatic thoughts of people who were depressed and, in particular, how these thoughts changed as a result of treatment. To explain the results of their study, they coined a new phrase—the power of non-negative thinking. In contrast to the slogan of the time, "the power of positive thinking," they found that when they compared the internal dialogues of depressed and non-depressed adults, and even the thoughts depressed people had before and after treatment, it wasn't the number of positive thoughts that distinguished the groups. It was their "non-negative" or neutral thoughts that made all the difference. Depressed people had more negative thinking than non-depressed people, but after successful treatment there *wasn't* an increase in positive thinking. In fact, positive thinking stayed about the same as before treatment. Successful treatment was linked to a reduction in negative thoughts. The take-home message from this seminal study: The *real* secret to mental health and well-being isn't to repeat positive mantras daily; it is actually to reduce the negative thoughts.

How do we best decrease the frequency of negative thoughts? By not responding to one negative thought with ten more, and instead by cultivating a new habit of practicing neutral thinking instead. It's a better use of our time. Remember that the brain gets better at whatever we do a lot of. So, if you are piling on negative thoughts, this becomes automatic. If, however, when you are having a bad day and you have one negative thought *(I'll never get this project done, and look at the kitchen, it's a mess!)*, you respond not by hammering away at yourself with more accusations *(I am irresponsible, I am incompetent, I can't get anything done)* but instead by simply reaching for a measured, accurate view of what's going on *(I am overtired, that's why my house looks like a disaster to me. This project is hard, and I'm tired and that's why this is overwhelming right now)*, that is how to teach the brain a better way of responding to temporary worries and doubts.

THE NEW DESTINATION: DON'T WORRY, BE ~~HAPPY~~ ACCURATE

According to researchers, at any given moment (and you have 20,000 such moments each day) your mind organizes your experiences as positive, negative, or neutral. Although our preference is to feel good and no one intentionally seeks to feel bad, the psychology is more complicated than you might think. With our engineered survival mentality, we are wired to remember negative moments most keenly. After all, we wouldn't want to make *that* mistake again, whatever that mistake may have been. Positive moments are stored as more of a flash in the pan and fade quickly, as they are important for our well-being but not required for our survival. So, the friend who snubbed us, the critic who panned us, and the soufflé that fell loom larger in our thoughts than the friend who was happy to see us, the praise received, and the gourmet dinner that worked. Neutral moments like the three meals you had today, on the other hand, are barely noticed.

Nudged by our propensity to think in opposites—black or white, up or down, good or bad—it makes sense at first that when your thinking is pulling too far in the negative direction, you frantically turn the wheel the other way, like a tactical ship trying to right itself. Even if you can do a momentary about-face on the surface, feelings don't lie.

The more you remember to go for neutral when you are struggling, the more your mind will remember that pattern, like a frequently visited website that your computer anticipates when

---

TRY THIS

Think about your day. When you start to feel yourself judge or criticize an experience, using words like good, bad, or awful, or when you make negative predictions or generalize about the future, pause, put the judgmental commentary aside, go back and just describe the moment. Tap into your neutral thoughts to ease your transitions. Think of it as doing some job training with your impartial observer. The investment of the training time will pay off greatly in your next "heat of the moment" moment.

Say, for example, your son brings home two C's on his report card. First thought: *He's going to ruin his life!* Pause and remember you have a choice. Rather than heaping on more negative thoughts or letting your worry and anger surge, go for facts: *My son is a good student; yes he got two C's. I don't know why. I'm upset because I don't understand. I need more information. He's probably not happy with this, either.* Notice how your ability to reach for neutral will save both of you the unnecessary trip to disaster and back.

---

you type in the first letter or two. Your mind will fill in, completing the trip on autopilot.

WHAT'S RIGHT ABOUT POSITIVE THINKING? MAKING GENUINE POSITIVE EXPERIENCES A STAPLE IN YOUR LIFE

If you take "truth" as your barometer, of course it's healthy and helpful to be positive, which is a natural, authentic reaction. There is nothing better than genuine joy and happiness dispersed in wonderful though fleeting installments. Whether you are moved by the birth of a baby, thrilled to be collaborating with a favorite colleague, or delighted to get an e-mail from an old friend, you feel it and it's good.

These spontaneous feelings are not manufactured in the factory of your mind. You don't need to stop and think how to react to these good moments; they move you without any effort on your part. Welcome positive thoughts that spring from the positive experiences in your life, but you shouldn't knock yourself out trying to fashion them out of thin air when they just aren't there.

Research has found that being in positive states is not just a *reflection* of satisfaction and good health. As we would expect, intentionally spending time in those states can actually *produce* a feeling of satisfaction and success. It cuts both ways. As you begin to rethink and devalue the benefit of chasing down everything that's wrong or could be wrong, you free yourself up to notice and cultivate deep connections with what is right and good. The benefits are immediate.

How do you translate this to your own life? What captures our attention most days are things going wrong. Occasionally, however, we find a clearing and sit out in our yard, or put a plant in our apartment window, and that simple gesture seems to transport us and create a dramatic shift. You can feel your mood lifted above the line of the status quo. When it's genuine like this, feeling positive has immense power.

If you know how good the positive experiences feel, don't leave them *only* up to chance. There is a time and place for everything. You can't always bring yourself above the line, and depressives should not make that one more thing to get down on themselves about. What you can do is to familiarize yourself with dependable ways to tap into that good feeling: singing in the car, watching Monday-night football with your buddies, reading with your kids at night, saying grace before your meal, walking with your family, volunteering, or whatever it is for you. To follow *your* bliss, you need to know where *your* bliss happens.

What's right about this is instantly clear, but it takes practice. Over time, having a life that includes these buoying experiences convinces us why that life is worth living. It teaches us how to lower stress levels, experience greater satisfaction, and have more to draw on. It exercises our cognitive flexibility muscles so that when hardship comes, we can be more resilient.

FIND WHAT'S RIGHT ABOUT
YOUR NEGATIVE THOUGHTS

An executive came in to see me after having a rough performance review. Yes, it was a recession, yes, he had some family stresses during the review period, but he was devastated by the fact that he didn't get the stellar, flawless review he expected. "Did you bring in a copy?" I asked him. No, he had shredded it immediately after the meeting, he didn't want anyone to see it. Like the children I work with who get upset about a test grade, then crumple up the test and throw it out, my patient was likewise depriving himself of the opportunity to learn from his mistakes.

Two things likely happen when we muster the courage to look at bad news. First, in hindsight, looking back on a situation, often things don't seem so bad. The initial assault of bad news might have surprised you, but when you get ready to experience it again and reread the e-mail or the performance review, the bad news comes in for a soft landing. It can even feel like you are reading

TRY THIS:
Balance Out Your Thoughts for the Day

You have a choice: Do you want a rundown of all the things you did wrong that day, or of the things you did right? When you find yourself spending time cataloging the negative, put a time limit on it—say, two minutes— and then see if you can turn off that faucet and give equal or more time to finding and naming the good in what you've done or experienced with others on that day. Notice what happens to your mood when you focus on your accomplishments, and the ways you may have made people happy that day or the positive things that others did for you. Make a habit of it. Remember if you're having trouble getting *out* of the negative—go through neutral first.

A Higher-Level Challenge

Have you noticed that when someone asks how we are doing—someone who is going to really listen to the answer—we start with what's wrong. Our problem-oriented brain is wired to make it very hard to note the good before listing the bad. But we can change this wiring and prioritize and highlight what's going well, rather than overlook it as inconsequential. Try it. When you do your day or week in review, challenge yourself to start with what went well or what you appreciate. Remember, it will feel strange, as though you are wearing your watch on your left wrist when you've always worn it on your right. But with regular practice this habit of focusing on the good will become stronger. In time you'll find that your retrained brain will start pointing out more good things to you: *"Hey, don't forget to talk about that nice thing that happened at the flower shop."* Then, for a nice change, you can thank your brain.

a different letter, your emotional reaction has changed so much. Why is that? By then, your amygdala's response has receded, making room for your rational mind to receive the news. Second, as there is no better opportunity for learning than from mistakes, courageously looking at what went wrong saves suffering in the long run. Imagine if doctors refused to learn from their surgery complications because it upset them!

Sometimes the negative in life isn't just a matter of perspective; it's real. None of us are immune from tragedy, trauma, hardship, or loss. Researchers have found that in fact, those who recover most resiliently and effectively from these challenges are those who are willing to make a closer inspection of what really happened.

Couldn't you do fine skipping over some of the suffering, putting on a stiff upper lip and moving on? Here's the problem: Pretending that something didn't happen creates a warp and torques the system. Part of you feels bad, another part tries to straighten the warp without acknowledging that it's there. You are depriving yourself of the wisdom or insight that experience has to offer. Don't feel, however, that you have to be stoic and let yourself be awash with your suffering in order to really face it. Breaking down your visits to those difficult feelings into small, manageable doses, as we've seen, is how we are best able to assimilate new information and adjust.

FREEING YOURSELF: IN ACTION

At age twenty-five, Kara had just finished graduate school and was applying for jobs in her field of engineering. Six months after finishing her program, she had no job. She'd moved back home with her parents to save money, a choice that proved both good and bad. They were supportive, but every day that she didn't have a job she felt demoralized.

Kara came to see me because she thought she was doing something wrong and that was the reason she wasn't feeling better. I

YOU AND BEYOND:
Help Spread This Way of Thinking

Sometimes it is hard to know what to say when a friend is either struggling or complaining. You may be tempted to be cheerful and dismissive, saying, "I'm sure everything will be fine." Or the story may pull you in and you might respond with, "Wow, that sounds really awful"—something no one wants to hear. Instead, reach for the middle faucet and reflect back more neutrally and without commentary the facts that you hear. Think to yourself how you would say this without the exclamation points and question marks. Simply hearing the information without the hype of emotion could allow your friend the opportunity to see different possibilities in her situation and save her unnecessary grief. She may say, "Right, I guess it is just one rejection letter," or, "It's just one bad date, not the end of the world." In this way, she can reach the conclusion that is most constructive without you having to do it for her. If you know the person well, explain your approach. That person in turn may save you one day by turning on the middle faucet when you need it most.

asked Kara to tell me what she was doing. Every day she was spending time poring over employment websites, e-mailing contacts, and writing cover letters. All good. She then explained that when she felt discouraged or worried about what was going to happen, she gave herself pep talks, saying it was going to be great, everything would work out. But she said, "The harder I try to make myself feel better, the worse I feel." Worrying that this meant she might be getting depressed, Kara came in for some coaching.

It surprised Kara when I told her that trying to be "positive" was not what she needed to do, especially since it made her feel more despondent. It didn't mean that she didn't believe things would eventually work out, but making promises made her feel uneasy. Kara was doing all the right things to help her situation, and that was the report she needed to tell herself—the status at the moment. Jumping ahead to promises of a happy ending, as likely as they were, made her uneasy because it wasn't true now.

Kara was relieved to know that there wasn't anything wrong with her. The fact that talking positively to herself wasn't working didn't mean she wasn't capable of being happy or that she was depressed. Her thoughts were just getting ahead of her in a positive way, which made her as uneasy as getting ahead of herself in a negative or anxious way. The answer lay in staying with what felt true and real right now: "This is not easy, I'm doing all the right things, I'm going to try to be patient and stick with my plan."

PART II

The Four Steps

The Master Plan for Overcoming Anxious Thinking to Create the Life You Want

> *Knowledge is power: when you know how your brain works, you can take whatever steps you need to anticipate problems and play to strengths.*
>
> —JOHN J. RATEY, MD, AND CATHERINE JOHNSON, PHD, *SHADOW SYNDROMES*

THE PAUSE THAT CREATES TIME, DISTANCE, AND POSSIBILITY

We are storytellers, constantly narrating the events in our life, and the four steps ensure the story is about *us* and *our* lives, rather than the extremes and magnifications of our untrustworthy imaginations. These anxious story lines can get stuck in our minds and multiply and therefore *seem* more important than they are, but with practice, we can learn to effectively shake them out of the net. The shorter their stay with us, the less trouble they cause. Imagine that the stories you tell yourself are written in pencil, not etched in stone; each one is only a hypothesis, a starting point to then be proven or dismissed based on further investigation. The overprotective brain stays ready to take the smallest slipup as an

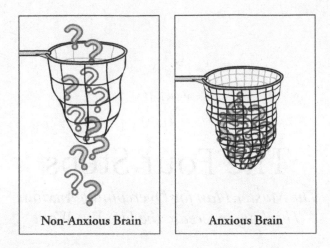

Non-Anxious Brain   **Anxious Brain**

opportunity to give us the boot. We need to look further and not be ready to give in so quickly!

How do you get from the noise in your head to the real situations you face? The four steps presented in this book help rework your hasty first takes on situations into the grounded, rational interpretation that is your path to a better life. As you've seen, the thoughts are natural first reactions to uncertainty or disappointment, one possibility among many interpretations of the moment. It's not about stopping these thoughts cold, it's about seeing them as questions or predictions to be proven or dismissed when synced with reality.

Stories have a beginning, a middle, and an end. Anxiety grabs the pen for the first lines. *This was the worst day of my life, I have no idea how I'm going to deal with this.* And so we are launched. It is up to you to change the plotline, to open up to possibilities rather than see your life as an open-and-shut case. The four steps presented in this part—relabeling, getting specific, optimizing, and mobilizing—will show you how.

1. First, pause and consider the voice—is it personally relevant to you? Or is it the universal first reaction when something

Step One:
Pause and Relabel

Don't just jump when anxiety tells you to do so. Consider the source, reduce its authority, and take a second to stamp the thought as an exaggerated reaction of the overprotective brain, signaling fear, not fact.

Step Two:
Get Specific

Narrow down the "everything is wrong" feeling to the one thing that might be.

Step Three:
Optimize

Expand the possibilities of how you are seeing the problem and the array of solutions to find the one that works best.

Step Four:
Mobilize

Get unstuck; decide which solution you are ready to implement. Get moving in a new direction one small step at a time.

goes wrong? Recognizing the voice of absolutes and recalibrating the significance of its message is called *relabeling.* Instead of stamping the message as *Urgent,* restamp it as an overreaction, a false alarm. This essential first step creates distance from your anxious thoughts.

2. You create context for your concerns by *getting specific,* seeing fears or doubts not in a vacuum, but in perspective. This

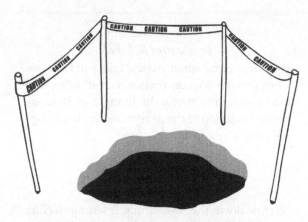

**YOU DON'T HAVE TO GO IN THERE—
IT'S YOUR CHOICE**

step is about narrowing down your focus to the actual issues
that you're facing and putting them into the smallest box,
rather than the large and unwieldy package that you are first
presented with: *Here's my whole life—I have to fix it!*.

3. We create choices for ourselves by *optimizing* or looking at
   our situation from multiple vantage points—invoking the
   voice of our wisest self, or others whom we trust, to weigh
   in. When you pinpoint what really deserves your attention,
   you want to move around to get the seats with the best view
   of the problem and the solutions. Your first seat may be up
   so close to the problem that it looks monstrous.

4. The last step is to release yourself from that stuck place by
   considering even one alternative to the gridlock that a worry
   or doubt can create. By understanding the problems and solutions, we create action by *mobilizing*, not just sitting stew-
   ing in our juices but taking steps to improve our lives. You've
   made the leap from unproductive thinking to embracing a
   more optimal and accurate perspective on your life and now
   you're ready to put that better understanding of your life and
   your choices into action.

Just because an anxious thought came to you doesn't mean you have to make a case for or against it. You don't have to go digging deeper in the hole of doubt or worry; in fact, following these simple steps will help you see your fear for what it is: not a sign of danger, but a signal of change and growth ahead. Instead of falling in to that hole, you may well be able to just go around it, confident that your attention and resources are free to be used elsewhere.

CREATING FLEXIBILITY: YOU HAVE OPTIONS

Think of these steps as a four-part harmony. Although they work together, at any given moment, one step may be more important to whatever you're facing. Because there are many different types of strategies for each step, you may want to read with a pencil or sticky notes on hand and keep track of the ones that you want to try first or those that work best for you.

Chapter 4

STEP ONE: PAUSE AND RELABEL (OR, DON'T BELIEVE EVERYTHING YOU THINK)

There's a name for it, and names make all the difference in the world.

—DAVID BYRNE

❧ *As soon as I think about what I have to do tomorrow, I'm instantly bombarded with everything that will go wrong—I'll be late, I won't get everything done, people will be angry at me, I won't be prepared. I can't stand the thoughts, but I can't get them out of my head!* ❧

WHO'S CALLING PLEASE?

We would all be a bit suspicious if our internal voice started saying things like, "Hey, you have absolutely nothing to worry about. Life is totally great! You are simply fabulous. Everything you do is perfect and gosh darn it, people like you!" We would want to see some

identification before letting those crazy ideas in the door. And yet, when our internal voice hits us with the other side of the coin: *What if everything you do falls through? What will you do with your life?* or *You totally blew this, you're a mess, you should give up!* we seem to hang on every word. These statements wouldn't make it past the sloppiest of fact-checking operations, yet these are the very stories we, prematurely, bring to press. These thoughts get the VIP treatment, gaining top-level security clearance to every nook and cranny of our existence: past, present, and future. Making their way down the hallways of our psyche, they trash the place. But hang on, weren't we just fine two seconds before they arrived, and won't we be fine again after we finally kick the stinkers out a few hours later?

If only anxious and negative thoughts showed up on the caller ID in the mind's eye—"1–800-Unreliable and Unrealistic," "Exaggerations-R-Us," or more to the point, "Knee-Jerk Reactions, *to go*"—life would be so much easier. The good news is that you don't have to stop anxious or negative thoughts from calling, you just need to know how to handle the calls. Relabeling is the caller ID. It puts the right tag on the thought, which instantly reduces the importance of the message, and that in turn decelerates the nervous system. We're all much smarter than our first thoughts. We just need to know who we've got on the line. You can't help who calls, but you can decide how long you let them carry on before hanging up. Not sure if it's worry or something real? Put that call on hold for a second. If you feel better, chances are it was not a call you really needed to take.

NAMES MAKE ALL THE
DIFFERENCE IN THE WORLD

When I was a child, my family took a boat trip to the Everglades. Our guide, eager to please his audience and make the trip worthwhile, would excitedly point to any dark-green blob along the shore and cry—"Alligator!" Then, as the boat got closer to the amorphous mass of stagnant material, he would correct himself resignedly and say, "Oh, no, my mistake. It's just vegetation." Our emotions were perfectly synchronized with our guide's proclamations. We got worked up every time it seemed like the real thing, but let go immediately when we saw there was no alligator. There was, needless to say, a lot of vegetation on that trip.

The fact is, names do make all the difference. Knowing what you're looking at and naming it appropriately is essential. We don't need to live life on the edge of our seats, especially because most of the time what's nipping at our heels is just vegetation— and it doesn't bite.

Whatever the "it" is that you encounter, you need to decide: alligator, vegetation, or something in between. Your first thought, courtesy of the amygdala, is usually like that jumpy tour guide— pointing out trouble at the least sign. It jumps in to surge our adrenaline with: *This is a terrible situation! Do something fast!* But unlike the guide, it does not correct false alarms or mistakes. That's where you can come in with your label maker. If you can pause and relabel the disaster as coming from a questionable authority, then you can decide if the problem truly exists. So you feel like the worst mom in the world because you forgot to give your child an umbrella and he got soaked? Just vegetation. Feel incompetent because your boss chose your co-worker's proposal and not yours? Vegetation again. Don't let those first thoughts question the entirety of your self-worth, which, by the way, was pretty much intact just two minutes before. Relabel the thought as unreliable. Because we're wired to jump at anything that looks suspicious or wiggles in the grass, somebody up there needs to be sorting the vegetation from the alligators.

YOU ALREADY KNOW HOW TO RELABEL

Relabeling is a skill that you do naturally. When you come home from work at 6:00 PM and see the clocks flashing 12:00, you don't run around acting like it's noon or midnight. You relabel, put a different caption on the picture you are seeing, and think, *power outage.* It's also how we discreetly tune out Auntie Maude's litany of health concerns because we've "relabeled" them, by chalking it up to Auntie Maude. We devalue or reduce the authority of the thoughts based on the source. Now apply it to yourself: You're not dysfunctional, you're *sleep deprived*; you're not incompetent, you're a *rookie.* Relabeling changes your *reaction* to the thoughts, which ensures that you don't waste time changing your behavior because of a false alarm. Instead of sending you spinning in spirals of fear and doubt, relabeling lands you gently right back to the point before the worry barged in.

The analogy of junk mail is my favorite way to explain the human capacity to relabel. Both worry and junk mail come in the same mail slot, both talk about serious matters—your future, your health, your financial successes—and both speak with great authority, noting, "This is your final notification! Don't be left unprotected! This is an offer you can't afford to miss!" Yet no matter how personalized the message seems to be, you know that junk mail warnings are sent to millions of people, so you throw them out and move on. Similarly, as you get to know worry, you can see that certain warnings—*that's a mistake, you'll regret it, what a fool, you totally messed up*—are also sent to millions of people every moment of every day across the globe. They are simply the universal, default messages that we all experience when we first encounter an unknown or a disappointment. Just as you sort junk mail from important letters, brain mail needs a similar filter. You don't need to believe everything you think. Keep the thoughts

that really matter, and toss the rest—don't waste time reading the fine print.

Relabeling doesn't make the worry thoughts go away—not right away. But, by changing your reaction to them, it changes their significance. If you don't get alarmed by them, you won't need to dwell or elaborate on them. You can instead carry on with what you were doing before you were interrupted by worry. If you discover a mistake or something that does require your attention, you can focus on it constructively rather than with anguish. Relabeling offers a powerful way to retrain your brain to learn what is worth your attention. Working consistently on flexing this sorting system in the brain means that over time, these thoughts won't appear as frequently or as urgently.

YOU DECIDE WHAT DESERVES YOUR ATTENTION

As you are reading right now, you are hearing your "reading voice" in your head. Meanwhile, there are likely other ambient sounds around you—children playing in the background, traffic, air conditioners, heating vents, subway trains whirring. Just as you don't

have to shut down those sounds in order to focus here, you don't have to stop the sounds of worry in order to think clearly. You simply need to classify and hear them more as background noise—and place your intention and attention elsewhere. In order to dismiss worry, you need to recognize the familiar sound track playing in your mind. Notice how your worry sounds the same as your spouse's or your friend's, which in turn sounds pretty much the same as people halfway across the globe. Because everyone's worry sounds similar, this helps assure us that its message means everything about the general nature of worry, and very little about the particular nature of us.

STRATEGIES FOR RELABELING THOUGHTS

Strategy #1: Rename the Narrator

Language is power. When the thoughts *What if I never get a job, what if I never get married, what if I never get anywhere in my life* fly into the inbox of our mind, our default processing makes us take those words to heart. They attack us when we're awake, they multiply in our sleep.

Who is talking to you that way? Must you tolerate it? Do they have the authority to make those sweeping claims and predictions? Short answer: no. Take the millisecond to recognize the telltale "oh no" and "what if's," stamp them as unreliable, and hand the microphone over to another voice in your head. Let your voice of reason take a stab at describing what just happened. When we say, *That's my anxiety, that's an amygdala surge, that's my inner pessimist pecking away at me,* or even just simply, *That's grossly premature,* we begin to have a choice in how we narrate the events of our life. We are no longer obligated to follow anxious interpretations simply because they get there first in our minds.

Putting a name on a potentially frightening or destructive process takes the mystery out. It also separates you from the thoughts, which allows you to begin to get perspective on them. By relabeling your *worst thoughts* as simply your *first thoughts*, the knee-jerk things we say to ourselves *without thinking,* you can save yourself the misery of the thousand recalculations of your self-worth, the speculations of doom and gloom, the stripping of your confidence.

For Caroline, naming her worry "The Perfectionist" helped her dismiss the running critique about everything she did in her day. Instead of feeling bad, as she had before, Caroline began to recognize that this was like a button that got pushed by accident. She stopped paying attention to the button and made a conscious choice to refocus on what she was doing. Says Caroline, "It hit me, I'm not a bad person—I'm careful. People who aren't half as careful as I am don't feel bad about themselves like I do. I thought I was making so many mistakes, but that's when I realized that *I* wasn't the problem—it was just these thoughts."

Luke called his worry "Existential Man" because the running commentary injected in his day questioned, "Is this really meaningful? Does this really matter?" The distraction demoralized him because in fact he liked his life, and it did matter to him. Rather than proving Existential Man wrong, Luke would just hand the thought back to its rightful owner, often with a wry "good luck with that one." He no longer felt that he had to stop and chew on

---

TRY THIS

Use clip art or your own sketching abilities to draw a portrait of your worry. What name best befits your worry's qualities: The Nag, Crisis Caller, Exaggerator Man, The Critic, Fido the Barking Amygdala? Hang it up on your wall, and when you get a "call" that doesn't belong to you, you can say with confidence: "thanks, but I'm not interested."

---

it himself. Relabeling frees you from your anxiety—you are no longer beholden to the thoughts. You are in charge.

Strategy #2: Hear It in a Different Voice

In one *Saturday Night Live* episode, the actor James Earl Jones, known for his distinctive bass voice, read from the Brooklyn phone book and made it sound like a haunting Shakespearean soliloquy. Suddenly something as benign as "Michael Smith, 1524 Silver Street, 718-555-0102" sounded like a terrible curse or a harbinger of the apocalypse. Tone captures all.

Imagine using this strategy in reverse. When your internal critic comes at you James Earl Jones–style, alternating between doom and gloom, dub in the voice of Adam Sandler, or the squeaky nasal voice of SpongeBob SquarePants. The way you hear messages goes right to your central information–processing desk in the brain and produces an instant emotional reaction. You can use that fact to your benefit by taking repetitive intrusive thoughts and having a more lighthearted understudy say their lines. We wouldn't dream of making light of important messages, but to unburden ourselves of unhelpful messages that only *sound* important, this strategy gives us the lift we need.

Vincent had incessant, intrusive thoughts about danger. Although he was now a parent himself, he would hear the serious voices that parents have—*"Watch! you could get hurt, Be careful!"*—over and over as he went about his day. It upset and embar-

rassed him, and he knew it wasn't normal, but it would often shake him up. We worked on changing the sound of the voice and even singing the warnings to "Row, row, row your boat" or "Happy Birthday." Embarrassment gave way to relief. Vincent had never thought that he would be able to free himself from these attacks. He didn't even need to sing the songs most of the time, usually just thinking *Happy Birthday* would help him move out of panic mode.

TRY THIS

You may feel a little self-conscious doing this, but go ahead and try it. Say the worry words in your head—or even out loud if you dare—in a different accent from yours, a Southern twang or drawl, a Surfer Dude, a jaunty British clip. It's not that there are no worries to consider, but you are receiving the hyped version, and you need to separate the problem from the hype. This doesn't instantly change reality any more than the negative voice does, but it changes *you*. You are effectively picked up and put back down at your starting line, instead of being placed at a disadvantage from your anxious or negative thinking. Now your clear thinking can begin.

Strategy #3: Separate Yourself from the Thought

If you want to get rid of the static in your head, you need to recognize that it's interference on the line, not the true message. Take a negative thought you are having—*I have so much to do I'll never get it done*—and now recast it from a distance. *I am having thoughts that . . . I'll never get my work done. My worry is telling me that . . . I'll never get it done.* Notice how this tiny tweak of semantics opens up working space between you and the experience you are having. It's no longer a done deal. *I'm a failure* is now merely one notoriously unreliable opinion.

Don't be surprised if at first this feels like cheating. This reaction is a result of having taken these thoughts seriously for so long, taking them at their word out of blind habit, not because of the payoff they've yielded. Keep going and notice day by day how much faster you seem to be able to switch off the worry track. It sells itself. Very quickly this won't seem like cheating at all, but instead will seem very wise, and the worry will feel like the voice that's pulling a fast one.

Strategy #4: Throw Back the Boot

When you are in the middle of an important meeting and think, *Lunch!* you don't
walk out of the meeting saying, "I hope
you don't mind, I'm hungry. Bye!" You filter the thought and get back to the more
important business at hand. We have
that capacity for selective attention, but

we don't think to implement that with worry thoughts because
they *seem* important. Attention-grabbing keywords like *disaster,
danger, ruined, horrible, idiot, fool* make it hard to pull ourselves
away from that plot line. But pull we must. Those key words don't
belong. Remember the amygdala's reactions can be overkill for
everyday life. If you imagine your inner dialogue as literally a
stream of consciousness, these thoughts could be considered the
random solitary boot or soda bottle that pollutes the stream. If
you saw a boot in your refrigerator, would you think, *Oh well, I
guess it's boot for dinner tonight*? Or would you think, *That doesn't
belong. I don't eat boot. I'm throwing it out!* Even if that boot ap-
pears in the fridge night after night, it doesn't make it any more
edible, and it certainly doesn't mean you're going to have to learn
to digest boot. Just because an extreme thought enters your mind,
even if it does so repeatedly, doesn't mean you have to grab hold
of it and change yourself or your plans accordingly.

Strategy #5: Downgrade the Worry

Remember the barking dog idea from Chapter 1? When worry
barks, just like your neighbor's mutt does when you get out of
your car, it plays with your emotions, putting you in a state of high
alert. You know you are safe, but in response to that alarming
bark, your adrenaline surges. To reset your baseline, it can help
to state the obvious. When you are upset, there is no sense of
scale or proportion; it's more of an on-off switch than a dimmer.
Create a numeric scale from 1 to 10, or use low, medium, high,

or color-code it, downgrading the risk from the red zone down to yellow, or possibly even green. The codes help you identify: Is this a big deal or a little deal? Say it in your head: "This feels bad, but it's actually just a 5." Either way, you will have relabeled an emergency moment, shut off the alarms, and gotten back to the business of your life.

HESITATION: IS IT OK TO RELABEL WHEN THE THOUGHTS FEEL SO TRUE?

When someone kicks you even by accident, it hurts. When you hear unpleasant thoughts even if they are unfounded, they trigger an emotionally painful reaction, too. When we think, *I am so lame, I can't carry on a conversation, I have nothing interesting to say, that person must think I'm a fool, that's it, I'm going to be alone* our stomachs go in knots, our heart beats faster, and we mistakenly equate *feeling bad* with evidence that these wildly distorted thoughts are true. It's natural to feel bad when you're being attacked, but it doesn't mean it was deserved. Just as feeling scared doesn't mean you are in danger, feeling discouraged doesn't mean you're sunk. Feelings are feelings, facts are facts. Like the sound track to a film, our feelings get manipulated by our extreme thoughts. We think: *I'm so upset, this has to be real, I must be right about this.* Time to push the mute button and let the facts narrate the story, not the feelings.

WHEN IT'S NOT ALL IN YOUR HEAD: WHAT TO DO WHEN THE MESSAGES HAVE BEEN SAID TO YOU

"What if you get hurt?" "Oh please, you shouldn't even try!" "You're not good enough for that." When the messages in your first thoughts are things that have actually been said to you in real life, this is what I call anxiety in stereo—you are hearing the same thoughts inside and outside of your head. But this doesn't mean

---

TRY THIS:
Consider the Source

Create a cast of characters to help you sort maladaptive thoughts from reasonable ones. Draw two boxes on a page. In one, write the names for the automatic negative thoughts you have. For example, The Magnifier, Disaster Guy, The Critic, The Alarmist, The Guilt Machine, Misery Man, or more factually, *unreliable, impulsive, amygdala-driven.* In the second box list the names for your logical, accurate thoughts: Logic Woman, Equanimity Man, Einstein, or simply, Voice of Reason. Maybe the first box is the Farm Team in sports—rookies that would swing at anything—versus the pros in the Major League who recognize the real thing when they see it.

Then, take a worry or criticism from today and run it by the narrators in each box to see how differently the stories are told. Notice how differently you feel listening to them. Just like you would hang up or roll your eyes when a telemarketer calls, as you start to relabel your negative thoughts in a humorous or derogatory way, you won't absorb them—you can dismiss them more easily and get them off the line. Next time you have an anxious or negative thought, activate your internal caller ID. Repeat daily! You'll be amazed how much faster you can end the conversation.

---

you can't relabel them accurately so that they have only the authority they deserve. Maybe the stamp is "My sister's overprotectiveness," "Dad's pessimism," "Mom's fears," "My brother's alcoholism," or "My boss's unbelievable ego."

You can authoritatively and even compassionately decide that these thoughts have little to do with you, and more to do with someone else's stuff. You don't have to judge others for what they may have projected on you, but neither do you have to be beholden to their projections. Just because Dad barrages you with pessimism, you needn't let it weigh you down. You have choices about how to proceed. If these perspectives are not just from the past but are in your current life and there is trust and room for levity, you could relabel "out loud"—"Wow, what you are saying sounds exactly like the critic in my head—are you two related?" Or, you may decide to create more distance in the relationship, even moving on from it in some cases. Whatever you do, know that you always have choices about what to do with thoughts— including the ones that belong to someone else.

In this chapter we have looked at powerful strategies that use re-labeling to take back control of the wheel when you have a worry or negative intrusion. With these general concepts under your belt, in the next chapter, "Step Two: Get Specific" you'll learn how to hone in on the real problem that got the anxious and negative thinking started in the first place. You'll become expert at shrinking and narrowing down the seemingly permanent, pervasive, personal problem to its actual temporary, specific, and often impersonal source.

FREEING YOURSELF: IN ACTION

As a forty-year-old successful executive, Steven thought he'd be enjoying the fruits of his labors more at this point in his life. He had a loving wife and four children, a solid career, and good health, but he was plagued by thoughts that he wasn't enjoying himself "enough." Especially when he was at a party, with his children, or playing golf, he would think, *Is this really fun to you? Maybe there's something wrong with you that you aren't having enough fun.* Then it would take root from there—*If I were a better father, I wouldn't be thinking about this. If I were more successful, I would just be enjoying things.* Steven could have been enjoying things much more if he hadn't been entertaining these thoughts.

YOU AND BEYOND

There are things that we can do, kindly, to save each other grief, like discreetly alerting a friend to the tiny but undeniable piece of green spinach lodged in his teeth. When you are witness to someone berating themselves with doubt and criticism, or spiraling with fear and worry, you can save them grief by helping them to separate themselves from their thoughts, rather than responding as if their extreme thoughts were accurate and cause for cheering them up. Try saying: "Isn't it amazing how worry can hit you when you're down?" As with the spinach, you can be a mirror for what's getting stuck. And that's a mirror we can all use from time to time.

We gave those thoughts a name: "Calculator Man." Rather than letting Steven stay in the moment, the thoughts ran a tab in his head, ringing up his total. It's not good for us to calculate our satisfaction quotient at any given moment. By giving that thought and experience a name, Steven was able to quickly dismiss these intrusions and stay more focused in the present. He was grateful to have an effective way of not having to detour out of the moment every time that thought came along. Instead, he could stay on the path that he was already on and experience it more deeply.

Chapter 5

STEP TWO: GET SPECIFIC

Narrow Down the Problem to the One Thing That Really Matters

No problem can be solved until it is reduced to some simple form.

—JOHN PIERPONT MORGAN

❦ *I need to know how to stop being nervous when I meet a new client. What am I worrying about? Everything!* ❦

WOULD THE REAL PROBLEM PLEASE STAND UP?

If worrying were an Olympic sport, then we could get awarded for imagining the most far-flung catastrophes or for executing the fastest downward spirals. But it isn't, so we don't. Whether it's opening a bill and thinking, *I'll never be able to pay this*, or getting a vague text from your girlfriend and thinking, *She didn't sound happy, she's going to break up with me*, or even having a friend's baby happen to cry in your arms and thinking, *If I made a baby cry, how will I ever be a good father?* we are exceptionally skilled

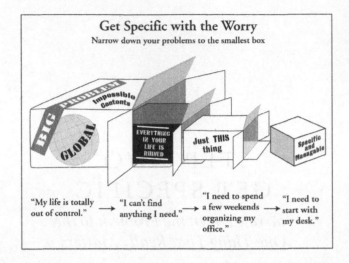

at jumping to conclusions based on that initial amygdala hijack in which our imaginations have run wild. We can't blame ourselves from wanting to predict what's next for us, but replaying over and over in your mind the exact way the lab technician said good-bye to you for clues about what your test results may be is not the best way to prepare yourself. How do we quickly snap back to reality? We need to reread the situation with the anxiety on mute to see what's really there. When you're upset or worried about *one thing*, the equivalent of a neurological flash-mob instantly assembles, creating a cascade of many possible things to worry about. Suddenly, it's not clear what the problem is and isn't, especially when every dreadful thought sounds so compelling and important. Your mood plummets under the weight of so much bad news.

Yet has any of this actually happened, or is it likely to? No. Somewhere amid the clutter of catastrophizing sits the actual problem, patiently waiting to be discovered. How do you break through? By getting specific. Rather than rushing in to solve the most global problem presented by the amygdala, the one that will only fit in a big box, you would be far better served by taking the

---

TRY THIS:
Go from the Biggest "Problem Box" to the Smallest
Remember the Facts and Feelings exercise in Chapter 2?
Feelings are in the biggest box. Let yourself go with the
feelings first, then work your way down to the specific
facts that fit in the smallest box.

---

time to narrow the worry to the actual problem, which most often
fits manageably into a very small box.

Albert Einstein is quoted as saying that if he had only an hour
to save the world, he would spend fifty-five minutes defining the
problem and five minutes on the solution. It's true that once we
reduce the initial daunting perception down to the matter at
hand, the solution is often obvious to us, and the problem resolves
quickly. The more your focus shifts to attend to imagined catastrophes, the more you shortchange yourself in solving real issues
that you face. And if those issues remain stealthy—bothering you
under the surface—your anxiety will have a constant trigger. Getting specific means locating the real problem that got lost in the
shuffle of worry. You can save yourself much anguish by slowing
down and finding the most accurate and adaptive interpretation
to match the situation in front of you.

Often, the real problem is surprisingly small, given the anxiety
storm it has triggered, but even when more serious challenges
exist, we will be far more effective in addressing them in their
most condensed form. We need to keep narrowing down our
fears until we find what is truly of value or truly at stake. So, rather
than stopping at our first impression, we instead need to persevere to find the issue at hand. Anxiety can dream big, and ratchet
up distress accordingly, but that doesn't reflect what is going on
in your life. No matter what real challenges you may be facing,
remember, anxiety's version of the story is always wrong.

IN SEARCH OF THE ISOLATED EVENT

When your thinking gets negative, the brain registers a small snag, glitch, disappointment, or discouragement as a signal that all is lost. To the outside observer, you were late for a meeting, or you fumbled slightly your introduction at the fund-raiser, but for you, these occurrences set off terrible consequences for the rest of your day—or even the rest of your life. It's not just one thing that went wrong, it's that the one thing set off a chain reaction like unstoppable dominoes tipping over and leaving your imagined future in ruinous shambles. Your reputation changed irrevocably, your opportunities were compromised. Wait, what happened to isolated events? The key is to shrink the problem back from the *everything* that is *ruined forever* to the one isolated event that may have occurred. After all, there may actually be something you need to learn or improve upon, and you'll miss it if you're looking at the whole picture being off.

YOU ALREADY KNOW HOW TO GET SPECIFIC

We all use this "narrow it down" skill on a regular basis. For example, think of the proverbial bad hair day. We don't think: *I have terrible hair and it will always look bad!* We get specific and acknowledge that on this particular day our coif is not cooperating. When the coffee isn't good from our favorite coffee shop, we don't think, *This place is horrible;* we just say, *That barista is having a rough day.* Getting specific means you don't change your theory based on that single event. You distinguish between trends and outliers or exceptions and limit the scope of something that went wrong to the situation at hand.

We tend to be great about getting specific with *other* people's fears, but this can be quickly forgotten when it comes to our own emotions. When a friend comes to you freaked out about an upcoming event like a party, a wedding, or the birth of her first child, you can see right through the tempest in which she's spinning. You know if she could just settle down for a second, she could fit

GETTING SPECIFIC WITH THE FUTURE

Ask yourself:

- What exactly are you afraid of?
- What are you picturing will happen?
- How much of you believes that is likely to happen?
- What other things do you think are more likely?

GETTING SPECIFIC WITH THE PAST

Ask yourself:

- What's the isolated event that just happened?
- What are you afraid the consequence of that will be?
- What do you really think the actual consequence of that will be?

what seems like a huge storm into a tiny teacup, and then she could tell you the one thing that she is *really* most afraid of. In this chapter we'll look at ways to develop that skill with yourself.

Fears start out either too vague, as in, *I'm afraid and I don't know why,* or too unwieldy, as in *What if nothing works, what if I am a total failure?* To right-size your anxiety, narrow down your initial take to the heart of the matter, so that you first see if it is even realistic, and then figure out ways to master the fear. When you stay at the unwieldy stage with your fear, you feel helpless to solve the problem and the helplessness becomes a sign to you that the problem really *is* hopeless. It's not hopeless; it's just not in a form you can work with yet. The problem is just in a box that's too big.

FREEING YOURSELF: IN ACTION

Christina walked into a session, plunked down on the couch, and said, "I have no real friends! Everybody is so self-absorbed and inconsiderate. I mean, they know what a hard time I'm having with my mom being sick. I'm done with them!"

KEY QUESTIONS FOR GETTING SPECIFIC

- What worries me the most?
- What exactly am I picturing will go wrong?
- How likely is that to happen?
- What is the thing that I really believe *will* happen?
- What are the steps I can take to make sure that doesn't happen?
- What is a more likely outcome?
- Is there anything I need to do to encourage that outcome?
- Does everything feel this way, or is it just one thing that does?
- Is this a temporary or a permanent problem?
- What part of this can I control, and what part is not within my control?

Because we had talked about this before, I responded, "Oh no, wait, smallest box, smallest box!" and Christina was able to start the work of figuring out the real problem. She was feeling very alone and despondent but also anxious, because she knew it would not be good for her to cut off from everyone now. In trying to narrow things down to the straw that broke the camel's back, Christina could see that one friend she reached out to was too busy to talk at a time when Christina really needed her.

When we went through the boxes further to narrow it down, the problem boiled down to the fact that Christina hadn't really told her closest friends what was going on. Christina needed to talk to one or two of her closest friends and tell them just how bad things were with her mother and that she might need extra support from them. So, what started as Christina's giving up on humanity got narrowed down to giving up, temporarily, on a friend in a bad moment. She now had a plan with some proactive assertiveness to prevent that situation from happening in the future.

Christina went from feeling hopeless to pinpointing what she could do. She could say, "I actually think they'll be really supportive." When left to choose between giving up on your whole life and giving up on the one thing that went wrong, think small. Give up, temporarily, on the smallest thing that you can fix.

WHAT ARE YOU REALLY AFRAID OF?

In the childhood story of Chicken Little, an erstwhile hero believes he must save the world when he feels something drop on his head. He immediately concludes the worst, that the sky is falling and the world is ending. In the end, when he is able to walk himself back to the initial data point ("something fell on my head"), he sees that the disaster was merely a small twig that the wind had blown down. You don't have to imagine and use your energy preparing for vague or remote scenarios. The more you focus on the right things, the better you feel and the more prepared you are for life.

NARROWING DOWN THE FEAR

Worry tricks us into believing that problems are bigger than life. You need to recognize the trick or tangle when it happens, and rather than assume that it's true, you can decipher what really belongs in your worry box. The strategies below are about separating the worry from the truth.

Strategy #1: Go from "What If?" to "What Is" to "What Else?"

In medical school, when faced with a list of a patient's symptoms, students are taught to think of the most likely scenario first (strep throat), not the most exotic or unlikely (malaria). Remember that entertaining the least likely scenario doesn't protect or prepare you. While you anguish over terrible consequences that haven't occurred, you could be preparing yourself for those that might, or better yet, be preventing them.

Do the side-by-side comparison from Chapter 2. Draw two lines down the middle of a piece of paper. Place "What if's" (the worries) in the first column, "What is" (the facts) in the middle, and "What else" (what you think is most likely) in the third column. The first column is born more in a haunted house full of things jumping from behind dark corners. The second and third come from a brightly lit conference table at a think tank with your name on the door. Where can you do your best work?

Strategy #2: Fight All or None Thinking

Getting more specific and narrowing down the worry means accurately assessing the degree of risk you take. We often say things like, "I have *no* idea how this will turn out" or "I have *no* idea what I'm going to do now," creating a limitless sky of fate's dark clouds, despite the fact that you have some pretty good ideas about what you'll do or what will happen. Risk-talk keeps the amygdala on alert and anxiety builds on the miscalculation of that risk. You need to be disciplined and manage that open-ended risk by right-sizing it. Reel in the astronomical risk and get it down to a 1-to-10 scale. Put a number on it. Just because risk exists, doesn't mean it's big. When the number-crunching, logical part of your brain is engaged, it shuts down the worry part. Another way that we get pulled into anxiety is by thinking that unless everything is good, it's bad: If I can't do this, I can't do anything. If she doesn't understand this about me, she doesn't understand anything. If my friend didn't invite me to the party, I have no friends. Take out the "Some Shaker" you learned about in Chapter 2, and remember that there are usually *some things* that are working even when *some things* are not. Look for them.

Strategy #3: Turn Statements into Questions

I hate my life. Everything is terrible. I can't do anything right. Case closed. Or is it? One way to undo the foregone conclusions is to turn these proclamations into hypotheses or questions that are open to interpretation. Do I really hate my life, or am I unhappy with what's going on right now? What is making me feel this way? Do I really feel like I can't do anything right, or is just one, or even a couple of things making me feel frustrated right now? Rather than argue with yourself, the questions engage you in a constructive conversation. If you find that your answers are all negative, then, like the child who refuses help, the best conclusion isn't that you're right about your life, it's that this isn't the right time to have that conversation with yourself. It will be unproductive. Tell yourself that you'll come back later and try again.

Strategy #4: The Paradoxical Approach: Expand to Contract

Sometimes the best way to back up and get perspective on a situation is to go *too* far with it. Imagine you are at a party and you blank on the boss's husband's name. You witness yourself being instantly catapulted into a black hole of shame and inadequacy. *Of all people to forget, now she'll hold it against me. I looked like such a fool.* Those first thoughts are gaining on you and you know that the longer you are tied up feeling bad, the less able you'll be to salvage the situation.

Rather than keeping that insult or personal attack at a low boil, turn up the heat, exaggerate, and watch this approach break the hold of that thought much more quickly. This technique is called flooding. By letting yourself get soaked in your fear or embarrassment, paradoxically, you can pull out of it sooner. So, if you thought, *"That was clearly the very worst faux pas ever committed, and it will certainly be emblazoned on everyone's memory from this day forward because people really do hang on my every word,"* after an initial surge in anxiety, the ridiculousness of the charge releases you. Sound strange? Try it now with something you're feeling uneasy about. Go overboard and blow the consequences of your misstep out of proportion on purpose. Nothing swings open the door to reason and rationality more than absurdity. It works very well with future events, too. *I will totally freeze up on that date. I will have nothing at all to say. It will be the longest silence in the history of dating, ever. It will be an Academy Award–winning performance of embarrassment.* Like the ping of a text message, reality comes to you: *It won't be that bad.*

An important logistical point with flooding is to not stop before you get the job done. Remember that desensitization works like a cold swimming pool. It feels uncomfortable until you adjust. Say you're feeling like a terrible mom because your child was the only student who didn't have his props ready for the school play in time for the dress rehearsal because you forgot. You can stay at a low level of recrimination for a long time, trying unsuccessfully to reassure yourself that it wasn't that bad, or you can turn it up and say: *"You are the worst mother. Your son will probably never forget this; he will be talking about it in therapy for years.* After the initial cringe stage, where you think, *Why am I saying this to myself? That's exactly what I'm afraid of!* the hold breaks and it sounds ridiculous. You are released. Often you can shorten future anxious moments by returning to a one-liner: *Right, Worst Mom of the Year Award today.*

Ralph's perfectionism was getting in the way of writing papers in college. He scrutinized every word, thinking that nothing he did was good enough. First, he tried the rational approach, reassuring himself of his talents and stressing that the paper was only one grade among many in his college career. That didn't make a dent. Taking the opposite approach, we came up with a single line: *Shakespeare would have retched reading your paper—that's how bad it is.* The absurdity broke right through the fear. His writing wasn't bad; he just needed to work on efficiency. From that point on, *Shakespeare retched* became the go-to concept to snap fear back to reality, and add a little levity on the side.

Strategy #5: Don't Zigzag—Don't Let Anxiety Jump from One Thing to the Next

Worry can be a magnet for other worries, and that makes it even more unwieldy. You could have handled one worry, but not the bunch of them. Many years ago on public radio, I heard a program on how to keep a clean and organized house. The expert cautioned against what she called "zigzagging," moving from one area to the next without finishing anything. When it comes to worry, zigzagging, or what one of my patients dubs "jumping anxiety" in which your mind jumps from *What am I going to do about my weight?* to *What am I going to do about my job?* to *Are my kids happy enough?* is similarly no good. The anxiety jumps around without resolving anything. Rather than allowing a moving target, make the worries get in line, one at a time. Nail down the most important fear and don't let it move. Focus on one topic at a time.

Strategy #6: Out with the Absolutes

You'll never get it right. You always mess up. No one cares about you. Although negative thoughts are unreliable, they command authority with their airtight proclamations. Remember, it's just the form taken by *first thoughts universally*. Rather than allowing the words *never, always, no one, everyone* to detour you, hear them as your cue to turn around and look for the one thing that warrants your attention. Psychologist Martin Seligman identified three qualities of negative thought that expand its impact. They are: first, making the problem or event seem more *permanent.* For example, burning the dinner doesn't mean you had a bad day, that would be too logical; it means you are fundamentally a terrible cook. Second, making problems seem more *pervasive.* For example, you're not just a bad cook, you can't do anything right in your life. And third, making problems more *personal,* assigning you with the fault. For example, it doesn't matter that the phone rang while you were cooking and your three-year-old was angling to rearrange your cleaning supplies, you are an incompetent disaster. The 3Ps, as Seligman refers to them, are an endless supply of what *not* to think if you want to get out of bed in the morning, and certainly not a good way to find the truth. For that, you need some other tools, and the exercises below give us just that.

Playing with permanence—it's just now, not forever: When you find that you're consoling yourself about one disappointment by predicting another: *Why should I work so hard, no one will ever*

QUESTIONS TO ASK

- Is this a forever problem or just a temporary one?
- Does this really always happen to you, or does it just feel that way?
- Is this what is going to happen in the future, or is it really just about now?

---

appreciate it? you have fallen into the trap of tagging the temporary as permanent. Although we might feel better for a bit by saying, *I give up, that's it, I'm not going to try anymore*, truly what will feel much better is the truth: Things change and we change right along with them.

After the first week at his new job, Fred decided it would never work. He'd come from an academic job and now worked in the pharmaceutical industry. He focused on one disappointing staff meeting where he had nothing to contribute and was ready to tender his resignation. He told me, "I'll *never* be able to be heard in this culture. Everyone talks differently from me. I'll never be able to make a dent. This always happens to me, this is why I left my other job, now it's happening here, too."

When we got specific, Fred was able to see that at his old job, he did have an impact and would just get frustrated when he didn't, which only happened sometimes, not all the time as he initially felt. Looking at his first days at his new job, he was able to see how he had had an impact in smaller conversations and meetings, so it wasn't across the board. Most important, he realized that his expectation for having the impact he'd like to *right away* was unrealistic for any new job—in any field. As he narrowed the problem down, he decided that he needed to be patient, that being a good listener in one meeting didn't mean that he would never have anything to offer. He was a newcomer to the culture, he would adapt, he just didn't have anything to say on that subject, *yet*. Rather than giving up on himself or the job, he was able to

put the problem in the smallest box and
say: I need to watch and learn the rules
of this culture so I can be effective in it.

*Playing with pervasiveness—is it just the
leaf or the whole tree that's ruined?*
Imagine if you found yellow spots on the
leaf of a mighty oak tree in your yard.
You wouldn't call in an arborist to chop
the whole thing down, you'd likely re-
lease an antidote such as a swarm of ladybugs to eat the aphids
that caused the problem. Yes, there is a real problem on that tree,
but it is limited and solvable. The roots, trunk, and branches serve
their purpose and the essence of the tree well. Similarly, when you
have a worry, a disappointment, you *feel* as though these isolated
events bleed down into the roots. That's the story you tell yourself
at the moment, but that's not the reality. When you are faced with
such a situation, imagine the tree, and like a professional diagnos-
ing the location of the problem, circle the source—is it everything
or just some things? Does it really go deep, or does it just feel that
way?

Now, if it is a leaf, but it feels like it goes to a deeper place, because of messages others have given you or experiences you have
had, try to visualize that warp or flaw as isolated from the rest of
the tree, or that it is present, but not a threat. Even if traumatic
events left their mark at certain points in your past, you have still
continued to grow to move beyond their impact.

Playing with personal: When something goes wrong, we assume
that it's all our fault. When people treat you badly, or not how you
expected, you think that they meant to do this personally to you
because they don't like you. Could it be that they were busy or in
a bad mood? When a situation doesn't go as planned, divide up
the pie to figure out what resulted from factors that you could
control, what came from another person, or what factors were

QUESTIONS TO ASK

- Is it everything that went wrong or just some things?
- What part of this worked?
- What part of this didn't work?

---

present that no one could control. As in the example below, you may find that yes, you were tired and could have prepared more, but the bulk of the reason your supervisor didn't respond well to your ideas is that she was very rushed and you presented them on the fly in a noisy hallway. Before concluding that you are incompetent or that your boss isn't interested in your ideas, identify the factors that went into the outcome of that moment that really had nothing to do with you. This will help you to assess yourself more accurately, but you may learn that next time you want to present your ideas to your boss, make an appointment to sit in a quiet conference room and get some sleep the night before.

Strategy #7: Bring Back the Isolated Event!

We all jump to conclusions. *This café stinks!* Why? *The table was dirty and they were out of chocolate croissants! I'm never coming back!* Never mind that it's your favorite caffeine joint and you nibble on a chocolate croissant at a clean table every day and you will no doubt be back tomorrow. Today, you've had it. It's easier to see your flawed logic when it comes to pastry supplies in coffee shops than when you're evaluating your own performance. *I didn't have the numbers ready for my boss and she's going to think I'm sloppy and incompetent. She won't trust me anymore.* Never mind that 95 percent of the time you're right there with the answers and have an excellent reputation as a most dedicated worker; in your mind, there's no room for error. The 5 percent trumps all success in your past work performance. To buffer yourself from *outlier logic*, you need to add certain terms to your vocabulary—bad day, bad moment, off interaction—and ask whether you really are a bad worker, or is this just a less than optimal moment?

PIE CHART OF RESPONSIBILITY
SITUATION: Disappointing meeting with boss

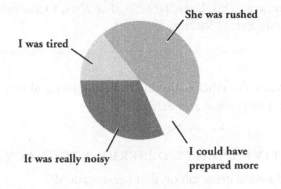

Strategy #8: Use the Red-Pen Edit

As we've seen in our exploration of the 3Ps, our negative feelings are manufactured in the workshop that specializes in specific patterns of distortion and misinterpretation. When the machine is fed the typical foibles, flaws, and missteps that we all encounter on a typical day, the other end produces a story of doom and gloom, with you as the protagonist *always* doing something wrong, *never* able to do *anything* right, and ruining *everything*! Take a red pen into the thoughts in your mind, or apply it to a written list of your thoughts, and rewrite the narrative. Remove absolutes and insert vocabulary from your new word bank. Once

---

QUESTIONS TO ASK
- Is it all about me, or not about me?
- What is my part in why things went the way they did?
- What parts belong to someone else (my boss, spouse, child was in a grumpy mood)?
- What parts belong to something out of anyone's control (it rained and we canceled the picnic)?

NEW WORD BANK

Some of the Time, Some Things, Right Now, At This Moment, This Time, Not Yet, For Now, Occasionally, Rarely, Partial Success, This Part.

---

you've made the edits removing the absolutes and inserting the truth, you can reread and exhale.

POSITIVE EVENTS DESERVE ACCURACY, TOO

"You did such a great job on that presentation!"

"Oh, no, it was nothing, I had a lot of help. I've done it before. I got lucky, really, my cat did most of the work."

You've all heard that before, maybe even from your own lips. Try as you might, you can't take credit for something that went well. Instead of experiencing success as a fluke when something goes right, you want to track down what worked, consider it a plan, and repeat it. So, acknowledging your success is not only a way of marking it but it also reinforces the steps you took to get there so that you can do it again. Sometimes you resist taking credit where it is due because you are afraid that in so doing, you raise the bar for others' expectations. If you claim that your success was accidental, no one can hold you to that same standard the next time. You would rather surprise others when things go well than disappoint because they expect more. But this assumes that it won't go well, and it locks in an anxious take on the story. In the process, you lose an accurate view of yourself.

Another obstacle is fear that taking credit means bragging. No. Exaggerating your success, rubbing it in someone's face, and going beyond the truth is bragging. Taking well-deserved credit for a job well done is a skill worth cultivating. Take a cue for those first-take interviews from some of the most amazing human beings on the planet—Olympic athletes. Note the lack of gloating. Note the specificity. They could have full bragging rights, but that's not how they play it. They talk details and strategy: I worked really hard on my pacing, I kept my knees together, I focused on the turns. Reaching for the truth when it comes to compliments sounds like this:

> I worked hard.
> I enjoy what I do.
> This project meant a lot to me and I really loved doing it.
> This is one of my strengths and it was great to be able to use it in this situation.

Instead of setting yourself the daunting task of solving the unwieldy problems your initial burst of worry or doubt constructs in reaction to an insignificant incident, we've seen how you can reduce your workload by resisting the urge to take on the whole world of impossibility and instead narrow down the problem to the real issue at hand. When you hang in there and get specific to identify the *right* information about what just happened, the most useful information, you find the part you can actually do something about. For those times when the worries you face go beyond the day-to-day snags of life, you may question whether narrowing down your burden is appropriate, given the magnitude of the situation you are in. Remember that especially when you are in the midst of real challenges—an accident, a loss, an illness—the most reverent thing you can do for yourself is to ease that burden. Finding the specific concerns that are most in need of your attention is the way to lift the weight of worry off your already strained shoulders and best work on your behalf.

FREEING YOURSELF: IN ACTION

Switching careers at mid-life takes a significant amount of gumption—it also takes good specifying skills. Renee had been a teacher because her parents had been, and she did enjoy her job.

TRY THIS
Practice Thinking Smaller Every Day

By practicing the discipline of narrowing down the problem to the smallest box with mundane annoyances, your brain will be in the habit of utilizing those same skills when more serious challenges come along. You head into your car Monday morning, proceed to spill coffee on your seat (and yourself) and think: *That's just great, what a way to start the week. Now my whole day is ruined!* Challenge yourself to persevere through the boxes: *It's a bad day, it's a bad morning, it's a bad moment, it's just a bad coffee mug design,* or even: *I just need to tighten the lid better.* You may find as you make your way down to smaller and smaller definitions of the bad thing that happened, that maybe, actually, it isn't so bad after all.

Think Smaller by Making It Bigger

The fastest way to make something smaller is often to stretch it to absurdity first and then let it snap back on its own. Think of something that annoys you right now—the soup is cold, the dishes are overflowing in the sink, or your kids were rude to your houseguests. Now, exaggerate those thoughts. *These kids are the rudest children I've ever met! Who are their parents? They have the manners of wild beasts.* The absurdity will help you snap back to reality. *No, actually, I just need to remind them to say thank you.*

Now try it on something closer to home—a criticism of yourself. *I'm the worst father in the world. I would rather play golf Saturday afternoon than play with the kids. I am a selfish louse who would rather play golf than watch* Barney *videos; every other dad would choose the purple dinosaur every time.* Ping: *Okay, I get it, I just need to plan some special time with the kids.* Stretch the rubber band of your fear to absurdity and watch it snap back into place.

YOU AND BEYOND

You know the scenes in movies in which a harried character has a big important meeting, is running late with
coffee mug in hand, frantically trying to find his keys. Papers and clothes fly everywhere, and then the wife walks
in, immediately spots them right there on the desk, and
says, "Looking for your keys, honey? They're right here."
You can help people see what is right under their nose.
When your friend, spouse, co-worker, boss, or child is
spinning with imagined, far-flung catastrophes, use the
questions in the Key Questions for Getting Specific box
earlier in this chapter to help them try to narrow the
problem down to the one thing that really bothers them
most. Help them carry their problems in the smallest box
and they will be most grateful.

But in the back of her mind, the business world called. Learning
of an MBA program that she could complete on nights and weekends, she signed up and took the plunge.

During the first class, a mock business negotiation, Renee did
poorly. Unlike the students who had undergraduate degrees in
business, Renee hadn't been schooled in the culture of playing
your cards close to the chest. Instead, she had learned that the
goal was to help students meet their goal. Discouraged, she was
ready to drop out: *I am not cut out for this, this was a total mistake. I'll never be able to do this. If I can't do a simple exercise, I'll
never be able to make it with clients.*

What had gone wrong? Focused on the feelings, Renee felt it
was hopeless. In talking it through and using the root-tree-
branch exercise, she was able to refocus on the part of the problem that needed her attention. Renee could see that she had
failed the exercise not because of something fundamentally
wrong or lacking in her, but because this was all *new* to her. She

realized this was a great learning experience because it illustrated why she needed to shift gears in her business classes. Her work with students would come in handy later in working with clients. But for now she needed to learn a new vocabulary and set of principles and that was exactly why she needed to stay in the program.

Chapter 6

STEP THREE: OPTIMIZE

Rethink What's Possible and Broaden Your Choices

> *Once you have begun to distinguish that it's all invented, you can create a place to dwell where new inventions are the order of the day. Such a place we call "the universe of possibility."*
> —BEN AND ROSAMUND ZANDERS,
> *THE ART OF POSSIBILITY*

🕊 *I know my fears probably aren't true, and things probably won't always look this bad. But how do I get to that point now?* 🕊

GIVING YOUR LIFE A WIDER BERTH

In the last step, you narrowed down your problems and learned to not let yourself be distracted or frightened by the giant shadows anxiety can cast. The next place we'll get unstuck from is the thinking that there is only one solution that can haul you out of a problem and that it has to happen immediately.

When in an anxious spin or a disappointment dead end, we often have a single, very narrow idea of what is going to get us out: *If I only got a new job, if I just earned more money, if only I ace the test, if he would only call, if I could just lose ten pounds.* Or we may have only one interpretation of what's going on in the situation: *If I can't do public speaking, I'm never going to be able to progress in my field.* The narrower the rescue pad, the more pressure to have that one and only. And the more it feels like when that *doesn't* happen, we're out of options. Instead of reducing our anxiety, we create more!

What's the alternative? Choices. Options. Possibilities. Second opinions. Just because you can't see them, doesn't mean they're not there. Optimizing is the way to expand your vision and perspective. It's about divergent thinking, generating the many different directions your next steps could take. Can you still hold onto that one solution you want? Yes, but once you start generating other possibilities, often you find you've already let go because something better has come into view. Either you find something you hadn't thought of before or you feel less stressed and more able to let things unfold naturally, without a need to know right now.

This requires us to step out of the strange "comfort zone of unhappiness" that worry paradoxically puts us in—*This is just how it is, I can't change my life, if I can't do X, then Y will never happen.* It entertains the possibility that things really can be different. Narrowing the problem down is a good thing, but narrowing the solutions is not so good. Getting your mind working on stretching and broadening the possible responses is the next goal.

YOU KNOW HOW TO OPTIMIZE— EXPECT CHOICES: MORE IS MORE

Worrying means getting trapped in one way of looking at a situation. Having one unreachable way of solving a problem depletes you, wastes your energy, and is rarely of any value. In contrast,

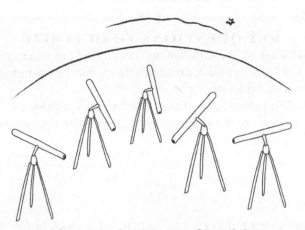

Looking into the Universe of Possibilities

optimizing is all about flexibility. Fear narrows our perspective; it literally narrows our field of vision. Taking the time to look at different interpretations, information, and ideas that exist just outside the quandary we perceive is boxing us in allows us to stretch outside the box. Rather than rushing to a solution that is fast but doesn't really fit, optimizing ensures that fear doesn't deprive us of the many possible ways of understanding that exist, and the many different directions we could pursue.

Imagine you walk into a paint store looking for a sunny blue for your bedroom, and the clerk hands you a can, saying, "Here's your generic blue paint." That's it? What, no Hydrangea blue? No Miles Davis blue? No Eleuthera blue? You mean I don't have forty different blues to choose from? In much of life you don't easily settle for one thing, especially not the first thing that comes along. Your natural instinct is to look for an array of choices. In this age of pull-down menus and limitless options for consumers, you insist on them. So you needn't succumb to worry's urgent, pressuring take on your life, which is notoriously unreliable and limiting. The fact is that we are natural choosers, and when we invoke that tendency in the emotional realm, too, the results bring much more satisfaction.

KEY QUESTIONS TO OPTIMIZE

- What are the different ways I can read this situation?
- If I don't read this situation with my fear, how different would it look?
- Who else do I want to call on to lend a perspective?
- What are the different ways this situation could be solved?

If you give a toddler a toy, he may bat it away, but when you give a toddler two toys to choose from suddenly you are a hero, and a deal can be struck. Researcher Sheena Iyengar, in her book *The Art of Choosing*, explains that our desire to choose is inborn. She describes a study in which four-month-old infants got upset if they couldn't pull the string to hear music, even though they heard the same amount of music when someone *else* pulled the string for them.

We all want to pull the string. And when it comes to our thoughts, we can. All you need is a willingness to go beyond the first thought and generate others. Second thoughts mean different kinds of thoughts. In this chapter, we'll look at mind-stretching exercises to do a 360° virtual tour of your situation.

WAIT FOR IT

When you're stuck at the crossroads with a situation or in the middle of a conflict with someone, patience can be tough to come by. It comes from being willing to look at your problems from different angles and reviewing many solutions before deciding on one optimal solution.

Moving from stalled to having options creates a neurological avalanche of the good kind, taking you from red to green. Even if you don't love any of the options, you will feel better just knowing you have choices. Optimizing is about seeing beyond the catastrophic thoughts in your head and letting other parts of your mind speak up to create these options. But remember that you don't have to overextend for unbelievably positive thoughts. Just reach for accurate thoughts that might even be hopeful thoughts. Realize that you don't have to be stuck in the corner. This is a time to be curious and leave the door open.

Imagine that rather than banging your head against the one thought that is positioned to get the best of you, you could have a veritable walk-in closet of choices. Rather than choosing the one thought that makes you feel terrible about yourself, you can find ten things that fit your life well.

If you can't think of the options now—this doesn't mean they don't exist. But the more you look for options, just by pausing and thinking the simple but in-the-moment radical thought "I have options. I have choices," the brain will learn the new habit of thinking in arrays, and they will appear to you more quickly when you are struggling. You will retrain your brain to shift out of the closed mind to the open mind.

Marian was always worried that people were upset with her. Out of very little data—a less than cheery greeting, a conversation cut short—she would stress about how she might have offended someone or made them angry and how she needed to fix it. She was in a constant state of stress, because there was always some interaction that left her with some doubt and a feeling of dread in the pit of her stomach.

We created a pull-down menu for Marian of other reasons a conversation might be cut short or people might seem irritable: They could actually be in a rush, having a bad day unrelated to her, or be tired or hungry, or maybe even just using their normal tone of voice, or yes, they might in fact be upset, but that in and of itself could be manageable. We also created a menu of ways to respond: compassion, humor, asking what's wrong. Rather than immediately jumping to the conclusion that she had done something wrong, she would visualize her menu and short-circuit her laps around the guilt and inadequacy track. Not only did this help Marian after such interactions, but during conversations themselves, she found herself able to relax and be less anxious and more fluid because she wasn't waiting for the other shoe to drop.

HOW TO CREATE OPTIONS: ALLOW YOURSELF TO BROWSE

One way of creating options has to do with perspective, generating different interpretations about the meaning, consequence, and importance of what's going on in your life. You can start by experimenting with different ways that you narrate the story of your situation. Say that a friend let you down. Think in menus: is it outrageous, thoughtless, or unfortunate? Do you feel: angry, hurt, or disappointed? Or, for example, if you turn down a request to volunteer at your child's school carnival and then feel worried that you aren't a good parent or that others are judging you, move your feet to stand in front of a different telescope and play with the array of interpretations: *As a working parent, I'm too busy*, or, *I don't want to help in this way, but I can help in other ways*, or, *I volunteer a lot in my life, I need to cut back somewhere*, or even dare to entertain the perspective: *I am selfish and I just don't care enough about this. I really hate carnivals and this is the last thing I want to do!* Try these options on for size and see what fits. Think of it as browsing. There is no obligation to buy, but getting to know your choices is a good thing. Sometimes by allowing yourself to go too far, you're able to find what fits just right.

Another way to create options is to gather other opinions on the matter, whether by picking up the phone to have friends or colleagues weigh in or just consulting them in your imagination.

A third way to create options is by identifying your hidden time lines. Often we get stuck feeling we have no choices when we decide that certain things need to be done in a certain amount of time or by a certain date: I have to get married by age thirty, I have to own a house by thirty-five. Are these time lines helpful goals, or do they pressure us by putting a hard-and-fast number on something that should happen more organically? Taking the problem of being lonely and wanting to be successful and adding an insistence that these problems be resolved on a deadline is not solving the problem, it's creating a second one. When you can look at that time line as an option but not a given, other possibilities emerge. Creating options means thinking in terms of activities that we can control, for example, deciding to date or save money for a house versus setting deadlines and end points that we can't necessarily control, such as getting married and earning X amount of dollars.

Another option-creating move is to have multiple ideas about what needs to change. We can unclutch and let go of the one big change we want, if it's out of reach right now, and identify smaller changes that can help. You may feel miserable in your job and the only solution may be to get a new one, but until that happens, there are other parts of the puzzle that can move: going for a walk at lunch, *taking* a lunch, connecting more meaningfully with colleagues, making changes *outside* of your job to improve your overall life satisfaction. When you are having the "anywhere but here" feeling, push the button to get outside yourself. It's okay not to know the solution. You have options.

Strategy #1: Open Up: Go on a Fact-Finding Mission

When am I going to_____? Let the blanks be blanks until you do some research to find the answers. The way to accomplish this is to turn your automatic statements into questions:

- I'm never going to get a job in marketing • How do I best get a job in marketing?
- I'll never be able to afford my own house • What are the different ways I could afford my own house?
- I'll never be able to start my own business • What are the different ways I could start my own business?
- I'm never going to be a good enough mother • Is there something I want to be doing as a mother that I'm not doing now?

KEY PHRASES FOR OPTIMIZING
- How would I like this to go?
- What are other ways to look at this?
- How would my friends look at this?
- If I didn't have anxiety, how would I see this?
- How would this look in my comfort zone?
- How would this look if I were more of a risk taker?
- How would this look in my wildest dreams?
- What will I do if I can't solve this situation the way I'd like?

As questions, they point to new possibilities that require some research, for instance, surfing the Internet, talking to others who are knowledgeable, and laying out a step-by-step plan, or even just having an open and honest conversation with yourself. It's possible these things may not happen, but if emotional reasoning has taken over, leaving you overwhelmed or discouraged, then you won't see that this problem isn't hopeless, it's just suffering from a lack of information or from misinformation. Sometimes optimizing means realizing that you don't have all the information you need. Then you either need to wait until you do, or go out and track it down.

Strategy #2: Consult the Possibility Panel

How can you expand your vision to see other points of view when the same negative feed keeps looping around in your mind? Imagine establishing your own board of directors, staffed with real or imaginary people whose perspective, guidance, and opinions, or even sense of humor you'd like to turn to in a tough moment. You can summon members' opinions one by one, or even let your panel discuss the situation among themselves and see where that leads. Who do you want on your panel? The Dalai Lama? Your wise grandmother? Your best friend, your dog? Your mentor from

Invite New Perspectives on Your Life

THE POSSIBILITY PANEL

the first job you ever had? A character in a movie that you admired? Bart Simpson or David Sedaris? The beauty of the assembly is that it is all in your head, and in this instance, that's a good thing. Just stepping out of your own spin of ideas for a moment to contemplate getting other opinions instantly frees you up. Any additional wisdom you may glean from these trusted advisors is gravy.

Consider summoning your patient, calm self, which also deserves a turn at the microphone. When your mind keeps spewing out the same answers—*You've failed again, this is a disaster, you'll mess up*—it's time to hear from some other voices. Exercise your authority and call on folks sitting in the back of the room, not just those front and center who have been reiterating the disaster warnings. Write down your panel members on a piece of paper and keep the list in your workspace or on your bedside table. Consult early and often.

Strategy #3: Challenge the Authority of Your Assumptions

I'm not the kind of person who could ever do *that;* that's not something I could ever ask for; there's no way I could ever live without. . . . Maybe these assumptions are true, but then again,

What Are You Walking Into?

maybe they aren't. Remember, peering over the fence of your givens to what might be on the other side is like browsing at the mall. There's no cost to try things on, and you may be surprised to find that outlandish things fit better than you thought. Without committing yourself too far, restate your givens in this way:

- If I were the kind of person who *could* do X, what would it look like for me?
- If I *did* ask for something like that, how would I do it?
- If I *could* live without that, what would I do instead?

If you can be courageous enough to just ask the questions, you may learn some valuable information about who you are and what you need in life. The real risk comes from letting fears prevent you from exploring the options.

Strategy #4: Consider Walking in Through a New Door

In a classic skit by the British comedy ensemble Monty Python, an unassuming man walks in an office door thinking he is going for civilized argument, only to be ripped to shreds verbally by his interviewer. It turns out that he walked into the wrong door, into the Office of Abuse. If only he'd known!

It is crucial to walk into the right room. Imagine how different you would feel sharing your concerns in the room of compassion versus the room of regret. When you hear worries and despair, perhaps you, too, have walked in unknowingly and need to find a more suitable place to park yourself for good advice. This exercise is especially helpful at night, when you find yourself locked in the anxiety room. Create your own set of doors and set it next to your bed, under your computer monitor, on your fridge. Change your doors frequently.

Strategy #5: From Here to Eternity Versus from Here to Absurdity

We saw in the last chapter how conjuring absurdly bad versions of your situation can release the grip of anxiety. Now go to the other extreme, to the absurdly good. You can break free from negative "worst-case scenario" thinking and get to realistic "most-likely scenario" thinking by taking a quick detour through the ridiculously positive. Make a chart with three columns on the page: worst-case scenario, ridiculously best-case scenario, and most-likely scenario. For example, when you're going to meet your mother-in-law and you think it won't go well, go ahead and have that picture of the avalanche of faux pas, insulting her alma mater, choking on her cooking, or using the wrong fork at the meal. Then imagine that your mother-in-law looks you in the eye and says, "I can't believe the incredible good fortune that you— wonderful you—came into our son's life." Indulge in that reverie. You couldn't possibly have asked for more. Here comes the sound of a record needle abruptly stopping. *Screech*! Okay, so you know that probably won't happen. But maybe you could have a little laugh at the expense of your anxiety. With nerves calmed by the comic relief, you can know that you may not walk out of that dinner having found your new best friend, but chances are there will be no major mishaps. Stretching to the absurd in either direction helps loosen up thinking to see the many alternative viewpoints between the poles.

Strategy #6: Hit the Newsstand

In his book *A Whole New Mind*, Daniel Pink gives several ideas for broadening perspectives, something he refers to as the skill of symphony. The exercise he calls "Hit the Newsstand" involves literally going to the newsstand looking for something new, something that you wouldn't normally ever pick up. Grab several magazines that you've never read before and scan them for what jumps out at you. For example, in a horticulture magazine, you can find something that helps you think about handling prickly people in your office, or in a sports magazine there might be a suggestion for how to handle your own fear of failure after seeing how the pros do it. Although this strategy was not specifically designed for getting unstuck from emotional entanglements, it gets the wheels turning in a new direction. Can't go to a newsstand? Go to your bookshelf, or even CD shelf, close your eyes, and choose anything. Close your eyes one more time, open to a random page and see what you find there. The key is that when you are spinning round and round in the same coordinates, completely random things can help open things up and move your mind to new hubs and directions.

Strategy #7: Fast-Forward to the End of the Story

Think about how most anxious situations turn out. We kick ourselves or preferably laugh at ourselves for how worked up we got over (thankfully) nothing. To fast-forward to that point, ask yourself: What would it look like if this problem were solved? What are the different likely ways this will turn out? How will I feel? To help that end point scoot a little closer, can you borrow any ideas from that picture now? How will you see this tomorrow? Borrow that perspective today.

Strategy #8: Switch Glasses: All Wrong and All Right

Be daring. Be radical. What if you decided—just for a minute— to see the situation that is making you miserable right now as good. What would that give you? What would you be able to see then that you can't see now? Imagine what you might be able to do with the information that comes from turning the appearance of a bad situation on its head. Is it possible that this is how visionary dreams are born? Hewlett-Packard was started in a garage; Microsoft was started during a recession. A key to success is being able to stretch and see the potential hiding in a lot of challenging conditions. But you have to look for it.

To exercise these optimizing muscles regularly, next time you find yourself being judgmental and you're thinking, "That person isn't smart or attractive" or "Their house is a mess," challenge yourself to see it as the opposite. Try to look harder at what people have to offer, what they do know about that is *different* from what you know, how their dirty dishes and dusty floors are more a reflection that they really value their other priorities—their devotion to their work, the time they spend with their children—rather than what they lack, in this case, neatness. We increase flexibility not by denying the flaws but by rethinking them as evidence of something different that isn't immediately apparent, rather than something deficient. Learning this type of flexibility will help you to be a less judgmental person, but it will also help you see something hidden in your circumstances beyond the flaws.

Strategy #9: Let It Be, at Least Overnight

Most of the time, the problem we went to sleep with doesn't seem as bad when we wake up. What felt impossible at 10:00 PM you may have forgotten when you get up at 6:00 AM. While you were sleeping, your brain, unhindered by your emotional reactions, figured the way out of the maze. The take-home lesson is: Don't stay up late trying to figure out a solution to a problem. It's more efficient to sleep and let your mind do the work without you. Remind yourself that whatever you are feeling now is likely to lift in a few hours—just as you tell yourself when you are down with the flu and look around at the piled-up dishes in the sink, the trash basket overflowing with tissues, the laundry, the mail, the backlog of your life will all seem much easier when you feel better in a few days. How much of what is going on now needs to be solved right now versus tomorrow, a week, a month, or years from now? This will help take the pressure off the moment.

TRY THIS

You walk into a newly painted room and see the cracks,
the drips of paint on the floor, the light-switch plate that
is slightly askew. Those observations will be helpful, but
they aren't the whole picture. Now go back in and find
what works about the room, what you like or even love
about it. Get yourself in the habit of being able to have
dark and light sit side by side. Picture the yin-yang symbol
of dark and light forming a whole circle, or even make a
quick scribble on a piece of paper. Fill in one side with
what's wrong first. Then fill in the other side with observations of what is good or neutral. Respect and value
both. Over time, you may find that your idea of "wrong"
shifts altogether, and rather than judging something as a
problem, you may just see it as different, or who knows,
it might even be something that you come to love.

Strategy #10: Switch Shoes

Often, distress comes from an interaction with another person,
be it someone important like a spouse or a boss or family member
or someone you will never see again, like the driver who cut you
off, the person on the other end of the phone at the insurance
company, the surly waiter who gave you the bad table (on purpose, when clearly the better one was available). You are convinced of those people's intentions, convinced that you can
accurately read their mind and know exactly what that look or
curt reply meant. You can even interpret an absence of data, such
as when you haven't heard back from someone. *She hated my pro-*
posal; he wants to break up with me; she's really mad at me and
doesn't want to be friends.

Do you really have a sixth sense, or would you prefer to fill in
the blanks with answers just to feel like you have more control?
Switch perspectives. Put yourself in that other person's place and

ask, "What might be going on with that person that has nothing to do with me?" For example, is the editor three months behind on manuscripts? Is your boyfriend, who never wrote often, on that work deadline? Maybe that waiter is getting flak from his boss about not giving the best tables to high-profile customers—or frankly—maybe he doesn't think it is a better table. Stretch, switch, and generate the calmer yin to the agitated yang of your first interpretations.

Strategy #11: Shift from Scared to Prepared, from "What If" to "If, Then"

A final way of shifting perspectives that may be especially useful in situations with a higher likelihood that the challenges you face may require action, follow your *what if* with an *if, then*. Rather than being stuck looking at the cliff-hanger perspective that anxiety gives you, it's okay to consult your competence and make a contingency plan. Show yourself that even if the unwanted scenario were to occur, you would have options about how to look at and handle your situation. *What if my wife needs surgery? What if my son's school can't handle his learning disability? What if we have to move out of our house? If* those things happened, *then* what steps would you take? What are the different possible steps you could take? You needn't be left teetering at a place of uncertainty when having a backup plan would bring you peace. This is different from spinning with worry; this is moving ahead by thinking linearly. Call on your logical self to sit down and have a conversation with your emotional self. Let your thoughtful, planful answers to those questions walk you back from the edge of that cliff to a place where you have solid footing, a much better place from which to view the work ahead.

Figuring out the optimal takes the flexibility to see beyond what is in front of you. It also takes patience to put in the time to figure out what's best. When you know that you can count on flexibility to stay calmer, then you do stay calmer and feel less impulsive and less urgency to do something *now,* no matter the cost. You feel more patient.

If you talk yourself into the importance of being ready to let go of one fixed idea to gain ten others, you'll let go faster to pick up more solutions sooner. It's what many of us were told by our parents: "The sooner you clean up your room, the sooner you can go play." The more you respond to fear and uncertainty with a mind open to the options, the sooner you rewire how your mind is programmed to respond. When you get in the habit of looking for multiple doors or multiple perspectives, you won't have to go searching for these options. They will look for you.

FREEING YOURSELF: IN ACTION

Talia was feeling very stuck in her life. She left her full-time job at an advertising firm after ten years to start a family, also hoping that it would lead to an opportunity to start her own company. She was a talented designer, but whenever she thought about starting her own company, the walls came up. She needed capital. She needed equipment. She needed to rent space. She and her husband's cash flow was all flowing into the mortgage and repairs on their fixer-upper house. She needed more time. With her two young children still at home, starting a business would mean putting them in full-time day care, and she didn't think they could finance it. Her picture of this company kept getting constrained by the realities of her current life. It felt like a Rubik's cube, with each step locked into all the others. Then there was the anxiety. Was she good enough to make it in her own business? But the more stuck she was, the more anxious she was, because on some level she knew that she was more afraid than anything else. Talia felt isolated because most of her friends were either working or happy to be at home, so she didn't think that any of them would understand where she was stuck.

I asked Talia to convene in her mind a group of people she respected and to present her situation to them; then she should tell

TRY THIS
The Possibility Panel

Sometimes your own answer base is limited, and it helps to call in a lifeline or two. Who is on your Possibility Panel? Think of the wise people you know or wish you knew. You might include celebrities, authors, inspirational speakers, or wise relatives. These people are your heroes, your guardian angels, the voices you admire and trust to lend sage advice and warm encouragement, or to light a fire if it is warranted. Keep the list in your desk, or if you dare, over your desk. Others may want to create their own when they see yours. For good measure and a little levity, keep a seat open for a wise guy. A heckler can point out to you humorously that this isn't the end of the world, and you'll be able to think clearly about what to do.

Just Say Yes: Dare to Create More Breathing Room for Yourself

When you are feeling upset or stressed about a situation, be willing to say yes to all of the different perspectives you have on the situation, even if some of them may be more frightening or less than flattering to you or someone else. Let's say you are very worried that you embarrassed yourself at a staff meeting by being unaware of a basic principle of medicine that would help your patient. You've challenged your perceptions enough to realize that it's not the end of your career, but you're left with some tough alternatives: *I could take this mistake with grace and learn from it*; or, *My colleagues will look at me differently*; or, *I have some blind spots in my training, I need to do something about*; or, *My chief may ask me to step down from my supervisory position*. Consider each of those options equally. Try them calmly, without exclamation points and genuinely ask yourself which fits best. Even if a less than optimal outcome occurs, you may be better prepared to take it graciously.

Or, imagine you yelled at your son before he left for a camping trip and now you're worried about having ended on a bad note. What are the different ways of narrating that story? *That was not a good parenting moment, I should have had more self-control*; or, *I was nervous about him going away and that's why I yelled*; or even, *He was being a brat and I'm glad he's going to be away for a few days*. Instead of feeling dreadful about having said what you did to him, you may feel liberated as you see that they are only words, and they may well *not* be the words that describe all of how you feel, just a part of how you feel—and that's okay. Daring to mention the unmentionables frees up the energy it takes to keep stuffing down those thoughts that may be one of an array of choices on your mind. But doing so may be the very thing that allows you to find the choice that really fits the best.

me at the next session what she had found out. When Talia returned, I could tell something had shifted. The first thing she did was show me a sketch for a logo for her company. "What happened?" I asked.

"Well," she said, "my group was all the millions of working mothers now and in history who would totally understand my dilemma. I realized what I was feeling was normal. And it made me think, too, that maybe I was putting too much pressure on myself to have everything happen at once."

Talia continued, "I thought about what my grandfather would have advised me if he were still alive. He always believed in me—he told me that I didn't need to think so big, that I should start very small. I hadn't thought about it that way. I was thinking I had to do the whole business—like it was one static thing and had to be this entity with an office and everything. I realized that businesses usually do start small, and then with advertising and word of mouth, they grow. It changed everything to think that way. I worked on a logo, I cleared out some space in the attic for a workspace, I thought about where I could place ads, and some old contacts I could reach out to. I think I was thinking about *someone else's* job or life—and I was anxious because I knew it didn't fit. Now I feel like I'm figuring out the one that works for me."

Nearing his forty-fifth birthday, Ted felt discouraged that his life hadn't turned out the way he had hoped. Although to all outside observers, he was a great success, having earned tenure at his university at a young age, there were certain goals that he had in his mind that would indicate he had succeeded and he hadn't achieved them. Prestigious grants and awards that he had envisioned in his twenties were creating a sense of failure for Ted amid so much success. He was so focused on how to make these awards a reality that it interfered with focusing on the very work that would make those awards a possibility. More than that, Ted doubted his path, thinking that because these milestones hadn't come in, he had made big mistakes. All of this was making Ted have difficulty sleeping, and he had been acting short with his family and stressed and anxious at work.

YOU AND BEYOND
Seeing Possibilities Compassionately

When people you are close to—a friend, spouse, or child—launch into a negative or distorted view of their situation, you may be tempted to say something like, "Well, it's your *choice* to see that you're going to have an awful weekend," at which point they feel like you've slapped them in the face, and all they can think to do is bite your head off. Instead of saying no to their view, say yes, in a comment that acknowledges their state. Keeping the feelings separate from the facts, you can empathize with their feelings but still shine a light down a path to the different possibilities of where to go next. "I can completely imagine feeling like that; I would feel the same way," or, "So true, no one is going to argue with feeling like that. I wonder, though, if there's any other way this could go." This way, they're not feeling that they've done something wrong; it's simply a matter of perspective, and the more possible angles on the situation, the better.

Ted was shortchanging himself, not because of the awards but because of his focus on them. We started to question his goals. How meaningful would they really be to him? Were they essential now, or was that more a youthful dream? No one he had ever known had won them—they were very rare. Ted tried different ways of telling the story: *I have to win these awards or my life has been a waste; I would like to get this recognition, I would feel proud; if I don't get it, I am not getting what I deserve; I don't really have to gain this recognition because I like my life even without these accolades.* Just allowing himself to entertain the range of choices by saying these things that he had been afraid to say was liberating in and of itself and helped Ted to see what really fit best. As Ted was willing to question some of these "givens" in his mind, he opened up space that had been closed for a long time. He loved his work, but he hadn't been letting himself engage with it and wasn't taking full advantage of some of the rich experiences he could be having now collaborating with colleagues and mentoring his students. Giving himself permission, thinking of what his own mentors had said and would say about his work, Ted realized that he needed to get back to work. The best part of this was that no one was getting in the way but himself. Maybe the twenty-year-old was naïve, and now some other part had to take charge—an older, wiser part. Ted couldn't control the awards, and that was making him feel anxious, but recommitting himself to exploring the work he loved was something that he could do himself, immediately. Likewise, the rewards of doing that work wouldn't be on hold until some future date, they would come forward right away.

Chapter 7

STEP FOUR: MOBILIZE
Don't Just Stand There, Do Something!

> *Even if you are on the right track, you'll get run
> over if you just sit there.*
>
> —WILL ROGERS

❧ *I know what I should do, but I can't get myself to do it. I make
these big plans to change my whole life and then I never take action
and I end up feeling worse.* ❧

SOMETHING'S GOTTA GIVE

There is a simple law of physics, or goodness knows, there should
be, that says if you want momentum, move something. Anything.
So if one part of your life is stuck, try to move it. If you can't move
that part, move another.

We all know what it means to mobilize. You do it every morning
getting out the door and every night getting off the couch and into
bed. Some days are easier than others. Yet mobilizing in the face
of emotional gridlock is more familiar as advice you give to *others*
rather than what you offer yourself. When children are frustrated
with math homework, it is often obvious to the parents that if they
would just stand up, take a break, and wrestle with their little

brother, they'd be in a much better mind-set to tackle it when they return in a refreshed state. When you listen to spouses or friends talking about needing to make a big change with their jobs, you wish that they would just be willing to let go of that big idea for a moment and think in smaller chunks, network with other professionals, peruse job websites, or clean up their resumé, and then they could untangle themselves from their unhappiness.

But when we are stuck in a corner of our own, we are bad at taking our own advice and instead seem imprisoned in our quandary by a seat-belt with a five-point restraint system. This chapter offers a multitude of ideas that can unbuckle the belts.

By this point in the book you've relabeled your self-criticism as an attack of your worry demons, you've gotten specific and narrowed the problem down to the true issue at hand, and you've broadened your options on how to optimally solve it. Now what? Maybe you don't feel sprung quite yet.

Mobilizing needs to happen next. First, you mobilize in the moment. When you get stunned by bad news, like a deer caught in the headlights, you're just trying to figure out how to shake it temporarily so you can go about your day. It happens as you reel from a jolting surprise in a performance review, learn of a job rejection, or feel jilted by a friend. You'll see below that when you are upset, overwhelmed, and disoriented thanks to the amygdala in overdrive, movement often starts, humbly, with a change of scenery to break out of the hold the moment has on you.

The second step of mobilizing occurs when you shift into problem-solving mode. The best mind-sets to overcome inertia in life happen when you venture beyond the moment to resolve or change a situation. Here, the unit of change is a series of small steps that won't overwhelm or perplex you.

There is a third aspect of mobilizing that comes from the realization that sometimes you *can't* change a situation. But there is still an action to take—acceptance. Although this meaning of mobilizing may not apply often, in certain circumstances it turns out to be invaluable.

STRATEGIES FOR GETTING
UNSTUCK IN THE MOMENT

Start where you are.

—PEMA CHODRON

Hildi was stunned when she got the news that her daughter hadn't been accepted to the magnet school that her older daughter attended. She could hardly speak when she got the letter in the mail. In a flash, a million ideas ran through Hildi's mind. She couldn't picture how anything would work out. They could never afford private school. How would her daughter take this news? She was such a light, happy child—would this break her spirit? This wasn't the moment for plans or solutions, this was simply a day to get through the shock and absorb the news.

Hildi didn't want to think about it, but she couldn't think about anything else, either. With high voltage running through her body, she just wanted to get outside herself to shake this feeling.

Whether you are upset about a conflict with a friend, waiting to hear back about medical test results, reeling from a supervisor's "constructive criticism," or wondering how you will pay the bills this month, getting stuck in the spin cycle does you no good. It does quite the opposite. Worry makes you a captive audience to your doubts. Just slowing down the spinning may be all that you are ready for *at first*. You need a way to return to your senses, and often that comes from making a change, any change.

A change of scenery allows you to break up the gridlock in the brain. It's not about distracting yourself from something unpleasant (which is more like playing hide-and-seek with the devil). It's about understanding that when your spirit seems like a windup toy wedged in a corner and spinning its wheels, no matter how much it spins, it can't move all by itself. It needs to be picked up and pointed in a new direction.

THE BLESSING OF A WELL-TIMED SNEEZE

Have you ever noticed when you have been in a terrible mood, just about to hit your breaking point, fate intervenes in the form of your cat, who has repurposed the crumpled piece of paper that you threw on the floor in utter frustration? He's batting it around in a one-beast game of feline soccer, and you are instantly released from your anger. Or maybe your child has one of those rare moments in which he isn't asking you for a snack or more computer time, but he just simply wants to know what hail is. Or maybe even your husband does something sweet or odd, like sneeze really loudly. Suddenly, like a hero in a play swooping in out of nowhere to rescue or release us, this random event somehow changes everything. Although you've been sitting there trying different combination codes to unlock the grip your thoughts have on you, suddenly you are sprung free. You couldn't have predicted it, but the shift between one state and the other is like night and day.

This is called *incidental* change. It proves two things: first, that we can get out of those dark moments even though when we are in them we are convinced that's impossible, and second, even a very small thing will do. It also illustrates that we all would be well served to learn how to do this intentionally ourselves, rather than counting on the incidental hero to sense our distress and send help or waiting for that chance breeze to blow us in a new direction. *Aaah-choo!*

Strategy #1: Let Go of the Rope

In a tug of war, when the enemy on the other end of the rope pulls you hard, if you let go of the rope you lose the competition, but you are also released from the pull.

Let's say you didn't get the business contract that everyone was sure would come through. You're shocked and know you've got to think it through, but you can't. Emotions hijacked, you're in overdrive, but you can't seem to leave your office, or even move. You're in a tug-of-war with your feelings. The longer you sit, the worse you feel, because now you're wasting time, too—*What's wrong with you?* you ask, adding insult to injury.

Consider who is at the other end of the rope: your own pressure to figure out how to fix things *now*, to control everything *now*. So make a deal with that pressure to walk away for a few minutes, but promise you will come back. The difference upon your return is that you will probably have a clear head and your feelings will have subsided to a manageable level, which will help you decide the next step. Movement shifts the moment. Rather than waste precious energies wrestling with your goals, you should let go, move, and take the small risk of walking away mid-process. Chances are that letting go of needing to figure it all out now will paradoxically allow you to figure it out sooner.

In the film version of neurologist Oliver Sacks's book *Awakenings*, Parkinson's patients who were frozen like statues suddenly came to life when a ball was thrown to them or music was played. By borrowing the will of the ball or the music, these patients were able to come back from wherever they were stuck. Although you are not physically frozen when trying to break out of an anxious spin or a downward spiral, invisible forces keep you stuck. On a small scale, getting up and moving clears your head. You engage different muscles, things immediately catch your eye. You don't have to push it, the mind naturally moves in new directions. You are no longer in a stranglehold with yourself. So sneak around the excuses—I can't move, I don't feel like getting up, it won't help—and just move. Borrow momentum from someone or something else. Pets improve health in part because they create action in your life that you don't have on your own steam. You can borrow will from any of these activities:

- *Listen to music.* Create a playlist of songs especially for these times when you need a lift or a push.
- *Get physical.* Go to the gym, go for a bike ride, dance in your living room, play basketball, or even throw rolled-up socks into the hamper.
- *Call a friend.* You might not even talk about what's going on, but connecting will help. You might think of someone who makes you laugh. Ask that person to tell you something funny.
- *Walk.* Get moving without planning or equipment. Go get a drink of water. Walk the dog, or just yourself. Look for beauty—it's everywhere. Find something that strikes you as if you're seeing it for the first time.
- *Look at pictures.* Flip through your photo album or electronic photo collection. Remember that the person you see there in happier times is waiting to reemerge.
- *Nurture your environment.* Do this even if you're not quite ready to nurture yourself. Water your plants, remove their dried leaves, reorganize the books on your coffee table—look at them. Do a small, manageable (five-minute) clean-up project like de-cluttering your bedside table, your entryway, or your car.

Strategy #2: Think Entry-Level

When the world feels like it is coming apart, you may not be ready to solve your problem, but you are ready to feel something different from what you are experiencing, so get moving. Start with the lowest-level operation. Do an errand or perform a small act of kindness for someone else. Although we may long for proof of "big" meaning or "big" accomplishments in life during these times, think of the Zen saying. "Before enlightenment; chop wood, carry water. After enlightenment; chop wood, carry water." It's best to begin humbly with the basics. Make yourself a cup of tea or a meal and clean up your kitchen. Put some music on to borrow momentum for these small tasks. When you see yourself moving, no matter how small the activity, it shows that you can move out of a stuck position. Often in the course of doing something mundane, a new thought may occur to you, or you might see something in your surroundings that strikes you as interesting, gives you a lift, and gets you thinking in a new direction.

Strategy #3: Realize What's Yours to Change

Our first house was a fixer-upper, a pattern we repeated with our second house, and if there ever is a third, I'm sure you get the idea. The realtor shook her head at the falling ceilings, peeling paint, and overgrown shrubbery. Well, actually she shook her head at us. We could hear her silently urging us to take our money and run. But it was a perfect location, so instead we moved in. One day soon after we took possession of the house, I was on the phone with my older brother, cataloguing the problems that we'd inherited from the previous owners, and then I said, "And on top of all that, they have this ugly red carpet in their front room." My brother, a man known for not mincing words, replied, "No, Tamar, *you* have an ugly red carpet in your front room."

Ouch. Even when we have identified our problems, we may stop just short of doing anything about them. "My kids *make* me prepare three different meals for dinner every night!" Red carpet. "I'm *stuck* making coffee for the office every day." Red carpet again. "Because of my anxiety, I *have to* sit in the last row right by the door, even though I can't hear anything the professor is saying!" Another red carpet. We complain, we agonize, we feel terrified thinking of what could be. But there we sit, with worry or negativity as an avoidance strategy. We somehow convince ourselves that anguishing about something is doing something. How is it, though, that when we are fully capable of identifying and even ripping up the proverbial ugly red carpets in our life, we don't just do it? To get moving, we need to sort out what aspects of our situation we really do control from the ones we don't. Once we see that the choice is in our hands, we are more likely to take action. What's the makeover strategy? Ask yourself, if I were in charge around here (and of course most times you are, at least in part), how would I be handling this situation differently? Remember that others around you who have benefited from your avoidance may not like the changes you implement, but that's up to them to do something about—that's *their* red carpet.

Strategy #4: Think Smaller

We think change has to be big and results immediate. When you're feeling very bad, you set your sights on big-ticket items— a whole new life, a promotion, a new relationship, a different body. And when that is clearly out of reach at 10:00 AM on a Monday morning, you start to feel like there's nothing you can do. You may think that until you know *for sure* that something will make you feel much better, you'll stay with the hand you're dealt, because you can't risk feeling more disappointment by trying something that might not work. Expectations about change can block your way.

We need to learn to think small. Thinking big often gets in the way of doing anything at all. We think that if we are feeling really bad or really scared, the solution must match that scale. That expectation keeps us from taking the very useful initial moves that are part of any process. The Zen saying does not state that all journeys start with a superman leap over tall buildings. The timeless wisdom is much more about a single step that reaches slightly outside your comfort zone. Once you have moved—even to go downstairs to get a snack, the situation has changed and so have you.

Small is also the operative word when you are making plans. Figure out exactly what your goal is and then break it down into small steps that you can tackle one at a time. Often, you take the fact that you don't have a plan or are stumbling with it as an indication that you shouldn't embark on it. Nothing could be further from the truth.

Strategy #5: Skip the Parts You Don't Like and Find the Moving Part

When you feel stuck, it may be that one issue that feels onerous is blocking you from taking on the other four that you could actually tackle. Rather than waste time locked into a staring contest with the one thing that you *can't* do right now, do what you can. When you come up against the chapter you *despise* in the novel you are writing, the aspect of your mortgage application that you *don't* understand, the part of your résumé that needs a new spin, don't let that one bad thing create a bottleneck for all that you could do. Give yourself permission to do things out of order. Skip over the problem to find the one thing that you are ready to do now. Once you're in motion on something, those intimidating parts may no longer look so daunting. Even if they do, when you see yourself accomplishing things in spite of the part you're stuck on, you'll get a lift. Be willing to skip, let go, and try again later—you may be pleasantly surprised.

Strategy #6: Cheat Motivation, Don't Wait for It

🍃 *I'll start that brief when I get motivated. I'll go to the gym when I get motivated.* 🍃

As much as we often sit gritting our teeth trying to will motivation into being, research suggests some surprising good news. Motivation *follows* behavior. This means that even if you sleepwalk to the gym, sneaking past your ambivalence, once you find yourself in a new situation or activity, motivation starts swirling in. So, find a way to bottle that idea for yourself. When my young patients are stuck, unable to get away from the television or out of the bathroom where they are excessively washing their hands,

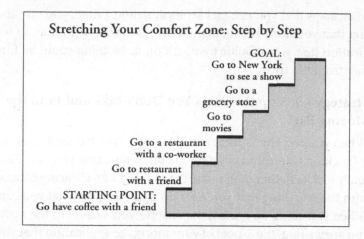

they imagine they are shooting themselves out of a cannon. You might think about taking off in your Ferrari, or simply pressing the eject button on your chair and going.

Legendary dancer and choreographer Twyla Tharp says that her morning routine of working out at 6:00 AM at a gym across town each morning doesn't come from motivation and discipline. It comes from the simple act of calling the cab to pick her up at 5:30 AM. Like the rest of us, she wants to go back to bed. But that one small phone call starts the train moving and then she can hop on. "The cab is moving. I'm committed. Like it or not, I'm going to the gym," she writes in her book *The Creative Habit*.

Once the first step is taken, it's harder to turn back. One small thing can kick-start the motivation. It's like a buy-one, get-one-free program for your neurology. Once the first step is taken, the others follow suit, effortlessly.

Strategy #7: Map Out Your Steps

You're ready for things to change in your life, but it feels like Ready! Set! Wait. You want companionship, so at the top of your stairs, you write, "finding a boyfriend, or a girlfriend, or even getting married." It's not like you can stop at a store on the way home from work and take care of that errand. You may feel discouraged because you can't will that big thing to happen; there's nothing

TRY THIS

Think of a goal that you have for yourself and write it at the top of a piece of paper. You might want to lose weight, deepen your friendships, increase social contact in your life, be less angry, be less shy, or be more assertive.

Write your goal at the top of the page. Next, write your starting point—where you are now—at the bottom. Draw a staircase between the top and the bottom of the page and think through the specific steps that you can take one at a time for a week or two, until you're ready to tackle the next challenge.

Remember the swimming-pool analogy from Chapter 2 for getting used to things? Each step you take may feel uncomfortable *at first*, but give it a little time and then you adjust and the water feels fine.

you can do but wait till it does. You have to look at the changes that you can make in your life to take you there. Take a minute to set your emotions aside, and instead tackle the situation in a matter-of-fact way, brainstorming and identifying the way an engineer would the small steps that are necessary to get to your goal.

When I work with children who are afraid to sleep in their own beds or go to the friend's house who has a dog, I always draw a staircase. We write the goal at the top of the stairs. Next, we write what they are able to do now, their starting point, and put that at the bottom of the stairs. Then I ask kids to name some of the activities that would be helpful for them to get from Point A to Point B. You can't fly up the steps. You take them one at a time. Whether you want to ask your boss for feedback (start with asking your wife or co-worker first, then approach your boss with something minor) or you want to shovel out the junk in your basement (spend ten minutes dividing the job into one-hour units, work for one hour on old tools, another on clothing, another on old toys, drive bags to The Salvation Army). The drawing helps us to visualize the possibilities from start to finish. Once the staircase is drawn, momentum begins.

FREEING YOURSELF: IN ACTION

Mitchell's best friend from college was dying of cancer. He had two young children, and Mitchell, with a family of his own, felt distraught about his friend and helpless to make a difference. Mitchell said that as irrational as it sounded, he thought that the only way he could really help was if his friend wouldn't die in the end. Focused on the sadness of that, he couldn't think of other things to do or value the things he was doing. In creating a simple list and placing the goal "I want to ease the struggle of my friend and his family" at the top, Mitchell was able to identify the very useful things he was doing that made a huge difference, such as playing with his friend's children, reading favorite *Science* articles to him, bringing dinner over for his family each week, being willing to talk about death. Looking at the list, Mitchell could identify what he *was* doing, instead of just what he *couldn't* do. This inspired him to think of even more ways to help. His feeling of powerlessness was depriving both Mitchell and his friend of the experiences that they shared in this difficult time. Being willing to take small steps made an enormous difference to both of them.

Bridget was having trouble with her teenage son Tim. Surly and dark, Tim was disrespectful and unappreciative, and this behavior wore on Bridget. "He won't say thank you, and sometimes he won't say anything. I have to tiptoe around him constantly," Bridget told me. She thought that her only choice was the big goal of getting her son to stop behaving like this, but she knew she couldn't control him. She felt powerless and depressed because she didn't like what this was doing to the family dynamic. Bridget usually responded to Tim by getting angry or saying nothing to prevent a fight. She was spiraling into a hole, all the while feeling that if she were truly a good parent, this wouldn't be happening.

We started to separate her son's behavior and dark moods from the choices she could make for herself, rather than seeing them as inextricably linked. Bridget couldn't force her son to be the moving part, but she had options about how she could move herself. Like the "Aha!" moment that parents experience when they realize that if their children won't go to time out when they are misbehaving, then the parents can actually take a time out and walk away temporarily themselves, the first step for Bridget was to imagine how she could respond differently. She realized that giving feedback was a choice that she had but hadn't been taking, and that she had a choice to not just stand there and listen to her son when he was being disrespectful. She began saying things like, "I'm sorry you are feeling bad," or, "I know this is where you are right now, but this isn't working here. This isn't how our family works. I want to help, but I just can't talk with you when you're talking to me like that. So if you are interested in working together, great, but if not, I can't help you right now." Not only did Bridget release herself from the trap of her son's moods, but her son started to respect her more.

Strategy #8: Put Time on Your Side: Setting Appropriate Goals

Often, what stops us from moving at all is that we have unrealistic time expectations in mind. A smarter part of us could say what my young patients say to their parents—"The more you rush me, the less I want to move!" Rather than get in a battle with yourself arguing over time, take the hesitation as a signal that maybe the timing needs to be the moving part. Is it the deadline or just making changes that is the most important part? Instead of saying, "I'm giving myself two months to get in shape," and then giving up after only one week because you foresee the failure ahead, ease up on the time frame and identify the new patterns you'd like to set day by day, week by week.

Strategy #9: Brainstorming Possibilities When You're Unsure of the Steps

The goal of brainstorming is to have a new direction, to get unstuck, and to move from problem mode, in which you feel hopeless,

---

FIVE QUICK STEPS TO BRAINSTORMING
- Step One: Identify the Problem
- Step Two: Brainstorm Solutions
- Step Three: Choose the Best Option, Rehearse
- Step Four: Implement
- Step Five: Evaluate the Effectiveness, Revise as Necessary

---

to solution mode, in which you shop for the answer that fits best. The neutrality inherent in brainstorming can be missed when people want the best answer right away. But that means they are simultaneously *analyzing* and *evaluating* when they should be neutrally generating ideas. Un-fettered generating of ideas comes first; analyzing them comes second.

To get more traction with the brainstorming stage, consider writing ideas on a handful of index cards. On each card, write down a possible next step, be it realistic or wildly unrealistic. Brainstorming is about generating heat and inspiration, not necessarily nailing down the next step, not immediately. By letting the cards do the talking, sometimes we feel that the choices are out of our hands in a helpful way and we just play it as it lays.

When Lauren, recently divorced, made the decision to do something about her loneliness, she was scared. She could now say that she missed having companionship, but she felt daunted by the idea of dating. After a decade of marriage, dating seemed like a universe in a different galaxy and she had no idea how to get there. We brainstormed on cards what other people might do—*not what she would do*—to start dating, and this strategy helped her come up with a variety of ideas. Shuffling the cards, as if someone else had made them up for her, she picked a card and talked about what that idea would look like for her.

Jesse used the same strategy for thinking about generating more business for his small real estate company. We wrote on cards all the different tactics his colleagues took: the ones he liked as well as the ones he thought he would "never" do. Imagining himself trying each approach, he was able to stretch and entertain new ideas.

Strategy #10: Barn Raising: Get More People Involved

One of the obstacles to moving forward occurs when you lack the information you need. You think that you *should* know everything already, so you neither move forward nor ask for help. Imagine that in optimizing you came up with the following analysis:

It's not that your business is a mess—it's that you need someone to do QuickBooks. Great. Now you need to find that person. But two obstacles to asking for help crop up. First, you may believe that you *should* already know the information yourself, so you don't ask.

Second, you think that asking someone for help will burden the other person. When you have figured out an option but don't know what to do next, reach out. Write this e-mail: "Hey, can I get your quick take on this? My mind is telling me this is crazy, but I wanted to get your perspective." Or even, "I'm having one of those days where nothing is working out—help!"

Soliciting new input can help, but don't choose an anxious or negative friend who will throw you right back into the mess you're trying to untangle yourself from. Choose a friend who can help you parse the details and identify the opportunities. If all your friends are anxious and negative, it may be time to revise your network.

You may also fall into the time-sink obstacle, thinking it will take too much time to do this—for you or for your friend. It will take time, but think of all the time it takes being inconvenienced by the problem. Often, we struggle for hours with something that a quick call could have solved in minutes. If someone called you and asked for ten minutes of your time, would you be annoyed, or would you feel useful and happy to help? Chances are that we all could benefit from the unspoken barter system in a good community or friendship.

Strategy #11: Going Through the Motions: The Power of Mental Rehearsal

Do you know why athletes are told to visualize running through a course when they can't practice on the track? Or why violinists can practice a concerto on a plane without disturbing the other passengers and without their instrument? Neuroplasticity suggests that when you're trying to master a skill, visualizing is the next best thing to doing it. So, if you're not ready to go in and talk to your boss about your co-worker who is consistently late, just imagine doing it. Put your boss in the chair across from you and direct the conversation. Try different approaches, start again, do it better, and imagine the boss's different responses. Keep at it until you can end on a good note where things work out. Especially if one of the things stopping you from taking action is how angry or upset you may get, these private rehearsals allow you to preview your reactions. By working some of that emotion out in advance, when you are ready to take action you will be clear-headed enough to say what you need to without fearing an unexpected burst of emotion.

A FINAL WORD: WHEN ACCEPTANCE IS THE ACTION TO TAKE

> *Teach us to care and not to care. Teach us to sit still.*
>
> —T. S. ELIOT

Sometimes, rather than spin around trying to wrestle a problem, we need to let go of it so that we can move on to something else. We get out of the way through acceptance.

When we encounter situations that we can't change, we shouldn't see that as an aberration. Life gives us both situations that we can change and those we can't. This is not necessarily a bad thing. In the midst of adversity, you often feel that you can do nothing, and as a result you want to give up. You might not

TRY THIS
Create Your To-Go Menu

Think about times when you've felt stuck in the past and how you've gotten out of them. Make a list of four activities to release you from the sticky place. Remember that motivation *follows* behavior, not the reverse. Do one thing, and when you see yourself moving, you'll feel motivated and capable of doing more. And remember the swimming pool that feels chilly when you first get in. The sooner you dive, the sooner you adjust.

Think of the first steps that lead to others. When you put your sneakers on, you're going for a walk. When you turn on your stereo or iPod, you move to the beat. When you walk toward the leash, your dog starts barking. These steps all set off an internal physical program that anticipates and readies you for the next steps, at no extra cost to you. Finding your first steps ushers you on your way.

Practice Letting Go of the Rope

Sitting for hours in front of a 1,500-piece jigsaw puzzle of the Eiffel Tower, you insist on finding the place for one particular piece that seems to be taunting you with its elusiveness. Then your child walks in and locks several pieces into another part of the puzzle. This apparently easier part would have been staring you in the face, too, if you'd only been willing to let go of the part that you couldn't solve at that moment and had instead searched for the part—the moving part—that you could. Initially, when we let go we may feel defeated—we think we should have been able to succeed, but with time, letting go of the stuck part in place of the part that moves feels better and better. Over time, because we anticipate the triumph on the other side of the (temporary) defeat, we won't have to work so hard on letting go; because we know it is actually the hidden door to moving forward, we do it automatically.

YOU AND BEYOND

When you help a friend who seems to be spinning his or her wheels, it's okay to stay out of their quicksand. Instead of spinning your wheels in tandem with theirs, gently suggest that a "walk away" often works for you to clear your head and see what the situation looks like when you return. Offer to take that walk with your friend, or even suggest something ridiculous or random to break the gridlock. "When I find myself in a sticky situation like this, nothing but dancing to the Rolling Stones in my living room will do." Your friend doesn't have to take your idea, but that picture may bump out the one that is stuck and suggest that this situation is manageable. In this way we can lead the change that others need to take for themselves.

A second way we can help others when they're stuck is to simply keep them company and make whatever task they're avoiding more of a social event. If someone you know is having trouble filing insurance forms, starting that new website, scouring the help-wanted ads, perusing dating profiles as a new single parent, or even just working on a stalled cleaning project, help your friend make an onerous task a little less so by showing up. Lend your momentum. Bring snacks and music. Your friend may return the favor down the road when there's something you can't bear the thought of staring you in the face.

---

wish for the choices you have, you'd rather not be in the situation in the first place, but short of fixing the situation, there are always ways that you can impact your life. As you've seen, the first level is how you narrate the situation. You can tell yourself that a situation is "the worst thing ever and unbearable," but after you start the story in that way, you can follow different paths by telling yourself, "This is my situation, it's not what I want, but I'm going do what I can to help myself."

If there's truly nothing you can do, then don't do anything. It's worse to keep reviewing and practicing the list of things that you can't do than to simply accept it. Put it in a box till later, when perhaps circumstances will change and you can try something different. Take action. Go back to the Try This strategies in Chapter 2 for worry time and worry vacations to help the worry stay in that box.

Executive coach Michael Bungay Stanier tells the story of an architect who designed buildings for a university campus. Instead of designing pathways between the buildings, he left it to the students to find the best paths. A year later, he returned to pave the paths the students had worn in the ground themselves. Although you may be impatient, sometimes letting go and giving yourself time to find that right path yields the best answer.

FREEING YOURSELF: IN ACTION

In college, Chris's friends knew him as an entrepreneurial go-to guy. His mind worked in big ideas, and he could instantly visualize success at the end of the arc. He planned to have his own business by age thirty. Yet, out of college and now age twenty-seven, in a place where he could make those dreams come true, Chris was getting depressed. He couldn't understand why he wasn't getting to those end points quickly and because he wasn't where he'd imagined himself to be, he felt he hadn't accomplished anything.

Chris thought that in order to move at all, it had to be a big step. He was so panicked about not meeting his longtime goal that his energies were being sucked into a black hole, rather than constructively deciphering whether this was really still his goal and what small steps he could take to get there. He was inundated with thoughts about being a failure and a fraud and not living up to anyone's expectations, especially his own.

Narrowing it down, Chris realized that he did want to own a business, but he hadn't learned how to do this methodically, creating a plan and smaller goals that he could feel good about when he reached them. He was still the go-to guy, but older and wiser; he now knew that small steps were the way to go.

Caroline was an engineer who also wanted to start her own business but couldn't seem to make any progress. She questioned whether she lacked the motivation. But it didn't ring true. Caroline was very self-disciplined. She had lost a significant amount of weight and kept it off; she had saved up methodically to buy her condominium, and she'd always considered herself a motivated person. So what was blocking her?

In talking it through, Caroline concluded that fear of failing or losing security wasn't the issue for her. The issue was figuring out where to start. Things like looking at office space, getting a business loan, creating a Web presence were spinning in her mind. She thought that because she didn't know what to do first, this meant that she was on the wrong path and the goal wasn't right for her after all.

When we started to brainstorm all the possible steps for starting a business, Caroline's strong, logical mind could assemble them in a way that fit for her. She wrote each step on an index card and then played around with the order until it made sense. There was still a lot to do, but she now had a plan and could begin to move forward.

Chapter 8

THE ANXIETY DISORDERS: WHEN YOU NEED MORE HELP

Your pain is the breaking of the shell that encloses your understanding.

—KAHLIL GIBRAN

WHEN DOES SOMEONE CROSS OVER FROM WORRY TO AN ANXIETY DISORDER?

What is "normal" worry? If you spend meetings stressed-out, are at a loss for words at a party, or feel a sudden rush of heat when you have to introduce yourself—does that mean you must reserve a place for weekly visits on the therapist's couch? The short answer is no. All of us have these experiences of anxiety some of the time. However, when worries become more than occasional in response to a stressful situation, and if they confront you at every turn, that's the first red flag of an anxiety disorder.

When you avoid important activities or situations because of fears of what could go wrong or simply because you know anxiety will make those situations impossible to manage or take all enjoyment or pleasure from the event, that's the second red flag of an anxiety disorder.

According to the psychiatric classification system used by health professionals, a disorder is indicated by the degree to which the symptoms interfere with social, occupational, or other important areas of functioning or cause clinically significant distress. In other words, when you have to make your plans or change them because of your worry or you suffer greatly getting through your day because of anxiety, you may have a disorder. If so, take heart, and take action. We live in a time when you don't have to suffer waking up to the weight of the world each day. All anxiety disorders are treatable, and with the right treatment, the prognosis is very good. You will find a list of organizations at the end of the chapter that will help you locate a therapist who specializes in the treatment of anxiety disorders in your area.

WHAT KIND OF HELP DO I NEED? THERAPY, MEDICATION, OR BOTH?

To alleviate the suffering of patients with anxiety, therapists today often choose cognitive behavioral therapy (CBT), the approach behind the strategies presented in this book, and with good reason. CBT is practical, easy to implement, highly effective, typically brief, and well liked by patients for all of those reasons. Decades of well-controlled studies have established CBT's success in treating anxiety and anxiety disorders. In fact, researchers have found that CBT is more effective than a placebo control (sugar pill) or analytic therapy and can even be more effective than medication for anxiety. Patients who have undergone CBT can maintain long-term gains that buffer them from developing depression or another anxiety disorder. The therapy also has short-term effects, enabling patients to learn a set of new skills for managing worry and the physical symptoms of anxiety, often within a few months of treatment.

Depending on how significantly your symptoms are interfering with your life, even if you start with a cognitive behavioral thera-

QUESTIONS TO ASK YOURSELF

- Do you often wake up feeling irritable, anxious, or apprehensive about your day?
- Do you make or change plans because you feel too anxious?
- Do you avoid situations or fail to enjoy them because you are distracted by worry and fear?
- Does life feel much harder than it needs to be?
- Do you feel tired or even exhausted from managing your typical responsibilities?
- Does stress make it hard to concentrate, relax, or sleep?

pist, together you may determine that medication would be a helpful adjunct to the tools you are acquiring in therapy. If anxiety interferes significantly with sleep, appetite, or mood, your therapist may recommend that you be evaluated for medication. CBT and medication work on different parts of the brain. Medication can be helpful in tamping down the limbic system—the emotional reactivity part of the brain—helping you feel calmer, whereas CBT changes the circuits in the cortex in response to learning new cognitive tools, helping you think more clearly and accurately. Medication can sometimes speed up relief and enhance a patient's ability to learn the techniques that will afford the long-lasting improvements.

There are two types of medication typically prescribed for anxiety that have very different actions and operate on different systems in the brain. The most common medications are selective serotonin reuptake inhibitors (SSRIs). These long-acting medications with brand names such as Prozac, Zoloft, Luvox, and Effexor, work on blocking the reuptake of the neurotransmitter serotonin to facilitate the efficient transmission of brain messages. The same SSRIs are used for anxiety disorders and depression. Typically, it takes anywhere from two to eight weeks before patients experience relief and the maximum benefit of the medication.

The second class of medications that are prescribed for anxiety, especially for panic disorder, are the benzodiazepines, with such brand names as Xanax, Ativan, Klonopin, and Valium. They are fast-acting medications that act to sedate or quiet down the nervous system, usually within an hour. They can provide a very effective short-term tool in overcoming anxiety, because they are temporary and have no lasting effects once they are out of your system hours later. Unlike SSRIs, which are entirely nonaddictive, benzodiazepines can be habit-forming, so your physician will carefully review your risk before prescribing.

WHAT ARE THE DIFFERENT ANXIETY DISORDERS, AND HOW DO I KNOW IF I HAVE ONE?

Obsessive-Compulsive Disorder (OCD)

People who don't have OCD say that everyone is a little obsessive-compulsive. In reality, there is a world of difference between wearing your lucky socks when you play golf or making sure you kiss your kids good night every day and the heavy burden of feeling for hours each day like the welfare of those you love rests precariously on your perfect execution of rechecking doors and stoves or counting the words you say to make sure you end on an even number. The primary difference between non-OCD behavior and OCD is choice. When you do things out of preference (you like counting your words because it's fun), this is not OCD. People with OCD do not recheck, redo, and apologize incessantly because it gives them a sense of satisfaction or feels good. They do this because they are seized by doubt about whether they actually completed the act in the first place or whether they executed it just right, without any bad thoughts or images that could undo the protection from harm that the ritual promises.

In contrast to event-specific, time-limited extremes that people without OCD sometimes experience, like double-checking all of the details of a wedding day's events or repeatedly securing the

WHAT TO ASK YOURSELF

- Do you have unusual, unpleasant thoughts and images (not simply ordinary worries) of harm, contamination, violence, scrupulosity, religion, or sexuality that you can't stop thinking about and that cause significant distress?
- Do you have rituals such as washing, checking, apologizing, or praying that you engage in to undo or prevent the consequence of the intrusive thought?
- Do you have specific ways of performing ordinary tasks that you feel you *need* to do that way, and can't skip, even when necessary?
- Do you spend more than an hour a day on obsessions or rituals?
- Are you late or unable to complete tasks because of fears of what might happen if you don't do them exactly right?

house before leaving on a long vacation, bizarre rules and beliefs ravage the life of the person who suffers from OCD on a daily basis. Rather than insuring their security, the constant belief that the outcome of their lives rests solely on whether they pictured a good thing when a bad thought comes to mind or that they opened and closed the cupboard exactly ten times (the number of grandchildren they have) leaves them in a constant state of just having barely dodged a bullet.

OCD is also very time-consuming. Perhaps all of us feel the need to recheck an item or two—the stove and doors at night, the hair-straightening iron—but nothing else; these habits aren't time-consuming enough to constitute OCD. A third distinction is that OCD checking routines become more and more elaborate, involved, and lengthy. Checking may become more frequent, often requiring total silence and concentration. If interrupted, they may need to be started again. People without OCD may have checking routines that are brief and potentially helpful. They check, and they're done. People with OCD come to a point where they've forgotten what constitutes reasonable checking, and they need to consult others to relearn what sensible precautions look like to the rest of the world.

Cracking the Code: Breaking the Rules of the OCD Tyrant Whispering in Your Ear

For thousands of years, OCD was a deeply misunderstood condition. Theories pinned blame on sufferers' need for control or perfection, on their overprotective parents, or long before that on being possessed by the devil. Neurobiology has replaced these destructive and archaic explanations, and we now understand that the relentless, intrusive thoughts are a nonpersonal, no-fault result of a clogged or faulty filtering system in the brain—the caudate nucleus, to be specific. Here, thoughts that should be edited get stuck and keep repeating. The repetition increases the credulity of the thought and the feeling of urgency to follow the orders—however bizarre—to perform rituals. Although sufferers feel shame and personal responsibility for the strange and even disturbing content of their thoughts, the basic themes of OCD (contamination, symmetry, aggression/harm/sexual thoughts, and scrupulosity) hold across all cultures and across spans of history. So, rather than being personal, think of OCD as a generic brain hiccup.

Once you understand that the reason you have these thoughts is because of a mechanical glitch, you can begin to relabel the OCD, demote its importance, and start trying to live your life the old way, the way that worked perfectly fine before OCD came on the scene.

Exposure and ritual prevention (E/RP) is the most effective treatment for OCD to create life-changing, long-lasting improvements. E/RP involves creating a hierarchy of OCD situations and deliberately facing first the lowest-ranking situation and resisting engaging in the ritual, because you've stamped it as unnecessary. It entails putting yourself into situations where rituals occur—

NORMAL "CHECKING" VERSUS OBSESSIVE-COMPULSIVE BEHAVIOR

Preferences	OCD
What I want to do	What I feel I *have* to do or something terrible will happen

using public bathrooms, not rechecking the stove—feeling the anxiety generated by the situation, and then intentionally *not* engaging in the ritual to see the anxiety break on its own because it was never necessary in the first place. When you feel anxious about the possibility of dirt on your hands, it's not that your hands are dirty, it's that the *all-clean* message hasn't gotten there yet. If you keep washing excessively, the brain will keep that loop going. It feels frightening to break rituals. Using E/RP in small steps, you see that not only does nothing bad happen when you break a ritual, in fact something very *good* happens—you regain control of your life.

Panic Disorder: An Anxiety Surge Without a Cause

I was totally unprepared when my boss asked me to do an impromptu summary for the partners—I panicked. We all use that term *panic* colloquially, but the rest of the story typically describes how the person pulled it together for a fine or even pretty great presentation. Someone with clinical panic disorder finishes the story differently: *Then I had to leave the room, I felt like the walls were closing in, I felt like I was going crazy, I didn't feel real. Everything seemed strange, I didn't know what to do, and finally I told my boss I was sick and went home. As soon as I got into my car, I started to feel a little better, and by the time I got back to my house, I felt relieved.*

WHAT TO ASK YOURSELF

- Does my anxiety hit out of the blue, or is there always a cause?
- Does it escalate within a matter of minutes, or does it percolate over hours?
- Do I have a feeling of dread like something bad is about to happen or that I'm going crazy, or am I just concerned that a situation will turn out badly?
- Do I avoid places for fear that I might have a panic attack?

Worry, even extreme worry, differs from panic in several important ways. First, by definition, panic has no clear trigger. It is characterized by a sudden surge of dread and adrenaline that hits out of the blue, even if you are in the middle of enjoying a romantic dinner at a favorite restaurant, engrossed in a fascinating film, or simply doing the grocery shopping. The fact that panic has no clear reason for appearing begins the fear, and that launches into more panic. You start to frantically, but understandably, ask questions—*What's wrong with me? Why is this happening? What's going to happen next?* Your body reacts to thoughts of threat with the default response—fight or flight. It pumps adrenaline into your bloodstream, makes your heart beat faster to get the blood flowing to arms and legs so you can run or fight for your life. This only compounds the distress, because, with no enemy in sight, you have gone from calm to full-blown freaking out, and have landed in an out-of-body experience in a matter of minutes.

If one difference between anxiety and panic is that panic occurs out of the blue, a second difference is that with panic, the physical reactions are as prominent as the disturbing thoughts. A third distinction comes in the speed of panic attacks. Whereas we could worry on a low boil for hours, panic attacks escalate within minutes of the first "Uh-oh, what's happening to me?"

A fourth and final difference is in content. When we worry, the parameters of our concerns may be distorted, but content-wise they are familiar and typical, such things as missing deadlines, getting a disease, or losing a relationship. In contrast, the fear in panic attacks isn't about making a bad impression or missing a deadline, it's about losing control and losing your grip on reality, going "crazy," or having a heart attack and maybe dying. Once you've had a panic attack, you never want to feel that out of control again. This in itself can create the very conditions that perpetuate panic. Then you fear going places, whether back to the movies where you had the panic, or anywhere, just in case it might happen again.

People who've experienced a panic attack become hyperaware of even the slightest changes in physical sensations. After that, small and insignificant changes in breathing or slight light-headedness, which would not have been detected prior to ever having a panic attack, can immediately launch someone into panic for fear that these are signals of another attack. Just the thought of having another panic attack can spiral into a panic attack. People with panic disorder never know when symptoms may strike, and they suffer from an utter feeling of being unsafe in their own body.

Although nothing is wrong with you physically, your complete incapacitation can be embarrassing and confusing to the people around you who say you are fine and question why can't you go to the party. Inside, you think, *Because I'm about to explode or die!* It's embarrassing and difficult to stay on home base or stay in touch with a person who feels like a lifeline to you, because if you're not in those safe places, you believe you're in danger.

Cracking the Code: Send Back the Fire Trucks, It's a False Alarm

In the comedy film *Analyze This*, Robert De Niro plays a Mafia boss who begins to break down under the strain of his line of work and have panic attacks. He rushes to the hospital one evening, convinced that he is about to die. When the unassuming

---

WORRY VERSUS PANIC
Worry
- Typically has a focus or trigger
- Waxes and wanes over time
- May or may not have physical components

Panic
- Occurs out of the blue
- Escalates and peaks usually within ten minutes
- Always has physical symptoms—heart racing, sweating, tingling, stomach churning

---

young resident reports that all the tests are normal and it is just stress, De Niro roughs up the doctor, knocks over some equipment in the examining room, and insists that there must be some mistake, that there is no way that what he was feeling was fake. In fact, De Niro was perfectly safe and healthy. The most important fact to hold on to when having a panic attack is that the symptoms are completely harmless and will pass on their own. They will resolve a lot sooner when we can understand why they are happening, and here's the answer.

Panic disorder can best be understood as a test of the emergency broadcasting system—except that unfortunately, it forgets to announce the test first. The sudden onset of physical symptoms is a perfectly logical progression of the emergency response (all it is missing is the emergency). But without knowing this, you misinterpret, understandably, the signals of racing heart, sweaty palms, light-headedness, and hyperreality or surreality as a sign of something very wrong happening in the body. So you ask, *Why is this happening? What's wrong with me? What's going to happen next?* These questions all serve to escalate the amygdala response. Thus, we misunderstand the original signal as a real alarm, the body keeps responding to our distress, our distress continues to escalate with the disconcerting physical symptoms, and the result

CHANGE THE MESSAGE
These questions stoke the fire of panic:

- What's happening to me?
- What am I going to do?
- When is it going to stop?
- Am I going crazy?
- What if everyone is noticing me freaking out?
- What if I lose control and start screaming?
- What if I need to go to the hospital?

These lines calm the panic:

- This is panic, it is uncomfortable but harmless.
- I feel scared, but I'm not in danger.
- There is nothing wrong with me.
- This will pass in a matter of time.
- I feel this way because I'm scared, not because I'm actually in danger.

is a vicious cycle of terror and dread. What stops it? Redirecting the cycle the other way. Instead of asking questions that send more juice to the amygdala, make factual statements that reduce the demand and thus the supply: *I am having a panic attack, I am fine, there is nothing wrong with me. These feelings are uncomfortable but they are harmless, if I help myself to stay calm, this will pass and I will feel better in about fifteen or twenty minutes.*

The treatment for panic involves *psychoeducation*, or a translation of the processes that occur, and *interoceptive exposure*, a desensitization to the physical symptoms of panic. In interoceptive exposure, you practice running or panting to see that when your heart beats fast, you can slow it down, it's not dangerous to you. In-vivo exposure, another component of treatment, involves gradually revisiting, in short stints that gradually extend, the situations you avoid, such as being in stores, restaurants, or movies, because of fear of panic attacks.

Generalized Anxiety Disorder (GAD):
Worry on Autopilot

We all have stressful days when the devil is in the details. Meeting deadlines, staying on schedule, and fielding a barrage of e-mails can feel like an episode of *Mission Impossible*. When these challenges are frustrating but manageable, we call this modern life. When instead of creating momentum they create a constant worry list about your current life, your future life, and the lives of others and that leaves you stressed, angry, or on the brink of tears, then something else is going on. If that is your experience more days than not, for at least six months, you may have generalized anxiety disorder (GAD).

Unlike typical worry, which ebbs and flows in reaction to the stresses in our lives, the worry with GAD is constant, uncontrollable, and exhausting. The first characteristic of GAD is excessive worry, from finding it unbearable to be late for an appointment to worrying about how you look, how you perform in your job, how your friends feel about you, what your financial and medical future will be. Another characteristic of GAD is that the consequences of any one minor misstep are seen as linked to inevitable and irrevocable consequences, leading to a catastrophic future. With many sentences starting with, "What am I going to do if . . . ?" each problem or hypothetical problem is complex and takes up far more time than actual problems, which are discrete and solvable. It is easy for people with GAD to feel consumed by worry that expands to fill every hour.

For those with GAD, a constant feeling of being on edge and braced for an imminent problem or disaster means there isn't a moment in the day free from worry. Daily tasks are opportunities for things to go wrong. People with GAD run marathons in their mind, constantly looping around all the possible ways bad things are happening or could happen in the future as a result, and physical symptoms such as fatigue, headaches, stomachaches, and even body pains are common. The amygdala is always turning on

ASK YOURSELF

- Does worry feel constant and uncontrollable and not just in response to specific stressors?
- Do you often feel tense and upset, have headaches, muscle aches, fatigue, or insomnia?
- Is it hard to enjoy activities because you are preoccupied with what could go wrong or what will happen next?

and mobilizing the system in response to fears of the worst consequences for small situations.

People with GAD truly suffer as worry wears on them cognitively, physically, and emotionally. They are hypervigilant, scanning the environment for signs of trouble, and have a general "what's wrong?" stance toward life. They may have trouble concentrating or sitting still, have frequent physical problems, and get upset or irritable very easily. If you perceive that things are constantly on the edge of going terribly wrong and you are responsible for preventing them, it is nearly impossible to relax.

Cracking the Code: Not Every Bell Tolls for Thee

People with GAD feel compelled to be on their watch constantly, but this means looping around hundreds, even thousands, of false alarms in the course of a lifetime.

Therapy for GAD involves challenging the perceived positive protective role of worry: If I worry, I can prevent bad things from happening, and if I don't worry, bad things will happen and it will be my fault. By changing their belief that worry serves a function, GAD sufferers can begin to see worry for what it is. No matter how strongly we believe our worry, deep down we know the truth: Worry doesn't protect or prevent, it simply makes us upset and takes an enormous toll for constantly being on guard.

A second element of treatment is developing a regular practice of exercise, breathing, and relaxation to help the body unlearn the high-alert pattern. A third element is learning how to be more present and aware in the moment rather than racing ahead to worst-case scenarios, Increasing awareness means not only noticing when worry is starting and giving yourself choices but also deepening your engagement in and appreciation of what is actually going on around you, which increases the meaning and satisfaction you derive from your life. The worry time and worry vacation exercises in Chapter 2 can help set limits on time, so you can begin to regain control over anxiety. Worry can't barge in any time, you're going to train it to be "by appointment only."

Social Anxiety Disorder

In one advertisement for a social anxiety medication, a person sits at a table in jail under a bare fluorescent light surrounded by intimidating people, like an inquisition. Then, the scene changes and you see that this is what it feels like to the person with social anxiety, but actually it is just a friendly conversation at a restaurant.

Although we all know the occasional moment of sudden discomfort when meeting someone, worrying that our palms are sweaty, that there will be dead air space with nothing to say, the feeling comes on and then it goes away. We warm up to the situation eventually. With social anxiety, this phenomenon is constant. Every moment is a performance with no backstage breaks.

WHAT TO ASK YOURSELF

- Do you feel nervous at first in social situations and then warm up, or do you feel unbearably self-conscious and do those feelings persist throughout the interaction?
- Do you often feel that you are being scrutinized, making it hard to focus or think?
- Do you approach social situations anticipating that you are going to do something embarrassing or even humiliating?

You believe people can see through you and there's no safe place to hide even when you are alone in your apartment. The critics have all sharpened their pencils and fixed their gaze on the smallest unit of measurement from our word choice (not clever, or even stupid), our appearance (that hair out of place, the blemish, the wrinkled shirt), our right to exist (who do you think you are?).

None of us would consider it pathological to want to make a good impression, participate fully in a good conversation, or be thought of as attractive or interesting. With social anxiety, the constant concern about being scrutinized by others creates the very conditions that make it hard to focus socially or give an accurate appraisal of how you come across.

Social anxiety disorder doesn't allow for any warming up slowly in a social interaction. You are instantly under those imagined hot stage lights until you feel and sometimes even appear so hot and sweaty that you may need to excuse yourself so you don't make a scene. You feel watched and evaluated all the time. Even driving in your car, getting the mail, and eating your lunch are fuel for scrutiny. As with many other anxiety disorders, the more uncomfortable the situation, the more you avoid it, and thus things like answering the phone, going out on dates, and replying to text messages may be avoided for fear of saying or doing not just the wrong thing, but a very embarrassing or humiliating thing.

What would that thing be? This is where the door of social anxiety needs to be opened. Awkward silences, stumbling over words, and blushing are all things that we all do at times. Rather than shine a bright spotlight on them, we can learn ways to laugh them off, ignore them, and move on. Not surprisingly, when you learn how to make light of them, they greatly decrease in frequency.

Cracking the Code of Social Phobia: Fire the Judge (or Turn Off the Judge's Microphone)

With a live-in critic scrutinizing and judging every move, no wonder you're afraid to do anything, even breathe (it might be too loud, or look weird). The very effective treatment for social anxiety involves cognitive restructuring, otherwise known as "firing the judge" and making your fears pass through a reality check. Instead of letting the scrutiny take all of your attention, demote the importance by relabeling the source as your overprotective brain and hear the running critique of your existence as background noise. Otherwise, it really will be difficult to concentrate on the conversation you are having. Maybe intuitively you know that you need to quiet down these thoughts, but there are two other steps in treatment that are extremely helpful. With the flooding technique from Chapter 5, Getting Specific, bring on the mistake and expand it until it feels ridiculous—*I am going to make a total fool of myself, I will have absolutely nothing at all to say, it will be the worst conversation in history, I will say something so bizarre and strange, she will run away screaming from me, hoards of people will follow.* At first, stepping into the flood will be your worst fear, but if you persist with it, you will desensitize and break the spell and hear it as the outrageous version of your life. You may come up with a shorthand flood—*Worst Conversationalist on the East Coast! Here goes!* to remind yourself that you're really not at risk.

Then you take the show on the road and practice these exposures in low-stakes situations at a store that you don't frequent or with solicitors at the mall whom you'll avoid next time anyway. Ask a question at a store, chose the safest friend to call on the phone, or better yet, practice with people you don't even know, calling random stores to ask their hours. Practice these exposures several times a week, and do several tries each time. Normally, after asking the first question you feel more anxious, but after asking the third one in close succession, you begin to feel a sense of mastery and accomplishment.

Post-Traumatic Stress Disorder (PTSD)

When you have or witness a near-death experience or something that you perceive to threaten your life or integrity or that of another person, you are stunned. The ability to process what you have felt, seen, heard, or smelled is overwhelmed by the enormous fear and intensity of the moment. Approximately 70 percent

WHAT TO ASK YOURSELF

- Are memories of the trauma taking over other aspects of my life and interfering with my functioning, mood, and enjoyment?
- Do I get very upset in or need to avoid situations that remind me of the trauma? Do these situations get easier with practice, or rather do I respond more intensely each time?
- Do I have nightmares or flashbacks in which I reexperience the trauma?
- Do I feel constantly irritable, on the edge of tears, unable to relax, and hypervigilant for signs of threat?

of adults will experience a traumatic event in their lifetime, whether it's an act of violence or violation, a car accident, a natural disaster, or a wartime experience. By definition, a traumatic event is one that is responded to with fear, horror, or helplessness. About 20 percent of those who experience such an event will develop post-traumatic stress disorder. It may seem difficult to distinguish between a natural recovery process and PTSD, but they are very different. With a natural recovery process, grief, sadness, crying, distress, irritability, and avoidance occur, but they diminish over time as you move through the expected phases of acceptance of the loss or event.

In general, as you work through traumatic events, you experience a gradual improvement, slowly returning to activities in life, finding meaning and connection. With PTSD, the grief or fear doesn't move. Instead, in a completely physiological and involuntary way, which is very painful for the sufferer, mind and body are programmed to remain in a state of readiness to cope, protect, defend. As a result of this, people with PTSD have reactions that are often extreme and unexpected—even to them. They are preoccupied with the trauma and may feel unable to think of

FINDING HELP

- Anxiety Disorders Association of America:
  www.adaa.org
  8730 Georgia Avenue
  Silver Spring, MD 20910
  Phone: (240) 485–1001
- Association for Behavioral and Cognitive Therapies:
  www.abct.org
  305 Seventh Avenue, 16th Floor
  New York, NY 10001
  Phone (212) 647–1890
- Academy of Cognitive Therapy:
  www.academyofct.org
  260 South Broad Street 18th Floor
  Philadelphia, PA, 19102
  Phone: (267) 350–7683
- International OCD Foundation:
  www.ocfoundation.org
  International OCD Foundation
  P.O. Box 961029
  Boston, MA 02196
  Phone: (617) 973–5801
- Mental Illness Research, Education and Clinical
  Centers (MIRECC), US Department of Veteran
  Affairs:
  www.mirecc.va.gov
  810 Vermont Avenue, NW
  Washington, DC 20420
  Phone: Crisis Line 1–800–273-TALK (8255)

anything else as the mind replays aspects of the event with precise details. They may have dreams or flashbacks about the event, and they find themselves constantly on the lookout, at the ready for any clues or signs of danger.

It is not unusual, therefore, for a person with PTSD to suddenly jump out of the way as if, for example, a car were about to hit them,

YOU AND BEYOND

If you suspect that a loved one has anxiety that goes beyond the normal reactions to a stressful life, you can encourage that person to seek help. No one likes to be told what to do, and this is especially the case when someone is already feeling stressed. Our suggestion of treatment will be accepted most openly when we approach through the door of compassion. Let that person know that you are feeling worried about his or her worrying. Share some information from this book, and wonder aloud if things could be a lot easier with some new ideas. Don't apply pressure or feel the need to rush the process unless there is truly imminent danger. Instead, know that for all of us, it sometimes takes several people mentioning an idea over time before we are ready to act on it. Even if your sharing your concern doesn't lead to immediate action, consider it loosening the jar lid; after a few more tries, it may be that things give way.

or have a sudden surge in adrenaline or a bout of uncontrollable crying. Although this may seem strange to people around them and even to sufferers themselves, it is completely logical and expected based on the brain's hair-trigger response to some signal it has detected that may be similar to some aspect of the traumatic event. Reexperiencing the feelings they had in the moment of the trauma, even though it isn't happening at the time, can be upsetting in and of itself, especially when flashbacks can at times appear out of the blue. As a result, those who suffer with PTSD will often limit excursions outside their small circle of safety.

A second consequence of being locked into the time warp of trauma is that sufferers experience a foreshortened sense of the future. They lose faith in their worldview and conclude it is futile to imagine that the world could be different.

Fortunately, there are extremely effective treatments for PTSD. Although challenging, treatment can often be streamlined and efficient, and sufferers are often incredulous that they can break free from what previously felt hopeless. They can grieve or respectfully process what actually happened without getting stuck in an infinite loop of terrified reactions.

Cracking the Code of PTSD: What Happened Then Is Not Happening Now

The brain has many ways of helping us understand and digest difficult experiences. Trauma researchers explain that because of the terror experienced in the face of life-threatening events, our normal equipment to process events is stunned, overwhelmed, and shut down. The brain prioritizes coping or surviving the event, and thus the emotional processing of that event must wait. As a result, data and details of the trauma are imprinted in the senses as isolated, static pictures without a narrative. In reaction to the overwhelming material they have lived through, sufferers have flashbacks or shut down and feel numb, or both.

With treatment, sufferers of PTSD are able to slowly, one picture or memory at a time, process and integrate the emotions that accompany the trauma to create a cohesive narrative and help their body and mind not react as if it were happening now. Another essential aspect of the PTSD treatment is that it helps to turn the pages in the narrative, rather than stopping at the worst part. Finally, treatment helps sufferers move to the resolution of the story, which may be about how they or others survived, creating understanding and acceptance for what they could not control.

PART III

Additional Tools to Free Yourself

"I think, therefore I am." So says Descartes. So far we've learned how to manage the anxious version of that, which is: *I think I am going to totally mess up, therefore I am going to totally mess up.* We know that thinking doesn't make it so, and the four steps help us move out of those initial fears, doubts, and recriminations and take care of the real business in our lives—the part that fits in the smallest box but opens up the greatest possibilities for us.

In this section, we look at other essential pieces of the puzzle for effectively freeing yourself from anxiety. These are:

Our feelings: When we're anxious, it's not just our thoughts we need to get hold of, it's the fire burning in our hearts or our bellies, whatever the case may be. Feelings can blindside us, and it wasn't a topic that was covered in school, but there are very effective ways of working with our feelings so that not only can we calm them down but we can identify what started them in the first place. That's our first stop in Chapter 9.

Our strengths and resources: Next, because anxious and negative thinking brings out the worst in us, or at least highlights our worst moments, we focus on how to locate and keep handy our strengths, the unique qualities that endure with us despite the ups and downs of life. Whether we take the time to get to know our strengths or not, they are there, so rather than operating in the dark, we take the opportunity in Chapter 10 to take stock of what we can rely on most in ourselves.

Our expectations: A third influence on our anxiety is the expectations we invent (often without knowing) about how we need things to go in our lives. We walk into situations expecting that people will love us and tell us all about it, that our days will go off without a hitch, that the job will come to us yesterday, that people will be so happy with everything we do. When expectations meet the world and somebody gets hurt, it's usually not the world. We learn in Chapter 11 how to make great expectations, meaning those that are actually great for our well-being. Though we can want to have people love us, listen to us, do what we say, expecting that it will actually happen (when others are involved) is a very different story. So, focusing on what we can control, we will learn how to be constructive with our expectations, and to match up expectations with accurate explanations for why things work or don't work—so we can get credit or direction for what needs to change.

Our goodness: Much of the hard work we've done so far is about what is wrong in our minds and how to fix it, so in Chapter 12, we look at the ways that we can bring meaningful experiences, such as gratitude, empathy, and compassion, into our lives on a regular basis, not only for our benefit but for the greater good.

Chapter 9

HOW TO OVERCOME YOUR FEAR OF ANXIOUS AND NEGATIVE FEELINGS

You can't stop the waves, but you can learn to surf.

—JACK KORNFIELD

Growing up with a father who had alcoholism and depression, Francis had a tough childhood. In addition to dramatic scenes, everyday life meant walking on eggshells, not knowing what mood his father would be in, what would set his father off, and whether his mother would be able to figure out how to keep the peace. Survival in Francis's family meant not showing emotion. Not only was nobody there to comfort you if you were scared, but it could start problems. Francis learned as a young child that showing emotion made you vulnerable and made other people angry, so he trained himself to keep a low profile.

Francis worked hard, took care of his younger siblings, and tunneled out into a good life for himself. But now his wife complained that Francis was emotionally distant. She might know that something was bothering him, but he wouldn't talk about it. When his wife was upset with him, or just upset, period, Francis felt overwhelmed. He'd learned emotion was too big to handle, and it led to bad scenes and bad feelings, so he shut it down. Although he was devoted as a husband and father, much was off limits in their marriage.

In sessions, Francis admitted that when something upset him he could feel his body bristle and tighten. He could visualize the wall going up. He didn't like how he shut down on his wife and kids, and he criticized himself because he knew he was the problem. This interfered with their closeness, and he felt inadequate, not knowing how else to cope.

Eventually, Francis was able to forgive himself and understand that what he had learned about emotion seemed "wrong" now, but that it had been the absolute right thing to learn to survive his childhood. He began to ask, *What if I didn't put up the wall, what would really happen? Would I crumble or would it just feel uncomfortable? They are just feelings and they're mine.* He started to picture a different kind of wall. Rather than the fortress he needed to protect himself as a child, he saw a moss-covered low stone wall, like those that lined the paths in his native Ireland. He felt safe behind the wall, but it was alive and permeable, with plants and vines growing in the cracks. He could talk to his wife over the wall without losing his footing. He started to use this image at work, too, when things got tense. Knowing that he could let in what was going on around him and not be obliterated by it made Francis feel much happier and connected. In the lexicon of CBT, he was "dosing himself" to feelings a little at a time.

EMOTIONS: IN THE WAY,
OR SHOWING THE WAY?

When my niece Allison was three years old, her brother, Isaac, was born. While driving home from the hospital, her father asked her how it felt to have a baby brother. Little Allison, sitting in her booster seat, paused thoughtfully and replied with all seriousness: "It feels like vomit." Out of the mouths of babes.

If you want to have control, feelings can feel like a problem. They are messy, unpredictable, and perhaps, like vomiting, *feel* uncontrollable and like something is very *wrong*. Something is bubbling up from deep within that shouldn't. Feelings often come out all at once rather than in manageable installments. We fear that feelings will envelop us, take over, and never end, so we try not to feel.

As a survival instinct, we don't take kindly to running head-long into situations out of which we can't later exit. From their hidden place, feelings threaten to jump out or slip out, overtake or embarrass us, and until they have been confronted, the coast is never clear. But ask yourself, are they really an emergency? Or are the feelings, however uncomfortable and at times even excruciating, really the best intelligence we can get about what is actually going on with us?

Maybe your experiences of feelings aren't as dramatic as Francis's above. They may not threaten to obliterate you, but still, you may experience them as unpleasant, embarrassing, or indulgent and want to avoid them as much as possible. But it doesn't really work, because in the back of your mind, the feeling nags. In this chapter, you'll learn that it is safer than you think to look those uncomfortable feelings in the eye and receive the crucial information only they can deliver. To do so, you need to learn their nature. You need to learn how to surf the waves.

Anxious feelings may strike us as an enemy attack, but really they are more like an interoffice memo from deep within. It's important to know what is registering in your emotions. You want to *strengthen* your internal communication system to receive the start of that thread. Trying to suppress or deny feelings puts us at a disadvantage. By understanding how feelings work, you can safely go into them and glean the information you need from that memo, knowing full well that you can find your way back out.

Otherwise, you generate more anxiety by thinking something is wrong that you must make stop. Feelings feel *in the way*, but truly, they *are* the way. It may seem too horrible to consider certain feelings—self-doubt: *I'm not as good as I thought, I'm a fraud;* grief: *My wife doesn't love me anymore, I'm going to be alone;* guilt: *The accident was my fault, I'm an irresponsible person.* But you need to keep returning to them because there they sit, waiting patiently to be understood. You might even find that the feeling doesn't fit anymore once you muster the courage to try it on. When you trust that you can ride out anxious and negative feelings, your perception changes. You move from feeling you are in an unmanageable situation to seeing yourself overcome.

In dealing with feelings head on, we learn a new association and start to see feelings as uniquely qualified messengers. Instead of running for cover, we shift to a welcoming stance. We look for the clarity that feelings can offer like nothing else. We anticipate the recovery, even the relief of knowing what's what instead of hiding from ourselves. We go from "I can't handle it!" to "This is what is going to help me handle it."

WHY WE FEAR FEELINGS AND WANT TO MAKE THEM STOP

❧ I don't want to feel any discomfort ever. ❧

None of us would want to admit to that extreme view, and yet, when we are upset, this thought hovers. When things feel bad, we want out, and fast. It feels like more than you can bear. *My mother is sick with cancer, my company is downsizing, I didn't get the contract, my husband wants a divorce, my child has diabetes.* You see that wave coming: You panic, then start to run the other way as though you can avert a disaster. If you let yourself feel the wave at all, you think it will knock you down. But what are you really running from?

Feelings are information. We brace ourselves against receiving that information and that is okay as a first reaction, but it doesn't make the information go away. Is it really the feelings that are so awful, or are your fears *about* the feelings the stumbling block? We get dragged around by our distress *about our distress*. Worry responds to the discomfort, setting off alarms, but matching one alarm with another won't do it. By engaging in a noisy reaction, you restrain the message from being delivered and then receding. The fears and beliefs make whatever was underneath seem so much worse.

It seems counterintuitive, but if we want to feel better, we need to learn how to manage feeling bad. Thus, the goal is not to remove the feeling, but to remove the fear of the feeling. Rather than approach negative feelings as something *wrong* that you need to escape, you need to learn to safely go in, receive important information that started the feeling in the first place, and then set about solving it. You don't want to scramble the message that started that feeling. You want to clear the phone lines in order to receive the call of whatever that feeling was—jealousy, frustration, sadness.

FEELINGS GET THERE FIRST, LEAVE LAST

Emotions arrive first and call the shots, causing you to react before you even know why. You run into an old friend and before you can think, *Hey, you snubbed my wife and me and didn't invite us to your wedding*, your chest is getting tight, your face is tense, and it's difficult to smile. You're mad before you can even remember why. In fact, you're madder than you would *decide* to be about the situation, given the chance to think it over. The brain is wired to feel before knowing.

We fear feelings because often they make the worst part of an experience appear before the rational mind catches up. You need to trust the notion that although reason may come late to the party, it always shows up. So, if you can hang on with the discomfort, your wise mind will be able to help you understand what just happened, and then you'll no longer feel enveloped by the feeling. You'll be on the other side of it, looking back.

STRONG FEELINGS PASS OVER TIME

The body operates on the principle of homeostasis—maintaining a steady state. Feelings rise quickly, then peak and start to resolve. Just because the start-up is faster than the resolution doesn't mean that the resolution won't come.

When we're scared, angry, or upset, our feelings heat up really fast. Although they take longer to dissipate, it is important to tell yourself in the middle of an intense feeling that *it will pass*. This will help bring the end sooner. When women are in labor, they often watch the monitor to see the arc of a contraction, so that when they hit the peak of pain, they know that they are in the clear and it's downhill from there. Although you can't carry a feeling's monitor around with you, remember that at the very moment when the feeling is most intense, just on the other side of that arc of pain or intensity starts an arc of relief as the feeling is resolving. The next time you are in an argument with someone and getting upset, try to tell yourself, *The way I feel now is not how I'm going to feel later.* Sometimes just this thought can cause a shift in your feelings, and you can let go of your half of the anger rope faster and work toward resolution. If your worry's take on the story is, *This is terrible, I can't take this, I can't do this. This shouldn't be happening*, generate a simple antidote with, *This is natural, this is hard, but it is true, and it is temporary. If I can listen to what I'm feeling, I'll know how to take care of myself.*

TOOLS FOR INCREASING
EMOTIONAL REGULATION

Strategy #1: Visualize Degrees of Separation

When you get swept up in emotion, it can frighten you into thinking that you are inseparable or indistinguishable from the feeling. We don't like to lose sight of ourselves. Instead, you need to de-identify from the feelings and see them, as meditation master and physician Jon Kabat-Zinn describes, as a fleeting storm passing

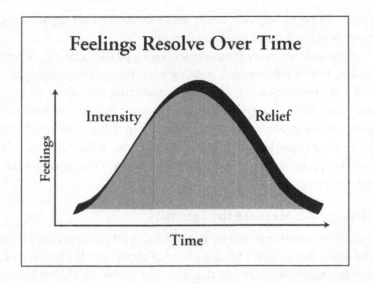

Feelings Resolve Over Time

Intensity   Relief

Feelings

Time

through your steady sky. The feeling is of you, but it is not you. You can picture noisy, messy storms with clouds, rain, thunder, and lightning. But just as they come, they go. Imagine what the sky will look like when the storm passes.

Imagine that the feeling you are having is a big storm cloud in the sky. What color is it? What shape is it? Are there birds in the sky, is the wind blowing? Look at the clouds and notice that they are moving. Look at the sky and see that it is still. Can you picture in your mind a gentle wind blowing the clouds away? Maybe there is a kite in the sky, drifting gently by. Maybe you'll fill in the land below with a mountaintop, a beach, your home, a field filled with brilliant wild flowers. As you engage your mind to paint the picture, you channel less energy to the adrenals, and with your breath and focus, you create a hub of acceptance and calm that you may find yourself circling around more regularly now that you know where to find it.

Imagine taking the feeling you are having and putting it on a stage or a movie screen. Can you describe it or see it in the frame of the screen? Can you put yourself farther back in the theater and sit in the middle row and talk to that feeling, saying, "I know you're trying to help me, but it feels like you're hurting me right now. What is it that I need to learn now?"

If you feel that everything is falling apart, picture a strong, woven basket, tightly intertwined, holding everything firmly together.

Or if emotions are thrashing and stirring you up, then step back and picture a gentle stream running in front of you and leaves flowing down the stream. Picture putting your troubling feelings on those leaves. The stream, like you, is flowing strongly and the leaves, like your feelings, are temporary disturbances riding on top of the stream.

Strategy #2: Measure the Intensity

Take your emotional temperature. When you are upset, and then still upset five minutes later, it's hard to appreciate the subtle shift that is happening—namely, that you may be feeling slightly better than you did five minutes earlier. You need tools to monitor the intensity of your emotions. Use a scale from 1 to 10, or low, medium, high. Monitoring the intensity of the feeling gives us hope that the worst of it is over and relief is coming. By taking note of these distinctions, it introduces the very hopeful sign that these feelings are changeable. How you feel now isn't how you have to feel; it's temporary.

Strategy #3: Invite the Feelings in That So Many Others Have Experienced, Too

Rather than feeling like emotion is crashing the party, you can root yourself in the fact that you are in charge, by being the one who invites the feeling in. It may be comforting to tell yourself that what you are feeling is universal. At any given moment, there are millions of other people who are having a similar experience. This normalizes what you feel and makes you feel less alone in the experience, whether it's connecting with others fretting about their insomnia, or others who are wondering how they are going to support their family when they've just lost their job, or others

WORDS OF ACCEPTANCE

- It's okay to feel this way.
- This is a natural reaction.
- It's normal to feel this way.
- This can't hurt me.
- It is uncomfortable but not unbearable.
- This is where I am right now.
- I will move through this.
- This will pass, but this is just how I'm feeling now.
- Millions of other people know this feeling and are going through this now, too.

who are worrying about their children. As varied as the repertoire is of human emotion and experience, so is it similar and shared.

Strategy #4: Empathy and Acceptance Starts with You

I hate the way I'm feeling. I shouldn't be feeling this way. I need to make this stop. When you already feel bad, the stamp "this is wrong" makes it all the worse. Physically, you are twisting the knot. Instead, coach yourself to accept the feeling with words like these below:

Without empathy, you've got an internal tug of war. One part of you says, "This is how I'm feeling," while the other part says, "I shouldn't feel this way." For many of us, the instant program of anger or sadness is left over from childhood, or maybe even a current feed from someone important in our life, like a spouse. Although these programs can wear deep grooves through the psyche, remember the miracle of neuroplasticity and our brain's ability to lay down tracks for a new direction. You may need to reeducate yourself, understanding that as difficult as it is to have received those unhealthy and unhelpful messages about emotions, those who taught you are in need of compassion, too. They

QUESTIONS TO ASK

- What am I really afraid of now?
- Does it make sense?
- Is it something I can handle?
- What am I really feeling?
- What am I trying to tell myself?
- What can I learn from this experience?

are stuck with this understanding of life and may be unaware that there are other choices.

Strategy #5: Breathing Versus Bracing

If clenching and bracing ourselves against a feeling is how we keep our fingers pressed on the "on" button for distress, then breathing is the way we turn it off. Go back to the strategies in Chapter 2 for intentional breathing. Feel your body, especially your chest and abdomen, releasing as you breathe. When your brain picks up on the calm signal, it will help reinforce or enhance that feeling by reverberating the all-clear signal through your body. Don't think "relax"; think "breathe."

Strategy #6: Be the Observer Rather Than the Participant

When you find a point of stillness and quiet inside, you are in a better position to observe the reactions you are having, rather than just reacting. In this way you are more likely to choose to have different ways of responding to what's happening. From that point of being the observer, you find that you needn't respond to every influence that goes by. In your thoughts, this means shifting perspective from acting out whatever is happening to you in the moment to being the observer who allows the feelings and directorial instructions to simply be information rather than directives. When you notice yourself starting to swirl with a feeling, don't fight it, narrate it. "I'm feeling upset now at my children for not listening. I can feel the tightening in my chest. It is okay to feel this way. This feeling, like others I've had before, will come and it will go. I won't feel this intensity for long." By narrating what's happening, what I call with my young patients, "Tell, don't yell," the feeling loosens its grip on you and you return to a place of being in charge of yourself.

FINDING THE MESSAGE IN THE MESSINESS

As you become more comfortable with your experiences, you can dive into the messiness, like a competent swimmer diving in to collect items off the bottom of the pool. You can get in there, and confident in your ability to survive, you can stay swimming in those choppy waters until you retrieve whatever information you need to find.

WHEN IT FEELS LIKE TOO MUCH

There are times when experiences are more raw than usual. When someone dies. Or you lose your job. The doctor tells you your cancer is worse. Or you find out you were rejected from medical school. These life-changing jolts to the system can't be absorbed quickly. The strategies that we've discussed so far can be helpful in these situations, however, with a few caveats. First, accept that whatever you are feeling is valid. You don't want to set off the internal "something's wrong" program about your reaction, ever, and especially when something *is* genuinely wrong. Second, you can remind yourself that intense feelings, like grief, come in waves, just like all feelings. So you may be startled to find yourself crying all of a sudden or feeling very sad. This is the body's way of pacing itself. Know that it will come and it will go. Third, you need to pace *yourself*. Give yourself permission to feel whatever it is, or you can give yourself permission to compartmentalize and take breaks from the grief by doing something ordinary like an errand. It isn't that you forget what is happening in your life. You are grieving *and* you are buying groceries, or even buying a pair of shoes. It's the double life. You are grieving *and* you are living. You can connect with a universal feeling of grief shared by millions of other people. In this way, at the times that you feel most alone, you can take some comfort from knowing that you are not alone as you go through this natural process.

A WORD ABOUT VENTING AND WHAT YOU DON'T NEED TO DO WITH FEELINGS

Some of us have been trained in the "Get your feelings out!" school of thought, in which a Bobo doll or some other such punching bag is required equipment for the process. Many books have advocated punching pillows and the like to help get feelings out. But research has found that this type of physical venting can be counterproductive to calming your nervous system. Punching and other activities pump up the very same adrenaline system that you are trying to calm, and that makes the problem grow rather than shrink. Yelling, a verbal punch of sorts, is in a similar category and will likely keep alarm bells ringing. Talking through what you are feeling, on the other hand, enhances the feeling of resonance and congruence. Other physical activities like walking, exercising, or dancing can help you feel emotionally balanced rather than leave you feeling off kilter.

FREEING YOURSELF: IN ACTION

For Susan and Bill, confronting infertility as a couple was painful. Five years of hope, pain, disappointment, and exhaustion had worn on them. Although both of them knew what this was like better than anyone, Bill and Susan couldn't get close to the pain. Yes, they'd cry, but they couldn't look in. Instead, they would get angry at each other, and that was a good way to keep a safe distance from "going there," as they referred to discussions about

TRY THIS

Change your greeting when a feeling comes knocking at your door. Rather than shutting the door and turning off the lights like nobody is home, consider putting out the welcome mat to invite that good messenger in.

This will help me, whatever it is. I am getting the message first. This doesn't feel good, but it is not dangerous, I can welcome it, slowly, and get to know it a little bit at a time. Keep visits short to start. Picture the wave diagram earlier in the chapter and realize that as much as the intensity of the feeling is building, just on the other side of that, the feeling will resolve; this is how we are built. The wave will come and it will go. You will still be standing, and you will have gained valuable perspective in the process.

---

their infertility. They had resolved that the infertility treatments hadn't worked, but they felt lonely and alienated from each other and didn't know how to get back to trusting each other again.

In therapy, they realized that they both wanted and needed to say things because not saying them was getting in their way. They talked about their own feelings of inadequacy and how they wanted to blame each other. They found that what had been terrifying for them to contemplate saying was freeing once they did. They both had thought it would be too much. But now, supporting each other, they began to feel that the infertility was not all about pain and loss because through it, they were finding a deep trust in each other. This was something they had.

When Justin even thinks about his job, he feels nothing but a blinding feeling of dread. He commented, "I try to avoid thinking about it. Whenever I do, on Sunday night or as soon as I wake up in the morning, it's there, like this dark force." The more Justin avoided thinking about his job, the more the dread increased. When he was able to bravely open the door and look at his dread,

YOU AND BEYOND

It's uncomfortable to experience your own feelings bubbling up, but the emotions of others can also make us uncomfortable. Remember that people's feelings are also *their* important interoffice memos. It is best that we don't stifle that, but we can help alter how the message is delivered. Remember that when messages come across in anger, it's often because the people delivering them are struggling with their feelings themselves. Rather than feeling attacked by them, realize that their intensity is coming from a beeping amygdala, too. Help your spouse, child, and co-worker to realize that you want to know *what* they're feeling, but that it's hard to hear it the way they are saying it because it's setting off your amygdala as well. Everyone will benefit from slowing things down. If your conflict is resolved ten minutes later, or even twenty, because you've both taken the time to calm yourselves down first, chances are the conflict actually *will* get resolved rather than escalating. The more they are able to get to the bottom of what they are feeling, the better for both of you. Empathize with them: "I know you're really upset. I really want to understand. Let's slow it down; I can't really hear you when you're talking this way. Can you just tell me what's going on? I want to work this out." They may be so surprised that you didn't just attack back that they may be instantly disarmed, and this will actually increase the chances for a peaceful victory for all.

he was able to see that, for him, it was just about the transition. He was fine when he got to work; it was the anticipatory feelings that overwhelmed him. Once he understood this, he could relabel that feeling as anticipation and know that it was temporary, and simply being able to give that experience a new and better meaning, gave Justin the ability to ride out the wave of transition, knowing it was temporary.

When you have that feeling of dread, you shut down as though it's a red light for your system. So, you can't figure out what it is, and you can't stay away from it, and that makes this a lose-lose situation. What if you thought instead, "I have some dread and that's okay." When you accept that this is how you are feeling (not that this is where you want to stay), then the program switches from red light to green light. The first step is to not say that what you are feeling is wrong. Next, say, "Part of me feels some dread and maybe another part of me could feel something else?" If you put the dread to the side for a second, what else is there? When you accept the feelings, they begin to dissipate.

Chapter 10

ROUNDING UP
YOUR STRENGTHS

Be yourself; everyone else is already taken.
—OSCAR WILDE

🐾 *Somewhere deep inside I feel like I should know my self-worth, but I don't.* 🐾

ARE YOU THE LAST TO KNOW?

There is a party game in which players have the name of a famous person written on a card and stuck to their backs before they can read the card. Everyone else knows who they are, and the object of the game is to go around asking questions about "you" until you can guess your identity. When it comes to our own strengths, many of us play this game every day without knowing it. Everyone else sees your uniqueness, abilities, the distinctive ways that you do the things that only you can do. You may feel in the dark about these things. Perhaps there are times when we catch these glimpses of ourselves. Often, however, our modesty, humility, or perhaps even our self-loathing gets in the way. Wouldn't we all do better if we could see what everyone else sees?

If you are going to bounce back resiliently from adversity, you must push off from your strengths to set that bounce in motion. So how do we grab hold of what eludes us, and why are we often so reluctant to do so? On the one hand, it's one of those uncomfortable touchy-feely exercises in a staff development workshop, the kind during which everyone secretly wishes they could slip out to make a call—or get a tooth pulled. On the other hand, just because something is uncomfortable doesn't mean it isn't valuable. When the focus is always on what's lacking, you can easily overlook your strong qualities, what's working well for you, the very things that can help you climb out of the negative mind-set. Knowing your strengths helps you better navigate your path in life in good times and bad.

If you are already comfortable with the idea of taking stock of your personal resources, then the ideas here can serve as a periodic inventory check. It is important to do this from time to time, as you may discover some previously unidentified facets. This is because as you continue to grow, there are shifts in what you appreciate and value. If, in contrast, you are more in the habit of chopping away at yourself, just remember that no matter how much you chop in your mind, it doesn't change who you are. Your basic nature remains whole. It's there whether you see it or not.

RETHINKING STRENGTHS: EVERYTHING COUNTS, EVERYONE COUNTS

Whether you cure cancer, teach elementary math to the child who will soon grow up to cure cancer, create the jingle for a breakfast cereal commercial, or provide nurturance and breakfast for your family, everything counts. Strengths are not based on some external market value like the net worth of your 401(k). You know that markets fluctuate, so that's not a steady star to which you can hitch your wagon. Rather, see your attributes as a way to be the truest version of yourself. Do you really want to be the last to know about who you are? By removing the calculation, the

judgment, and the comparison to someone else, you can take this deep opportunity to reflect on the unassailable value that is yours.

The freest appreciation of each other (and ourselves) is outside the framework of comparisons. If every time we feel inadequacy or envy, we pause, and instead of digging deeper into that dark hole, we relabel that first reaction, then we might find the supremely reassuring fact that we are surrounded by spectacular people. What starts as an uncomfortable moment could actually unveil *more* that we like about our life and identity. Think to yourself, *I get to work with these people, I get to learn from these people, how fortunate.* And just as you do this quick recalibration invisibly in the privacy of your own mind, others may well be doing this with you. They notice your sense of style, your kindness, and instead of being threatened, they enjoy it and try to emulate you. Imagine the potential of this contagion of appreciation.

TURNING THE MIRROR MORE FAVORABLY

Given the chance, we can all rattle off our flaws and foibles. But notice how when given the same opportunity to itemize your positive attributes, an awkward silence falls over the room. Part of the problem is that you may not even be sure of your positive attributes. Being aware of your vulnerabilities is essential information for self-protection and recovery. But that awareness is about self-protection alone. It doesn't help you thrive, grow, find optimal friends, living situations, partners, or satisfaction. Connecting the dots of your flaws doesn't lead there. In the late 1990s, the young field of positive psychology readjusted the mirror for self-reflection. Instead of focusing on weaknesses, shortcomings, or pathologies, the new angle values being able to quickly put your fingers on the aspects of your life that are in good working order. Although not a solution to life's problems in and of itself, the strengths-based approach helps to balance out the picture.

This is about being accurate and factual and taking inventory. For all of us raised to bristle at anything remotely resembling pride, don't worry. This isn't about tooting your horn, this is about balancing a distorted picture. Knowing your strengths helps you seek out the situations where you will thrive and have your best resources available during challenging times.

BUILDING AND BROADENING THE STRENGTHS VOCABULARY: GETTING OUT OF THE RUT OF "SMART AND SUCCESSFUL"

*I am the only child of parents who weighed,
measured and priced everything; for whom what
could not be weighed, measured, and priced,
had no existence.*

—CHARLES DICKENS, *LITTLE DORRIT*

When we set out to look for something, it helps to know what it is. There is a myth that the Eskimo have 100 different words to describe snow. In reality, it may be more like seven. When it comes to our search for our strengths, we may be limited to just a couple of words that provide narrow definitions. For example, in children, the narrow definition for a strength is usually being *smart* or *athletic.* For adults, *smart* stays in the running, but *successful* is the other narrow category, and usually *successful* narrows further to a single data point: our *income.* We focus on salary like students focus on SAT scores, and yet statistics tell us repeatedly that over a certain level of income (in some studies this is marked at $75,000), golf club memberships, fancy cars, and precious jewelry do not ensure happiness. Even when people win the lottery, after the initial windfall, they return to their prior baseline level of happiness. So it turns out, money can't buy love or happiness.

We can cheer on our smart and athletic children and praise our smart and prosperous adults, but then together, let's search for value far beyond these limited categories. Only when people find their unique ways of creating meaning and purpose in life do cultures and civilizations continue to grow and innovate. The fact is, we all benefit from expanding an appreciation of a broader array of perspectives, sensibilities, and gifts. We need to do this for ourselves and for each other.

STRATEGIES FOR GENERATING YOUR OWN STRENGTHS LIST

Approach this exercise with the facts (and paper and pencil). Then you can get curious and interested and be less likely to trip over your criticisms, doubts, and judgments. You will be more likely to then take what you've got and put it to the best use for yourself and beyond.

How Are You a Key Player?

If you want to know the role of the shortstop in a baseball game, remove him and watch how everything changes. Imagine a day where you are unavailable. What would be different in the lives of your family, your friends, your co-workers? You may get urgent calls like, "Wait, how do you boil an egg again?" or "How do you close out the register?" But aside from these, how do conversations at the office, gym, or the coffee shop happen differently without you? Think about what kinds of requests have been made of you in e-mails, by phone, and in person, and what kind of information people share with you. What perspective and observations do you

TRY THIS:
Expanding Your Strength Vocabulary

When you compliment or envy others, what are you focusing on? Beauty? Wealth? Don't let yourself get into a strength rut. Diversify your focus to notice the effort that others make naturally. Appreciate how a friend helps her elderly neighbor with her gardens. Mention how a child has a keen eye for observing lizards, frogs, and all things reptilian, how a colleague has a knack for making everyone feel included in a discussion. Not only will you make their day, but notice how quickly the glass fills up for you.

The goal is to stretch beyond "successful" and "beautiful" to a broader vocabulary of strengths. At your dinner table or office conference table, work on constructing a strengths synonym list. Everyone at the table can write down ten positive attributes, such as open-minded, purposeful, creative, persistent, detail-oriented, big-picture oriented, compassionate, or thoughtful, on a piece of paper and keep them handy for easy reference. When someone slips back into the old standby of smart or successful, pull out the list and stretch!

bring, and what does that say about you? Are you the one who keeps morale going at work? Are you empathic and the only one to ask others how their day is going? Are you the organizing whiz, the keeper of information? Are you the problem solver, the mediator, able to see things from many perspectives? Although you may have a first thought that anybody could do that, think again. Nobody would do it quite like you.

What Do You Lose Yourself In?

Are you a weekend warrior who loses herself in being productive, innovative, and maybe even adventurous with new household projects? Do you love conversations, listening attentively, compassionately, and contributing articulately? When people become completely immersed in an activity, the focus needed to concentrate erases the commentary of self-consciousness. You *do* rather than think about doing. You can't go lose yourself in every activity, so take a close look at what you are doing when you do hit your flow. What does that experience say about you? Write down some adjectives to describe what enabled you to do that or what happened when you were in that state.

Get a Second Opinion

When you are stuck and can't solve a problem yourself, what can you do? Get a consult. Ask a good friend, spouse, or a trusted colleague to do a "strengths swap" in which you each take turns talking about what you admire, appreciate, and enjoy in each other. You can also do this exercise in your imagination. If your best friend, spouse, employer, or co-workers wrote five words about you, what would they be? Think about things that have inspired people to compliment you or thank you. When do you feel most comfortable with yourself around others? What words describe that experience for you?

Parents can think about how their children would describe them. If the children were writing a personalized Mother's or Father's Day card, what memories would they talk about and what would it reflect about you as a parent?

Behind the Scenes: How Do You Do the Things You Do?

"That five-minute promotional video I did? Oh, thanks, it was a piece of cake."

"The dinner party for twenty-five? No sweat."

"The family room addition that I built on weekends? It was easy."

Yeah, right. They were easy because of who *you* are. They wouldn't have been easy for just anyone. What is it about you that made that moment possible? Think about a proud moment or

accomplishment that you feel exemplifies you. It could be something big and tangible as in the examples above, or it could be an
e-mail that you wrote to a friend, a great conversation you had
with a colleague, a visit you paid to an ailing relative, or even a
great walk you shared with your dog. Write the moment at the
bottom of a piece of paper. Now reverse the trip. Start at the top
and jot down all the attributes it took on your part to get to that
end result—equanimity, daring, willingness to ask for help, compassion, ingenuity, humor, and generosity? Try it again for a few
more events and create your list of personal attributes that you
can count on at all times because, with no additional supplies
needed, you've got them.

What Part of You Doesn't Show Up on a Test?

For many of us, our work is just one part of life, and though we
try to make it fulfilling, it isn't the full reflection of who we are.
It's good to work toward having a job or daily work that makes
full use of our gifts, but other essential aspects of our personalities
might not be tapped into when we punch our time cards. Describe what is important to you outside of the job you do each
day.

Strengths out of Struggle

Sometimes when we struggle—whether it is with our emotions
or situations that we find ourselves in—we can overlook what we
are asking of ourselves just being in those situations. Are we
courageous, patient, devoted, generous, compassionate, honor-
able, and dependable?

Anyone who has come through a personal challenge like caring
for an ailing loved one, surviving an illness, or losing a job may
know that these are just crossroads. Having been taken down to
the mat by life, we find deep within ourselves resources and con-
victions that were always there but previously untapped. We
emerge, resolute, making important discoveries and decisions
about how to live our lives more healthily, more meaningfully.

If you have been through a life-changing event like this, realize that you were the one who took this opportunity to make changes. If you are in the midst of an experience like this, think about what you are bringing to the table now to manage and address the situation. Try not to discount your efforts by saying that this is what anyone would do. The fact is, this is what *you* are choosing to do. Often unforeseen at the moment, anything we invest in gives back.

OVERCOMING OBSTACLES TO SEE YOURSELF ACCURATELY
Old Tapes: Hand-Me-Down Negativity and Pessimism

🍃 *Why would you ever think you could do that? Who do you think you are?* 🍃

Sometimes those aren't just knee-jerk accusations, but playbacks of things that we have been told by parents, by spouses, siblings, or even teachers. Especially when we were young, we would likely have been ill-prepared to realize that comments like that reflect most directly the sender, not the recipient. The sender may have heard those messages from unhappy people in their life, and so the pattern goes. We may have incorporated these negative predictions into the chorus of our own negative thoughts, sight unseen. We were told not to dream, not to brag. Return those tapes to their rightful owners. They don't belong to you. For your sake as well as future generations, start a new hand-me-down of *permission* to value yourself and others, to accurately speak the truth, and maybe even to revel in it.

What Are You Waiting For?

One of the roadblocks to identifying your strengths may be that you are waiting for something else or someone else to point them out. This is what psychologists refer to as an "external locus of

control." We look to our paychecks or material possessions as evidence of our worth, or to praise from authority figures, friends,
maybe even the clerk at the video store, to tell us if we are okay.
Because you can't control the whims of these inadvertent judges,
who may be having a bad day themselves, you are bound to feel
bad if nothing happens to make you feel good. Can you imagine
the insecurity you feel when your self-worth is contingent on the
mercurial moods of a boss or mother-in-law? It's much better to
be the keeper of your own worth. Your strengths are not situa-
tional, like a currency that only works in one country. Your worth
is a constant; it only increases over time, it doesn't fluctuate.

WEAKNESSES WITHOUT SHAME: WORKING WITH WHAT YOU'VE GOT

Some of you may read through this chapter holding your breath
because just hearing the word "strengths" immediately summons
up distaste or an insecurity that you have none. Now that we are
talking about weaknesses, you can exhale. Having love, compassion, or just plain awareness and acceptance of our blind spots or
weaknesses is important, and a strength. It's not just the good
parts, it's the full monty. If you've got good, healthy relationships
(and if you don't, this is one more reason to look hard for them),
they don't look at you as a mathematical equation like the character in *Little Dorrit*. These weaknesses are not taxed or sub-
tracted from your absolute value. It's an all-inclusive package deal.

The fact is that you set the tone for how others see you. If
you're feeling badly about where you are in your life and say as
much, others will see you at a disadvantage. If, instead, you can
relabel and demote the significance of these self-doubts or even
simply accept them as part of the process, folks will follow your
lead. For example, during a difficult time in your life, you might
say: "I'm in transition. I'm into building character right now instead of capital. I'm hoping it's just a phase." Humor isn't always
possible, but it can help.

WHAT'S LUCK GOT TO DO WITH IT?

After working in the private sector as a graphic designer for over a decade, Chloe decided that she wanted a change and began applying for university positions. She had always wanted to teach, and at this stage of her life, while she raised her children, it seemed to offer the most flexible schedule. With her great talent and experience, Chloe was able to get a tenure-track position. A colleague in her new department kept saying, "Do you know how lucky you are to get this job?" It made Chloe feel uneasy, as if she had somehow snuck in by luck or a fluke. After the fourth time the colleague said this, Chloe nailed the problem and said, "You know what? It's not luck, I earned this job!"

Was Bill Gates lucky? Was it just luck that made The Beatles the Fab Four? In the book *Outliers: The Story of Success*, Malcolm Gladwell answers the question with a yes and a no. Bill Gates came of age right at the time when computers were taking off, and he was able to dedicate thousands of hours exploring the possibilities of the nascent electronic world. How many hours? According to one theory that Gladwell describes, it takes 10,000 hours of hard work to reach a level of mastery. So whether you are looking at your own accomplishments or looking at someone else's ability to pull things off, remember that far beyond luck or coincidence, success requires the strength of *perseverance* to take you beyond your gifts and good fortune.

IT'S NEVER TOO LATE TO GET SELF-WORTH RIGHT

Like the labels "shy" or "quiet," the tag "low self-esteem" has a way of boxing people in. That's tough news for someone whose hope of improvement is already in short supply. But if you look back at the Getting Specific strategies in Chapter 5, you can understand that the term "low self-esteem" reflects a pattern of misattributing *specific* limitations as something permanent and global. When

TRY THIS
Create a "Strengths" Memory Box

If you are suddenly being visited by "Measurement Guy" in the middle of a group at work, at a party, or with your extended family as you hear someone's successes listed and feel that you come up short, make an accurate description of several people around you, including yourself. Don't glorify unless you are willing to shine that light on yourself, too.

When you are struggling with a sudden plummet in confidence, rather than fall deeper into the depths, look around for evidence that your life is of value even though a blogger or a boss panned you in one way or another. Just like children need to learn that when they make a mistake, their parents may be upset with them temporarily but still love them, we need to remember that bad moments don't make a dent in the bigger picture of who we are.

Keep a folder, box, or computer file of experiences that you feel really good about. One friend calls it her "Atta Girl" file, another the "Break Glass in Case of Emergency" file. It could be compliments you've gotten from others, e-mails of thanks or appreciation that others have sent, photographs of moments that you helped create, or the time you gave that speech at your cousin's wedding and everyone commented how beautifully you tied together all the themes of their relationship. Take ten minutes right now and start that file. Take your list of adjectives from the strengths exercises in the chapter and put that in the file, too. Picture your "suitcase" of strengths that you have with you at all times.

By being able to right yourself again, you may see whether there is anything constructive to take from the "panning," but you'll be considering that information from a position of go rather than a position of stop.

Although circumstances don't always enable you to push off from that stance of strengths, they are always at your disposal. Practice being in that mind-set by giving the moment a name, like "Charlie's Wedding." Visit that place often in your mind, and your physiology will remember what that was like and will reward that trip with a feeling of rightness and productivity.

Rather than focusing only on what's next in your life, take stock and savor what you've already accomplished. You're not just as good as your next accomplishment, you're all the things that came before. Look at your accomplishments and remember that success isn't an accident. It comes from you.

one thing goes wrong—say, having trouble finding someone to have a relationship with—the default conclusion is that you are no good across the board. This couldn't be more wrong. If you have thought of yourself as having low self-esteem, think again. Keep your attributions accurate, and rather than have labels box *you* in, see yourself as having limitless possibilities, and put your specific problems or challenges in the smallest box.

WRAPPING IT UP

Anxiety overestimates the risks in a situation and underestimates your ability to cope. Rather than feel diminished or intimidated by your anxiety, you can be in charge. By having your emotional résumé in hand in the form of your strengths, past successes, and experiences, you will be ready to tackle worry challenges, knowing exactly what you bring to the table. As you identify your strengths, you will find ways to make this information as accessible as knowing your shoe size.

The goal is to connect with your resources and strengths, including those that don't match up with what someone else has in mind. As you go through this chapter, you may see the ways that your day-to-day life does draw on your strengths, or you may find that some of your strengths don't yet have a way to flow in your life. This may encourage you to pursue activities or relationships that tap into those more.

When you haven't identified your strengths, they are like the baggage on that closed circle of a conveyer belt with the one unclaimed suitcase circling around and around. Maybe you forgot you had it, so you never go to pick it up. Well, pick it up! It is waiting for you to claim it.

FREEING YOURSELF: IN ACTION

Katja, a graduate student in her late twenties, was living paycheck to paycheck emotionally, waiting for endorsements from her

YOU AND BEYOND
Show the Seams

The reason we love to hear behind-the-scenes stories of celebrities and heroes or even our neighbors is that we can then demystify the process of their seemingly painless rise to stardom, or their seemingly charmed life over the backyard fence. When you watch people juggling their lives so well, keeping all the plates in the air, but then hear, "I have such a migraine," or learn "I got fired from a job" or "I ate a lot of instant ramen noodles for dinner before I got to this point in my life," it does three important things. First, sharing a vulnerability or mistake offers a window into someone, and a human connection and the beginning of trust. Second, it also demystifies the process of success and shows it is safe to try something without knowing exactly how it will work out because taking risks is how you grow. And finally, the more we are all willing to show our seams, the more we won't waste so much precious energy trying to pretend that everything's perfect in our lives. So for your own sake and that of others, show the seams every once in a while, feel the instant connection, and who knows, you may be encouraging the other person to take a risk in their own life that will have great benefit for all.

boyfriend, her professors, her family, and her friends. Her strengths didn't seem legitimate to her unless an acknowledgment came from someone else. Perfectionism and anxiety prevented Katja from trusting herself, and she felt it was safer to not stick her neck out with her own judgments and opinions. Although enviably competent, kind, and beautiful, Katja was growing more depressed and reclusive and withdrawing from social contact. She was preparing herself for the worst rejection because she was counting on others' acceptance so desperately.

Taking the first small steps meant identifying her own strengths to see that these were permanent features unaffected by temporary fluctuations like a grade on a test or whether she was clever at a party. Thinking of the tree analogy (which we learned about in Chapter 5), she began to discipline herself to identify the mistakes or less-than-perfect moments as leaves, and stop hacking away at the trunk and roots. Although her first thoughts continued to be harsh, as in *I'm completely useless*, she rephrased them, as in *Right now, I'm having a thought that I'm completely useless*. She realized then that these ups and downs were caused by her interactions with others. Some went well, some didn't. But the "success" of the interactions wasn't all on her shoulders. She also realized that these bad feelings didn't signify something deeper about her, they just affected her deeply. This distinction made a big difference. By thinking, *I'm feeling this way, right now, but this can change*, Katja was able to be more present with others, enjoy herself more. and count less on the reactions of others because her own contributions were beginning to stay with her in her mind. As a result she felt less anxious and was able to talk more in class, and at parties. The positive feedback arrived without her trying so hard. She still had to discipline herself to not let her internal doubter ruin the moment for her, but she was striking more of a balance, which was a good start.

Chapter 11

DISAPPOINTMENT PROOFING: HAVING BETTER EXPECTATIONS

Expect nothing. Live frugally, on surprise.

—ALICE WALKER

🌿 *I feel like other people control my emotions. Everybody's always letting me down, and little things really upset me. It doesn't bother them: They have no idea. I feel devastated on a regular basis. How can I have more control?* 🌿

THE NATURE OF THINGS: ARE YOU EXPECTING TOO MUCH, OR IS YOUR FOCUS TOO NARROW?

We all know the joke about the guy with a broken arm. He goes to the doctor and says, "Hey, Doc, so I'm going to be able to hit backhand like John McEnroe after this heals, right?" The doctor replies, "Well, could you hit like John McEnroe before?"

Sometimes expectations have much more to do with what we *want* than with the reality of how things are. What happens next is the clincher. We create needs out of wants. We insist on the picture we have in mind (even if it has little to do with what we actually need or what's available), and our wishes turn into demands. Or even into bizarre, irrational requirements and ultimatums. "I have to hear back about that job *today*! There's no reason why I *shouldn't*, I sent in the application *weeks* ago!" We demand a refund from life, as if we feel we've been denied something we are owed. And because there's no one on the other end of the line eager to take our call, we're just stuck brooding over it ourselves.

Welcome to the tricky business of expectations. It's human nature to want to have control, to predict what's going to happen next, and there's nothing wrong with that. But things often don't go as planned. We get outbid on houses, passed over for jobs, rejected in love, and contend with serious illnesses just when we had other plans in mind. Although there's nothing wrong with dreaming about the future, we must watch carefully and prevent the wants and dreams from morphing into expectations and demands. When that happens, your very happiness and well-being become conditional. The if-then statements begin. You start thinking that if things don't work out just as you envision, then you will be miserable. Not so fast, that's not how it works.

FINDING THE MOVING PART—*YOU*

To avoid inadvertently setting yourself up for major disappointment with expectations that don't match reality, you must learn to find the moving part—you. Rather than wrangle with reality, you can get flexible and change your expectations. A friend once told me that she would never date a man who didn't have good shoes. Whether he was nice or handsome or smart or generous, no matter—if he didn't have good shoes, forget about it. We may laugh or shake our heads, but take a closer look: We all have the good-shoes test in one form or another. As a result we've all missed out on opportunities that didn't conform exactly to our

mental picture. Allow for some give in your expectations. Who knows, you might overlook the man in the chewed-up sneakers coming down the road on his way to the shoe store, who stopped, captivated, expressly to have a conversation with you.

SAFER EXPECTATIONS, SMARTER EXPLANATIONS

Is there a safe way to be proactive in your life without setting yourself up for crushing disappointment or for missing out on opportunities that might be great but weren't exactly what you had in mind? Expectations need wiggle room, so that you can manage more resiliently when things don't go as planned. Keep your expectations simple, real, and flexible. This can range from the everyday moments (Must you absolutely have the best table at the new Italian restaurant or do you just want to have a great night out with your friends?) to the big picture (Do you truly need to be married by twenty-five, own your own business by thirty, have it go public by thirty-five? Or is a more reasonable expectation to have a fulfilling life with a family and your own business and let your hard work unfold over time?).

Expectations create the landing pad for your life. If they're really narrow, it's going to be mighty hard to land safely. Broaden the pad.

There will be times when you're willing to take it to the mat for what you want, and that's fine, but often a little latitude with the picture you have in mind will allow you to find the opportunities hidden in what the Dalai Lama's wisdom articulates: "Sometimes not getting what you want is a wonderful stroke of luck." Another element that can help protect you from disappointment is to pinpoint the real reasons when things don't turn out as you expected, what we'll refer to here as good "explanations." You might think: *I have a new baby, this was supposed to be the happiest time of my life—I just feel depressed and miserable. I must be a bad mother.* Well, the fact that you understandably haven't slept for three weeks may have something to do with why you're just not feeling happy about it. Or you might be thinking: *I thought I was perfect for this job, and I'm totally overwhelmed, so I must not be very smart.* Well, maybe the fact that your boss threw you in with no training or orientation, has made you work fifteen-hour days, and has been basically unavailable since you arrived could be a factor. Or maybe it's this: *I went to such a good college, I should be a shoo-in for a job, but I'm still unemployed six months after graduating. I must be a total loser.* Maybe the fact that you are entering the job market in a deep recession is a crucial piece of the puzzle. Buffer yourself with good explanations.

When someone else lets you down, you may misunderstand their actions, too. You may think: *She should have called me back hours ago, she's angry at me for how I acted on our date,* only to find out that she was stuck on a conference call and couldn't get away, or even that she's not a phone person and she was never going to call, but she e-mailed you and you never thought to check. People usually aren't trying to let us down or disrespect us; they are just operating on a different set of principles than we had expected. So, before we go on a manhunt either to turn ourselves in, or someone else, it's important to get the story straight. We'll first work on how to fine-tune expectations, and then we'll look at how to generate the best explanations for when things don't go as planned.

CREATING SAFE, RESILIENT EXPECTATIONS

- Keep it flexible.
- Keep it real and reasonably realistic.
- Keep it yours (make sure these are your expectations and not someone else's expectation for you).

The mind-set for resilience is keeping clear goals for what you can control and flexibility for what you can't.

At age thirty-five, Sven had one goal. He wanted his company to hit the $1-million revenue mark by the time he was forty. He had been an inventor since he was a child, so when he finally hit on a winning product, he was eager to see its success (and therefore his) soar. Watching the bottom line every day and not seeing it budge very much, he began to think he'd never meet the goal. Instead of relabeling that sluggish trajectory as the normal initial growth in a business, Sven would catastrophize about the future and blame himself for being inadequate. This would then set off a spiral of procrastination, and he wouldn't get any real work done for weeks.

What was the moving part? What part could Sven control? He couldn't make people buy his product, but he could change what *he* was doing to increase business. I asked Sven to focus not on what would happen if he didn't meet the goal about revenue, but instead on how he could increase the chances that the revenue would go up. He needed to shift his expectations about what success looks like, to not interfere with his chances of being successful.

He was very indignant at first, assuming that I, as a non-business person couldn't appreciate the idea of revenues. But as we discussed resilience in business and concluded it meant remaining flexible, he decided to reshape his goal to be about the number of companies he contacted and offered to do presentations each month. Rather than being discouraged each month that he wasn't where he wanted to be, Sven could feel good that he was doing what he could to get there. The rest would follow.

Strategy #1: Make Expectations About Things You Can Control

Often when I teach this idea to my patients in the business world, they bristle at the thought that there *are* things out of their control. Yet heeding this one idea could prevent so much anguish. So I give them first an example from my practice that is far removed from their own lives, to make it easier to elicit objectivity. I tell them about students and grades. When I tell my high-strung students, and their high-strung parents, that it isn't going to be helpful to say "I have to get straight A's (or else)," they are ready to pack up and find another therapist. Do I want their child to be a slouch, a failure? This is not about lowering your standards and failing out of school (though by the time these words leave my mouth, their worry is already flooding), it's about basing your goals on what you can control. You can control *effort*—how much time you put into your studies and whether you get help from the teacher—but you can't control the *outcome*, which in this case is the grade. Why? Because you never know what tricks may be on the test. Some teachers even advertise that they don't give perfect scores because they want kids to strive for something. But just because you can't control the grade doesn't mean you shouldn't try.

Apply this principle to something in your own life. You may have a number in mind for your sales target for the month, but you'll be best off if you set your expectations on how many cold calls you'll make, how many times you'll follow up with existing clients, and how you can revamp some of your brochures. These are the cards you hold in your hands.

Expectations that are based on things we *can't* control can create skewed explanations. "If I don't get a call back from the audition, then I have no talent. If I don't get into the master's program, I'm not smart. If he doesn't call me after that first date, I'm unlovable." Push pause and rethink your conclusions. Use the Get Specific step to narrow the problem to the smallest box: If you don't get the part, maybe you weren't right for it or could have rehearsed more thoroughly; maybe the program only accepted 20 percent of applicants, so it was a stretch; if he didn't call back after the date, well, did you think there was any chemistry between you? You need to be able to get yourself up for a second and third round when life knocks you down, or simply goes slightly off the tracks. This is resilience. Having room to absorb some of the disappointing news and attribute it accurately is crucial in staying on your feet, especially because we don't hold all the cards.

Sometimes our expectations for ourselves are altogether unrealistic and create a sense of failure, simply because what we were asking ourselves to do wasn't possible in the first place. Mara felt like a failure because she couldn't make her elderly parents feel better. Burdened by physical challenges, their quality of life was suffering. Mara would leave visits with her parents crestfallen that they didn't smile when they were with her. They were so preoccupied with their ailments, they couldn't focus on anything else. A devoted daughter, Mara loved her parents and wanted them to feel better. But expecting that she could somehow reverse the aging process, bring them back to health, and relieve their burdens was of course not in the realm of possibility. When she worked on the optimizing step, considering what friends and even her parents would have said to her when they were in a better state of mind, she realized that the one thing she *could* do that no one else could do quite like her was to be there as a listening ear for her parents.

Strategy #2: Break Down Expectations into Reasonable Parts

> *Man wants to achieve greatness overnight, and he wants to sleep well that night too.*
> —RABBI YOSEF YOZEL HORWITZ, THE ALTER (ELDER) OF NOVARDOK

Patience is a virtue—this we know, but let's be honest, don't you wish you had already finished this chapter? Don't I wish when I started writing that it was already done? We may think of learning to wait as a child's assignment, but with technology that offers immediate answers through search engines, instant gratification is the norm. Researchers have found that when we feel satisfaction, we get a chemical "dopamine squirt" in the brain, a neurotransmitter hit that we come to crave, and we are irritable without it. This is not a good habit for the brain, given that lots of things in life—other people's motivations, Mother Nature, and the laws of space and time—won't bend to the instant satisfaction template.

What does learning to wait have to do with anxiety? At its essence, waiting is about tolerating some discomfort in the uncertainty of not knowing exactly what is coming next. As we've seen, it's also about *refraining* from filling in that gap and uncertainty with an anxious or pessimistic ending. If you set unrealistic expectations, you build a stress machine with worry on the one side—*What if I can't do it, how am I going to do it?*—and discouragement on the other—*I didn't do it, I'm a failure.* The person didn't fail, the goal was a miscalculation.

Establishing small goals that we meet more quickly is how we generate momentum. So even though we're impatient and would rather set a big goal, in fact, we will have more satisfaction more frequently if we break down the big goal into smaller reasonable steps. As you see yourself take those steps, you are propelled forward to bigger goals.

TRY THIS

Think about an expectation you have for yourself, for a relationship, for a friend or spouse. Write it down. Spot check to see if it is possible based on the factors you control, and if not, rewrite it so that it is possible.

For example, about practical matters:

> *The original:* I expect my house to look neat even though I've got three kids.
> *The rewrite:* We will all (including my kids) do five minutes of cleanup before dinner each day.

About emotional matters:

> *The original:* I expect that everyone will love everything I do.
> *The rewrite:* I don't need everyone to love what I do. I am going to work hard to do a good job; some people will like it, some won't.

If the notion of small goals gives you pause because you have great expectations for yourself, remember what you learned in the last chapter about successful people who put in their time. They are workhorses who believe in themselves, but who believe in their perseverance above all. They may think big, but their goals tend to be stepwise and methodical. Reasonable goals are the goals of champions.

Strategy #3: Turn Demands into Preferences or Requests

How quickly does something you want turn into something you need? Like kids who spot a new video game, they don't just want it, they *need* it or they just can't live. A demand sounds like this:

I need to_____or else_____.

I need my parents to understand how hard our lives are, I need my boss to appreciate what I do. I need my kids to stop fighting with each other. The hidden "or else" assumption is that if this doesn't happen, life is intolerable, or that if people aren't coming through for you on this expectation, they can't come through on anything at all. Hold up. Your amygdala is beeping.

A slight red-pen edit could help switch those ultimatums into preferences and reduce the suffering that comes from having too rigid ideas about how to reduce suffering in the first place.

I would like to_____. I can try to make it happen by _____.

When you swap out demands for preferences, you don't sit idly by with an unhealthy situation, but rather you regroup, see that situation as intolerable or not preferable, and then constructively take steps to improve it.

The less time you take lamenting how this day doesn't measure up and is all wrong, the sooner you can salvage the day you were given. It's not going to be this day that I planned, but it's going to be another day, so let me see what the possibilities are. As writer Joseph Campbell suggests, "We must be willing to get rid of the life we've planned, so as to have the life that is waiting for us."

Strategy #4: Make the Covert, Overt

❧ *I wish my husband made plans for us more, I wish my friends checked in with me more, I wish my children were more organized, I wish my sister helped out more with the kids.* ❧

Sometimes even you don't know what you are expecting. You don't realize what the expectation was until afterward, when it's not met and you're crushed. But when you expect things of others, it is important to make sure they are in on the plan. Forgo any demandingness in favor of a friendly or simply assertive request. So,

ENSURING REALISTIC EXPECTATIONS

- Is the expectation under your control?
- Is it too big or too specific to be realistic?
- Can the expectation be broadened to make a bigger box or greater chance that things will go as planned?
- Can the expectation be broken down into smaller steps or goals?
- How important is it to you that this expectation be met?
- Is it really your goal or someone else's goal for you?
- Are you ready to analyze accurately what happened if things don't go as planned?
- Is there room to let go and let some things unfold?

for example, you're tired of calling a sitter and making dinner plans for you and your husband, and you wish that he would do this himself. Let him know how great it is to go out, and even mention the last outing you had—the movie or restaurant. Then say, "I'd really like it if *you* made the plans sometimes—maybe every other month. Can you do that?" Be open to the possibility that your husband may say, "I can't, or I can't without a reminder," and then you can brainstorm together on how to perhaps use the calendar on his cell phone to remind him to make a date. Be careful not to misinterpret his hesitation. It probably *doesn't* mean he doesn't care, it more likely means he's not a planner. End on a good note: "Our adult time means so much to me." Or maybe you'd like your sister to help out with the kids, and every time she *doesn't* offer, you feel more angry about what you've decided is her lack of concern. Instead of counting on mind reading as a means of communication, pick up the phone, write an e-mail, tell her what you'd like, and chances are she'll be happy to help and will likely say something that reveals something about the nature of her expectations of you: *You seem so together, I had no idea that you needed my help!*

TRY THIS

Make a side-by-side comparison by taking your first thought and doing a red-pen edit. So,

My husband should know I need a break from the kids when he gets home, or else if he doesn't, then he has no respect for what I do as a mother.

becomes

It would be greatly preferable if my husband ~~should know~~ knew I needed a break from the kids when he gets home, ~~or else if he doesn't, then he has no respect for what I do as a mother~~ but I know he does care and it's up to me to tell him what I need.

Another example:

I have to do a stellar job on my presentation on Friday or I'm going to lose my job.

becomes

It would be preferable if I did ~~I have to do a stellar job~~ a great job on my presentation on Friday ~~or I'm going to lose my job~~ and the chances are that I will do well because I've prepared, but I won't die if I don't, and they are not going to fire me if it's not stellar. Very few presentations at work, maybe none, are what I would call stellar. I'll just be disappointed, and I can deal with it.

When you read these two through, watch what happens to your body. You tighten on the first take, and the tension begins to release when you read version two. As you get used to doing the rewrite, not only will the words come more rapidly, but version one will begin to sound extreme and lose credibility. Remember, always keep your red pen handy.

ROOKIE ERRORS: WHEN YOU'RE NOT USED TO THINGS NOT WORKING OUT

Some of the most vulnerable people I've encountered in my practice are not the folks who have more than their fair share of problems. Those people have learned well how to survive. It's those who, for a variety of reasons, have had an enviably good life. They've had such smooth sailing on so many fronts that when they suddenly find themselves in a situation where they can't just make it work, they're stumped and panicked. They take aim at the nearest target—themselves. If something is wrong, it must be them. Maybe they haven't given it enough time, or they need to ask for help, but they never needed to do that before, so that seems like a very bad sign to them. Because they've always succeeded on their own wits, they assume, first and foremost, that their wits have let them down.

Take Dante. At age forty, he had enjoyed a meteoric rise in his career and quickly built himself a reputation as the genius of finding untapped resources in arts organizations. He was charismatic, passionate about his beliefs and causes, and no one could resist him. Hired by a struggling museum, he assumed that this job would be no different and he would quickly begin to turn things around. But several months in, nothing was turning. Dante had never met a situation that he couldn't fix, and quickly and masterfully, at that, but he was hitting dead ends. Although his boss had said nothing, Dante began to doubt himself, second-guess his moves, and find he couldn't think as clearly. He started to spiral downward, thinking: *Maybe you've always overestimated your ability, maybe you should never have thought you could do something so hard or so great.*

Dante was expecting another meteoric rise and couldn't see that this was an outlier, a temporary lapse caused maybe by the learning curve of the job and the fact that the economy was in a recession. Had he gone in with a more flexible time line, or with the belief that he would have eventual success, he could have more easily weathered the challenge. And most important, he could have realized that his boss was not disappointed. The boss hired Dante because of his skills, not because of his speed, and he had faith this project would succeed. Dante needed to separate out his performance from the outcome so that he could look at what went wrong and attribute responsibility accurately.

Was there a goal that you had in the past that was reasonable but perhaps not one you were ready for? What did you or could you learn from this situation that would serve you well in your next move?

EXPLANATIONS AND GETTING THE STORY STRAIGHT

Just like finding the lost mate to a shoe, when you have an expectation that doesn't work out, you need to match it up with an accurate explanation. Otherwise, the conclusions you reach may be unfounded and lead you astray. The more we relabel our first automatic explanations as the knee-jerk universal reaction to disappointment (we've failed), the more we can save ourselves the detour through that irrational explanation and learn the right things—the things we need to learn—about what actually went wrong.

For a long time, Aviva wanted to broaden her practice as a therapist to include support groups. Having been a one-on-one therapist for many years, she was nervous about whether she could handle the dynamic of multiple people in a room at one time. When the day of her first group came, she approached it with great trepidation. This was going to prove whether she could really run groups, or whether she simply wasn't cut out for this kind of work. Having made a schedule and agenda, things started off well, but then one of the members of the group kept sidetracking and even hijacking the agenda, addressing the group as if she were the leader. Aviva was devastated. It took days before Aviva could even tell anyone what happened, and when she did, she said, "I'm incompetent, this was such a mistake, I am not cut out to do this, I never should have tried, people won't respect me." But she considered her agenda good, and others in the group responded to it very well. The only problem was this one group member, who clearly had her own issues that didn't have to do with Aviva at all.

The problem with anxiety and negative thinking is that they shine a spotlight on what you conclude makes you a failure. Instead, you need to get specific and learn the right things from trials in life so that you can see what you want to do about it. Aviva expected that she should know how to handle everything as a group leader, and when she didn't, she labeled herself a failure. But on taking a closer look, she realized she was beautifully prepared for *many* things. The one thing that she needed to learn was what to do with hecklers.

Strategy #1: Do the Math, Slowly

Often, the quick math we do when something doesn't go our way is along the lines of "It's all my fault" or "It's all his fault." But accurate math means making sure that your explanation adds up with the facts, rather than being based on emotions. You may feel upset initially when things don't work as anticipated, but as you have learned, no matter how strongly you feel something, that doesn't make it true. Once the wave of emotions passes, you need to go back and reconstruct what really happened. As painful as this may be, it could lead you to the learning that will help prevent the situation from recurring in the future.

Strategy #2: Understanding the Behavior of Others

When we are disappointed by interactions involving other people, our first reaction tends to be an exquisitely, elaborately personalized explanation. *He was so rude at dinner, he must not respect me. He doesn't understand anything about my life and he doesn't care about me.* Then, the next morning, after you've huffed and puffed again, you come to the same conclusion you did the last time he was rude at dinner: news flash—he's rude. It has nothing to do with you. If you can store that essential information on a microchip bearing his name, the next time you are at dinner and he's rude, not only will you not personalize it, but you may be free to reach further into curiosity. *Why is he rude, what is it about his life that let him settle on acting this way?* You may even reach as far as compassion: *This must be a hard way to live, only knowing this way to connect with others, but wanting to connect so badly. He must be in pain, or it causes him pain to act in these ways. I'll send him the reassurance that he matters. Maybe he can relax and not be so rude.*

Bottom line: Sometimes you need to look for explanations that are about *them.* They are not setting out to drive you crazy; this is just who they are.

The second thing you can do is to better prepare yourself the next time you see that person. Don't expect the worst—that does no one any good. Be realistic. Chances are that you won't have a warm and fuzzy evening. Maybe position yourself to sit elsewhere if he really bothers you, or simply keep these thoughts in mind: He can't be giving to me, and that's okay. I have other places where I get my needs met, I don't have to have them met all the time . . . and I don't need them to be met here.

FREEING YOURSELF: IN ACTION

Cassie, a best-selling author, had arranged a book-signing event at a yearly book fair. Expecting her usual full-house crowd, she didn't do any publicity to announce it. When the day arrived and only a handful of people showed up, Cassie's first thought was, *Nobody is interested in my book anymore, I'm done.* Looking next for the accurate explanation, she asked herself, "What's different here?" and realized that she hadn't taken steps to get the word out. She was able to conclude quite solidly that publicity works, and moreover that she's good at it, so she needs to continue those efforts. If there had been a dangling expectation without the

Expect This, Not That

If you notice that you are continually being disappointed by people, it's probably not the people who are the problem. Ask yourself what you were expecting of those people. Chances are, who you are hoping those people might be is not really who they are. What you are expecting those people to do is not really what they can do (at least not now). And repeatedly coming up short is likely wearing everyone down. Although you may be grieving or angry, and rightfully so, for the ways that a person has let you down, consider this: Is it doing you any good to hold onto this expectation? Would shifting the picture you have in mind actually allow you to enjoy what that person *can* do, rather than only lamenting the things he or she can't do? Like forgiveness, changing an expectation for someone in your life is truly a gift that you give to yourself first. After all, that person isn't suffering with who he or she is—you are! Carry with you these simple instructions: For faster relief from a situation that is disappointing you and making you feel miserable, rather than clutching onto the idea that the situation must change, be the moving part. Let go of what isn't, in exchange for what is. You will likely be instantly rewarded for your flexibility.

When Others Have Impossible Expectations for Us: Return to Sender

There's a favorite Jewish joke in which a mother gives her son two neckties for his birthday. The next day, the son comes downstairs wearing one of the ties and the mother says, "What? You didn't like the other one?" If you notice that you are, to your surprise and in spite of your best efforts, continually disappointing someone in your life, maybe it's not you who needs to change; it may be the other person. Because we know that we can't just make that happen, we need to buffer ourselves from taking responsibility for something that doesn't belong to us. Rather than get defensive, we can try to hand the dilemma back to the other person by saying things like: "I'm not sure what you want me to do here, I'm getting the feeling that there's nothing I can do to make this right. Can we try to make this work for both of us?" Because few of us intentionally angle to create impossible situations for each other, at least not most of the time, if you can simply and nondefensively "return to sender," the sender may even be able to see the impossible situation he or she created and graciously revise the request.

YOU AND BEYOND
The Gift of the Wrong Cheese

Your husband comes home with the wrong kind of cheese for your fussy middle child who refuses to eat anything but the kind with the train on the wrapper. Picturing the meltdown that middle child may have, you are ready to pounce on your husband, but instead . . . you pause. Wrong cheese, yes, but was that intentional to set off a cascade of disaster in your house, or an honest mistake? Stop and consider the possibilities. After thanking your husband for trying, for remembering to get the cheese at all, this could be the crisis-opportunity moment for your child to try something new.

Sometimes innovation and growth are the outcomes when the wrong thing happens. So, as much as you need to factor in some margin of error in life, you may want to relabel some of those errors as opportunities for change. When something doesn't go exactly the way you expected, don't immediately protest; step back, consider how this seemingly wrong thing *could* actually work, albeit differently. It may not, but interesting things can happen when things don't go exactly as planned—think of the millions and millions of visitors to the leaning tower of Pisa each year.

---

proper explanation, this would look very different for Cassie. She could have stuck with that first thought and given up altogether. How wrong that would have been. Look at how far off track from the truth we can go when we don't mind our explanations.

Roberta's constant disappointment in people made her feel stressed and angry a lot more than she wanted. It took a long time to recover from each disappointment, and it often seemed that one event would spill into another. *Everybody is always letting me down. They never do what I want them to do, or what I would do. It is so frustrating.* Although with a red-pen edit she could eliminate the absolutes in the statement, Roberta's life was still too much of a roller coaster because too much of the time, she was counting on people acting in certain ways and often they didn't. Instead of seeing the moving part as flexing her expectations, Roberta would become more insistent that others change: Her colleague *should* get back to her the same day, her husband *should* pick up after the kids without reminders, friends *should* make weekend plans days in advance rather than at the last minute.

I asked Roberta if there was another option. What would it be like for you if you put a middle step between expectation and outcome—call it a feasibility check? There's nothing wrong with wanting what you want, but if it is unlikely to happen, it's not really helping you, or others, to expect it. She was hesitant at first, still feeling like she was right in what she wanted, but after a couple of weeks of pausing and readjusting her requests based on what was likely, an interesting thing happened—she noticed she wasn't mad. She felt happier. It hadn't occurred to her that shifting her expectations wasn't only about letting people off the hook. It was about saving herself from getting hung up, too.

Chapter 12

CULTIVATING EMPATHY, COMPASSION, AND GRATITUDE

The actual beneficiary of the practice of compassion and caring for others is oneself.
—DALAI LAMA, *ILLUMINATING THE PATH TO ENLIGHTENMENT*

Ben was experiencing a lot of frustration in his life. Currently unemployed, he wasn't happy with himself, and he was disappointed in people around him. He needed a job, that's what everything came down to. Every day that he didn't have one, he grew more angry at the world. Although he felt entitled to his anger, he also felt trapped in it. Nothing positive was happening in his life, he told me. Without a job or potential work, he felt no spark.

In our sessions, we talked about how beneficial the simple act of gratitude can be. Ben decided to start writing to thank the people who were trying to help him out with networking leads, letting them know that this was a hard time for him, but knowing that they were willing to help him meant a lot. He returned the next week buoyed by the replies he had gotten to those letters. "I didn't feel like there was a single good thing coming my way, but I think I was just feeling like a non-person. Having people say really supportive things made me feel normal—they weren't seeing me as a loser." The thing he was waiting for was a job. The thing that he didn't have to wait for was finding goodness in what was going on around him. His gratitude was the moving part.

CREATING NEW HUBS AND DESTINATIONS THROUGH POINTS OF CONNECTION

So far on our journey engaging the mind to remap the brain, we have swapped out maladaptive automatic patterns for healthier explanations and ideas. Treating thoughts as questions or as just words rather than proclamations gives you the opportunity to nudge yourself out of those unlikely but powerful downward spirals and into new probabilities and possibilities. These pages are filled with what we might consider effective weed control: identifying harmful thoughts, preventing them from taking root, not inadvertently propagating the bad seeds. This is an essential way to improve the quality of your life, but it's only half the picture. We need to deliberately plant seeds of goodness in our days.

Of course, we don't want to just *eliminate bad feelings*, we want to feel good. When we feel love, connection, compassion, and gratitude, we transcend ourselves, moving to new places and deepening our shared experience of life. The good news is that you don't have to wait by the side of the road for these experiences to come along and lift you up. You bring your own transportation. Rather than thinking, like Ben did, that you need something big to happen to change your situation and make you feel better, you can learn to intentionally travel in your mind or with your feet to these destinations and create moments of connection and appreciation. The more you make these ideas visible, the more you'll find yourself naturally heading in these directions. It feels good, and it does good.

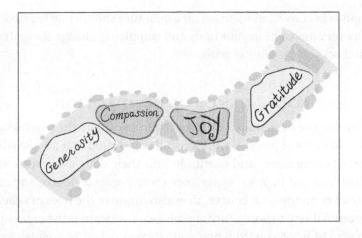

As you invest in this facet of living, you'll find that it is contagious. It tends to broadcast outward, opening up feelings of well-being to be shared all around. It is like a relay. Although there are times when, deep in the hole, it will be hard to be touched by someone's random act of kindness, but most often a broad smile, a warm comment, a small gesture sets off a chain reaction that you then relay by giving a gentle nudge to someone who may need it. Just at the moment your loving impulse may be waning, someone else's may be just warming up, and shared with you. This is the way the world heals itself.

THE PHYSICS OF SCALE

One more thing before you start. You needn't look for big things to be grateful for, like the college acceptance, the new car, the job offer, or the positive pregnancy test. In fact, the astonishing power of these experiences is that they operate on a homeopathic principle: Small doses have a big impact. No matter how enormous the bad feelings are, it only takes a tiny drop of gratitude, typically found in the smallest everyday moments, like a kind glance from a stranger, a heartfelt thank you, or a meeting of the minds in conversation, to set off a quantum shift in one fell swoop in every molecule in your body and completely change the system and set you on a better path.

THE SCIENCE OF CONNECTION

In recent years, researchers have begun to explore the psychological benefits of positive emotion and have found that people who bring compassion and gratitude into their daily awareness are healthier and happier, experience more positive moods, and are more contented. Of course, they also improve the lives of others around them, to boot. Turning the focus outward is the exact opposite of what you do when you worry. Locked in anguish and self-recrimination, the crosshairs of worry focus narrowly on you, but when you open up to compassion and gratitude, your view on life broadens.

It will come as no surprise to those of us who have spent time under the vice grip of our own scrutiny—and haven't we all?—that researchers have also found that excessive self-focused attention is part of a vicious cycle in anxiety and depression. The more self-critical we are, the more anxious we feel, and the more anxious we feel, the more self-critical we become. The narrower the focus, the narrower our bandwidth for joy and well-being. When you are so preoccupied with your dissatisfactions or stressing about a future event, you may be oblivious to the needs of others around you.

Given the physical toll that worrying takes, it's not like all that attention on ourselves does us any good in tending to our needs, either. In fact, knowing how to zoom out from the auto close-up is so important to mental health that one measure researchers use to gauge successful treatment for anxiety and depression is by a *decrease* in self-focused attention. We certainly don't gain by turning the scrutiny screws tighter on ourselves. We'd love to unlock the grip and turn the spotlight somewhere besides our own spinning worry and incessant self-criticism, but we just don't know how to do it. Empathy and compassion are one more way to step off that ride.

PROACTIVE WELL-BEING: COMPASSION PREVENTS MISUNDERSTANDINGS

Another compelling reason to learn the mechanics of compassion and empathy is that one of the most powerful, and most frequent, sources for anxiety and negative thinking is misunderstanding others' intentions toward us. We anticipate others' disapproval or get locked into battles with the imagined reasons why people make our lives miserable. *What if he's mad at me? What if he thinks I ruined everything? Maybe she hates me, he thinks he's better than me, I'm not important to them.* It is only later, after you've been to hell and back, running with the ball of someone else's supposed judgment or bad intentions for you, that you find, thankfully, you were wrong, *again.* There was no headline news story; they weren't mad or trying to hurt you; they do care; it was a misunderstanding. Being able to empathize, you can instead short-circuit the fear, outrage, or hurt. Seeing situations from another's perspective not only benefits others, but it is yet another very powerful way to shorten the detour and save you from unnecessary anguish: You become a better reader and interpreter of human behavior.

DISPENSING WITH THE GUILT TACTICS TO LOOK BEYOND YOURSELF

For some of us, positive, generative emotions come easily and are part of daily rounds. Others, and this is even true for all of us at some time, have a childlike knee-jerk reaction to the idea of being grateful. It can seem not only impossible but just plain wrong. *I hate myself right now. How can I give when I am lacking so much? This couldn't apply to me.* If you are feeling this way, this chapter is especially for you. It may feel like a contradiction: You are down, you have nothing to give, and even trying is one more way to highlight your inadequacy. But seeing yourself as excluded won't help either, and simply isn't true.

For generations, our understanding of generosity and thankfulness often came from a place of guilt and limited resources. The lecture went something like this: "We *should* share, because if not, shame on us, we were selfish and depriving someone else." Hold on. This is not your father's Oldsmobile. Sharing is very important, yes, but fortunately we've come to learn that it also just feels very good. So, thankfully, we can dispense with the guilt tactics once and for all and walk into gratitude and generosity through a new door—the door of mutuality, the two-way win of empathy. Because, in fact, in those times when negative experiences threaten to bring you all the way down, often gratitude and compassion provide the secret path to the light and to a place of feeling better. Sometimes with gratitude, that light can be blinding and splendidly so.

COMPASSION AND EMPATHY

I do not like that man, I need to get to know him better.

—ABRAHAM LINCOLN

Entering the empathy door means that instead of asking "*Why* did you do that?" you say, "You did that; I'd really like to understand that, can you help me?" Rather than insisting that you are right, you stretch to grasp something that doesn't initially fit with your view. When our younger daughter Raia was four years old she insisted on keeping her shoes lined up side-by-side *outside* of her cubby instead of in a basket *inside* her cubby where we each keep our shoes. I repeatedly reminded her to put her shoes away, but they would always end up in the same place. Thinking that she was being defiant or a little bit like the children I treat with obsessive-compulsive disorder, I said, not so patiently, "Why do you keep doing this!"

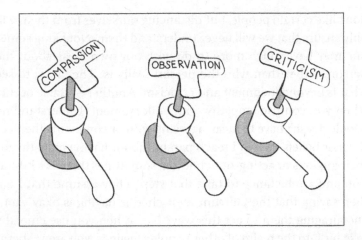

She started to cry, and then she explained: "Because if I don't keep them side by side, I can't tell which one is the right one and which one is the left." Even though her behavior hadn't seemed reasonable to me at first, there was a reason, and if I had put myself in her shoes, almost literally, I might have been able to figure it out myself. If you take the time to understand, most conflicts happen as a result of people doing reasonable things, or things for good reasons, the logic of which is not yet shared (or revealed).

As a starting point, we understand that we come into the world pre-wired for connecting with others. We see this best in the first five months of life, when babies, watching you smile, mirror your emotion by smiling back. Of course, it is a two-way street. Babies can make even the grumpiest person smile, and melt into that feeling. But there are two parts to empathy. The first is tuning in to what someone is feeling, and the second is deciding what to do with those data. Do you lean into it and connect with it, or do you stay distant and hold it up to your scrutiny? Thinking of our faucets from Chapter 3, here we can refashion them to find there is criticism, there is compassion, and there is the simple act of nonjudgmental observation: the key to accurate understanding.

Often, what gets in the way of empathy is judgment. Maybe we don't like what someone is doing, or even, as Mr. Lincoln says, we don't like certain people, but distancing ourselves from them will only ensure that we will never understand them. Not liking someone may have much more to do with our own ideas about the person, rather than who the person really is. The key is to see what is beyond judgment and criticism. Another obstacle occurs when you confuse empathy with endorsement. Understanding people doesn't have to mean agreeing with or condoning their actions or beliefs. When I teach parents about having empathy for their anxious or acting-out children, sometimes there is a hesitation and a reluctance to take that step. They assume that I am then saying that the tantrum their child is having is okay. Am I encouraging them to act this way? No. When you use empathy to enter into the realm of other people's feelings, you aren't standing back in judgment of the worthiness or rightness or wrongness of that viewpoint; you are stepping into their shoes and trying to see things the way they do.

The purpose of empathy is to evoke the recognition that a person—sharing a common humanity—is like you on a basic level. Empathy is not endorsement, empathy is recognition that a person could feel the way he or she does for whatever reason. When you don't accept a person's right to exist, you are filled with negative feelings yourself. You may be less accepting of your own unacceptable thoughts, blaming yourself, defining yourself by these minor weaknesses, rather than accepting them as part of the human condition.

Can Empathy Be Cultivated? Thinking Good for Others Is Also Good for Us

Like anything else, empathy starts at home. So, when you are frustrated with your spouse, kids, or even your dog, you can pause and instead of questioning, "Why aren't they acting the way *I* would?" you can consider their point of view and try to understand why they are acting the way *they* actually are, because there is probably a good reason for it even though you can't see it yet. This is a very good start.

To further deepen your skills and allocate more neural surface area to look for ways to feel compassion for others, consider the work of researchers Geshe Lobsang Negi at Emory University's Center for Collaborative and Contemplative Studies and psychiatrist Charles Raison, director of the university's Mind-Body Program, who have studied the benefits of compassion meditation. Different from traditional forms of meditation aimed at quieting the mind, compassion meditation challenges you to go outside of your comfort zone to people you may know but don't love and perhaps don't even like. When researchers teach compassion meditation, participants do a daily practice of feeling compassion for people they love, people they ignore, and people they don't like. Studies have found that those who engage in this practice are less likely to cling tightly to people they love, and also to not reject so strongly people they dislike. They were also, in general, more likely to be more present and aware of all people. And health benefits come as an added bonus. Students who practiced compassion meditation in a twice-weekly, six-week course showed a reduction in distress and inflammatory reaction in response to stressors.

It would make sense, given our understanding of the amygdala and its role in regulating our reactivity, that the more we train ourselves to see more friend than foe in our midst, the fewer unnecessary firings there would be of the sympathetic nervous system—the fight-or-flight reaction that triggers so much anxiety and negative feeling.

It may be easy for us to feel heartfelt compassion for a friend or loved one in a difficult situation because we understand that we are all in the same boat, and next time it could be us. However, it may be more difficult to tap into compassion for someone when you are angry at them, or simply don't like them. But if you want to get limber—this is exactly what you need to do.

Think of the many things that have caused a person to behave in a way that stresses you. Temperament, daily stresses, childhood experiences, socioeconomics, and more can all impact a person's behavior. After you have done the stretch of understanding—see if you feel differently: about the other person as well as yourself.

Empathy in Action

In my years of trying various ways to convey the concept of empathy to patients, one young man did so more poignantly and effectively than I ever could. At age ten, Ezra was struggling with the fact that he was always jumpy, fidgety, and unable to sit still, much to the disapproval and chagrin of others, especially his older sister. I suggested to Ezra that perhaps his sister didn't know that it is just his temperament to need to move around a lot. I asked Ezra if he knew what I meant by temperament. He said, "It is what your soul wants you to do. And because it's your soul, we need to respect it. We need to respect each other's souls."

Ezra's words spoke right to *my* soul. After that session, I immediately thought of the ways that I am critical of my husband. I bristle at his irksome habit of leaving every drawer, cupboard, lid, and bag open, and leaving chargers, long abandoned by their phones or computers, plugged into the wall. He leaves the caps off pens and often leaves a path of unfinished thoughts. When I followed Ezra's suggestion, I realized that my husband's soul is about creation. He is a visionary, a starter, and that's what his soul wants to do. And really, that's what I want him to do, too. The foundation of creativity in our household is built, in Ezra's terms, on my husband's soul. And so I unplug the charger, and close the doors and drawers, and reunite pens with their long-lost caps. But thanks to Ezra, I now do that lovingly, appreciatively, and without judgment.

Try it for yourself. Think of an irksome habit or complaint about someone close to you—your difficult teenager, your messy spouse, the cat who sits on whatever you are reading. Try to see that small behavior as part of a bigger picture that makes sense. Maybe your teen wants to be outspoken—a good quality—but isn't good at it yet. Maybe your spouse is not a detail person but is always there for the things that really matter. Maybe your cat is

TRY THIS:
Practicing Empathy: Let Go of
Judgment and Let In Compassion

When certain people are different from you and you can't understand the "why" of their behavior, stretch and take it as a given that it is right for them. Urge yourself, compassionately, to find the answer that fits in their world, even if it wouldn't be the way you would operate. You'll find that understanding doesn't only feel better all around, it is often a much more interesting endeavor than the open-and-shut case of judging each other.

When someone is distressed, imagine that you are that person—what would you want? How would you want someone to approach you?

In an argument, pause and instead of pushing your point, listen and imagine how the opposing point of view is interesting and true.

---

the most loyal of companions and just wants to be with you all the time. Even if after you do this empathy search, the irksome behavior remains a problem for you, this work was not for naught. Going in compassionately rather than with a hidden dagger attack will surely improve the outcome of your discussion about why you're asking someone to change.

GRATITUDE: THE POWER OF GIVING, AND GIVING THANKS

Most definitions of gratitude belie the power packed into the simple words "thank you." Gratitude comes from the Latin root *gratia*, meaning grace. In that moment of giving and receiving a heartfelt thank you, grace abounds. It feels good all around.

To some, gratitude invokes inner calmness and a letting go of tension. For others, it is a lightning rod for tension itself. If we can set aside the unpleasant memories of being scolded for *not* feeling grateful and the shame and embarrassment engendered there, we are free to see that gratitude has nothing to do with wrestling thankfulness from us. It is born, freely. When you find yourself engaging in a random act of kindness such as helping someone avert a spill, or clean it up after, helping a lost child reunite with a nearby parent, you feel good. When researchers at the National Institutes of Health studied the brain scans of volunteers deciding whether to keep or donate a sum of money to charity, they found that the altruistic group activated a part of the brain that usually lights up in response to food or sex. The central pathway to making these decisions of placing the interests of others before their own is empathy. When we put ourselves in the place of those less fortunate, we make these good choices. These studies suggest, however, that whether we are aware of it or not, making these choices has biological roots.

We may be more keenly attuned to meeting the basic needs of food and sex, and not need to consciously remind ourselves that if we met these needs, we'd feel better. After all, television advertisements drive those messages home every six and one-half minutes. To be proactive in feeling satisfied by helping another—the profit margin doesn't exist, so we must be the ones to remind ourselves of that.

Research has found that grateful people experience higher levels of positive emotions such as joy, enthusiasm, love, happiness, and optimism, and that protects a person from envy, resentment, greed, and bitterness. Researchers Robert Emmons of the University of California at Davis and Michael McCullough of the University of Miami looked at what happens when people of no particular religious background begin a habit of gratitude. In one study, several hundred people were divided into three groups. One group was asked to record the events of the day; the second group recorded unpleasant experiences; and the third listed the things each day for which they were grateful. The gratitude group reported higher levels of alertness, enthusiasm, determination, optimism, and energy. They were less depressed and stressed, and were more likely to help others.

If introducing a daily practice into your already full life doesn't sound feasible, don't worry. Another study found that people who kept a gratitude journal once a week reported higher levels of happiness than those who wrote daily. Making it a regular practice but not a chore makes all the difference.

When is the right time to be grateful? Sometimes with your sights set high, you don't feel that anything *counts* until the ink is dry on that deal you've been waiting for. You hold out for what you feel is your due. You've seen the bumper sticker "Don't Postpone Joy." But big-ticket items in life—the promotion, the record deal, the house, a baby—tend to be few and far between. So, cultivating a practice for living graciously by appreciating the smaller moments—a car that starts, a roof that doesn't leak, a note from a friend—brings feelings of well-being on a regular basis. Over time, you get less concerned about the meaning of gratitude and simply feel it spontaneously and even crave it because it delivers such peacefulness to you.

What are the right things to be grateful for? There are no wrong answers, and the list is endless. You read a good book and you are grateful to the author for telling the story. Your eye catches a glint of winter sun coming through the bare trees. Although banner days can be good to highlight by jotting down a few notes of gratitude, you may actually find the best use of this practice on the days when many things go wrong. On these days, we especially long most for a way out of the grip of frustration and disappointment. Often, on these days nothing breaks through like finding the place to exhale and appreciate what is.

What You Give, You Receive

• Facilitate the flow of everyday life: thank people, warmly, for everyday gestures.

- Write thank-you notes or e-mails when someone compliments you.
- Create a daily or weekly gratitude practice in writing or in your mind.
- Start a journal or a computer file to keep track of gratitude findings. You can be poetic and just write brief descriptions, such as "deer running through the backyard." Or you can write out the longhand, describing beauty, kind gestures, and awe that you noticed throughout the day.
- Establish a weekly or nightly ritual with your family, looking for the funny, the interesting, the moving, the good. Share the wealth of your observation with others.
- Remember that it takes about three weeks to establish a habit, so even though the first bit of time may feel effortful, it will become more second nature when you practice it regularly.

SAVORING THE GOODNESS OF THE MOMENT

Just as chewing on anxious and negative thoughts deepens their impact, *savoring* means to multiply the impact of a meaningful or pleasant experience by thinking about it. This means finding the "moment," as poet William Blake said, "in every day that the devil can not find."

You might stretch ahead to a moment and anticipate with pleasure how it will be, or stretch back to enjoy something from the past, or simply enhance your experience of the moment as it happens by commenting about it or quietly being with it for all its good. Start right now. Think about an experience where you felt moved or happy and recount the details to yourself. Perhaps it was the lunch you had at an outdoor café on a late winter day when the thermometer reached 70°F. Recall the feeling of the first hints of spring in the air, the trees preparing to bud, peeling coats and layers off to bask in the sunlight. Notice the ease that comes over your body as you settle into an easy breathing pattern. Imag-

SAVORING: BORROWING AHEAD ON ENJOYMENT AND MEANING

Imagine if each day, or even each week, you engaged in a savoring practice. That guarantees dozens of pleasant experiences each year that wouldn't otherwise occur, and *you* are the one who can make them happen. Psychologists Fred Bryant and Joseph Veroff describe three ways that savoring can multiply the benefit of the moment.

Anticipatory: Think ahead about an event you are looking forward to and tap into the excitement in advance. Begin imagining the positive feelings that you have about the people you will see and the activities you will engage in.

In the moment: Briefly step back from what you are doing and appreciate that it is happening—like the family dinner that is going great, even with its chaos. Savor the vitality of that chaos.

Reminiscent: Go back to a positive event and let your mind trace over the moments and experiences you enjoyed.

ine what would happen if you took these excursions in your mind more often, maybe even every week or every day while eating your ten-minute lunch at your desk. You could go back to your work refreshed from your journey. As with any new regimen, this will seem effortful at first, but whether you choose to take spontaneous savoring moments or link this practice with an existing habit such as doing the dishes or walking the dog, the more you engage in these excursions, the more they will become automatic and effortless destinations.

FREEING YOURSELF: IN ACTION

In the midst of a heated divorce, Peter and Nan were locked in raw, painful conflict with each other. Even sitting in the same

TRY THIS:
Finding Goodness

How do you generate good feeling even when no one is around to play? The idea of a gratitude journal made its way quickly from the research lab of Robert Emmons, author of *Thanks!* to Oprah and her viewers. This can mean anything from jotting ideas in a journal to a dinner-table ritual a few times a week. One of my friends has a gratitude partner, like a pen pal, and commits to texting or e-mailing her gratitude list a few times a week. When others are involved, it's more likely to happen.

The list can include gratitude for things others have done for you, gratitude for who they are, appreciation for the staples of life (food and shelter, a loving family), and finally, make sure to include yourself on the list. Appreciating how you've contributed to your good experiences this week is important, too!

---

room, on opposite couches in my office, the tension was palpable. And yet they had come together because despite all the ways they felt hurt by each other, they knew that carrying these wounds visibly into their new, separate lives only threatened to perpetuate the hurt by involving their kids. They wanted my help, but they couldn't conceive of how to break free. They cared deeply for their children, and the place where they could be generous and grateful to each other was in how they felt about each other as parents.

I asked them each to say what they appreciated and were glad that their children would get from the other parent that they themselves were unable to give. The initial awkwardness of the exercise gave everyone something to laugh about, but quickly that gave way to other feelings. Nan was able to tell Peter how much she appreciated his willingness to be whimsical and create spontaneous adventures with the kids, making forts, planets, snow caves. She liked how this expanded their worlds and sense

YOU AND BEYOND
Small Things Often

Remember the homeopathic principle of meaningful experience? Big gestures are great but aren't necessary. The smallest of moments are those that shift the system. Consider an extra word of appreciation, sharing a compliment rather than keeping it to yourself, clicking reply on an e-mail to say thanks, looking up and smiling when you're walking rather than looking the other way. We don't become immune to these gestures, no matter how many times they happen. They feel good and they may even feel unexpected. So don't hold back—do just a little bit more and know that you are responsible for the good ripples out in the world. Chances are that soon enough, you'll see that they find their way back to you.

---

of possibility. Peter knew that the children could always count on their mother to know what they needed, and he was relieved to know that even though his emotional radar didn't tune in well unless things were brought to his attention, his children would have a mother who would always provide that. Brought together in that time by their love for their children, they agreed that they would really try to preserve each other rather than hurt each other, so they could each do their part to give their children a whole life.

PART IV

Shortcuts

How to Find Your Way Through the Detours of Life

The peace you long for also longs for you.
—GUY FINLEY

DON'T CHANGE THE SUBJECT

We saw in Chapter 9 how your reactions to your feelings add roadblocks to managing the feelings themselves. Clutching negative feelings about feelings—*I shouldn't be feeling this way*—detours you and changes the subject. It becomes the new path. You are no longer thinking about whether your co-worker really meant to hurt you and how to fix that; instead, you are anxiously trying not to feel how much that hurt, or punishing yourself for how much you hate him right now, or worrying about what you're going to do when you next see him. Wait—what happened to the real issue of how to fix the situation with your co-worker? It got lost in the stampede of feelings and efforts to block feelings. You need to recognize the error, turn around as soon as possible, and take care of the business at hand rather than be led astray by anxious commentary.

This book is about getting from fears that block you from processing your real life to courageously opening the door to see what's there and discovering that you can manage what you've found. In these next two chapters, you will learn what happens when the first results are not in your favor and how to swap out your thinking about these inevitable snags of life for healthier choices. First, we'll tackle universal inevitable feelings—anger, jealousy, loss, and shame—and second, we'll look at what you might consider the human-made situations of perfectionism, procrastination, failure, and more.

Peace will find you sooner if you know where to look for it and meet it halfway. Often, the initial peace you think you seek, say, when you're in an angry moment (*May you rot in hell, enemy!*) is not where you find lasting comfort. The destination will be different through second-thought, closer inspection. You'll trade venomous first reactions with more peaceful reactions such as, "We're not understanding each other—let's figure out how to make it work." The sooner you can set your GPS to that destination, the more direct your journey and the sooner you will arrive.

If you are not in any particular quandary at this point, skim these pages, but make a mental note so that when you find yourself stuck with a negative feeling or in a negative situation, you can head back to your bookmark. It will help you understand the combination of feelings, expectations, and circumstances and also provide the blueprint for how to map out your exit.

Chapter 13

THINKING DIFFERENTLY ABOUT ANGER, JEALOUSY, LOSS, AND SHAME

Where you stumble, there lies your treasure.
—JOSEPH CAMPBELL

KEEPING OPEN THE LINES OF COMMUNICATION WITH YOURSELF

In Chapter 9, you saw that feelings, although they *feel* like a meteor coming toward you, are more like a satellite transmitting important information. No one wants to be the last to know. Rather than working against yourself anxiously and questioning how you will manage to *not* feel this, you can change your perceptions going into these feelings. You can unclench and choose to keep the lines of communication open, and then see that contained within this sometimes very painful package is a truly unique opportunity to greatly improve your life.

Difficult, big feelings typically emerge out of our interactions with others. Often you feel that something has been "done to you," and thus the only solution is to wait for those same people to "undo it." As we just saw in our discussion about expectations, depending on the cooperation of others for your happiness is not going to serve you well, since they may not realize this is what you need. This chapter reveals how big emotions like anger and jealousy work, and it provides the GPS out of the tangle of those emotions. You will no longer be afraid and will be able to stay with the feelings as long as you need to in order to get the right things out of them.

ANGER: THE FIERY MESSENGER OF THE NEED FOR CHANGE

If you are patient in one moment of anger, you can escape a hundred days of sorrow.

—CHINESE PROVERB

The Anatomy of Anger: The Savage Overrides the Sage (Temporarily)

Here's the challenge. By the time you realize you're getting angry, it's already too late. If anxiety is fast, anger is even faster. And "angry" people aren't the only ones who get roped in. Some of us keep anger tucked in better than others, but everyone at one time or another gets thrown into a seething, biting internalized fury. It happens with people close to you and with people you'll never see again. For example, it might crop up when your son-in-law doesn't like the meal you cooked for him, when the man at your dry cleaner swears he doesn't have the suit that you need for an interview tomorrow, or when your boss completely pans the proposal you've been working on for the last six months and acts like it is no big deal. Your cognitive switchboard gets flooded with a million simultaneous messages, all of which narrow down to some version of: "This is completely unacceptable, you must pay." As rational as you are, some part of you is still saying to fight until just one person remains standing—*you*.

BOTTLENECK BELIEFS:
This Shouldn't Have Happened and It's Your Fault; Now Fix It!

If we were to take a poll of all humanity and determine the causes of our anger with others, whether sibling spats, marital conflicts, or workplace disagreements, it would undoubtedly boil down to one of three assumptions.

1) Others *should have known* what you wanted and you're angry that they didn't.
2) Your way of doing things is right. You are angry that others have clearly done the *wrong* thing.
3) When people do the wrong thing, they are obliged to make things right. Now.

What just happened? Your amygdala has spoken. The body's superspeedy first reaction says, "Attack! Defend yourself!" But it also says, "Get a grip, don't embarrass yourself, you are totally out of control." You don't want to advance because that picture of your uncontrolled rage also frightens you. The more these messages urge you on, the more you are rattled and overwhelmed, and that causes the amygdala to protect you even further. The more adrenaline you feel, the more confusion you feel. The walls are closing in and you don't want to retreat, because the one thing you know for sure is that there's a problem.

Welcome to the World of Anger

How do you get a grip on the part of yourself that operates independently of reason? The crucial step for reining back the anger is to relabel your feelings. You need a quick way of recalibrating and contextualizing the intensity of your reactions to something that resembles you *before* the anger hit. When it comes down to it, you don't really want blood. Relabeling or putting a tag on anger separates you from that animal reaction and helps you connect with your higher faculties more quickly.

In the children's animated movie *Madagascar*, a group of talkative, city-spoiled animals escapes from the Central Park Zoo to an island where they discover some surprising things about themselves. In the wild, the lion, Alex, returns to his savage ways and starts to see his beloved friends not as faithful, furry creatures, but as slabs of juicy steak. Alex is both charged up and horrified by his animal nature. We like to think of ourselves as civilized and refined, but when anger strikes, even our loved ones can look like meat. Suddenly, the teeth come out and we're ready to bite. When I share this story with my adult patients and tell them to relabel their angry, animal moments as a temporary lapse where they see the world as steak, they're relieved and can distance themselves from the sense that they are monsters. Just because we see meat doesn't make us beasts. It just makes us human. Step one, relabeling, is the most important step in anger because we take the intense physical response we are having as a sign of how important or justified it would be to take aim and fire. We and our physical responses are not to be trusted in a moment of anger.

Once you are able to pause, cool your jets, get your composure, sit back in your seat, and exhale, what's next? Whether you try to work things out in the boardroom or at the kitchen table, the next step is about construction and communication. Anger happens when there is a misunderstanding or a disagreement. What does it look like when situations are resolved competently?

Maybe on the other side of this misunderstanding or disagreement is an important item that you can check off your list. You won't have to argue about *this* again, because you've successfully figured out a plan. Instead of peering into the dark abyss of conflict, know that there is a bridge to resolution. The goal is to change the perception of what happened from threat to misunderstanding, and ultimately to an opportunity for better understanding.

BETTER BELIEFS:
See an Opportunity for Resolution, Not Revenge

The best way to have patience in your one moment of anger is to be aware of your bottleneck assumptions and replace them with more accurate alternatives:

1) Behind the other person's "attack" is a need for you to understand.
2) You have options about how to perceive or respond.
3) Your goal, always, is to make things better.

Rehearse Your New Understanding

When someone does you wrong, it can feel outrageous, unforgivable, and irrevocable. Sometimes these words do describe the situation, and sometimes they just describe how it feels. Whichever the case, they will only keep the adrenaline flowing, and they won't help you to regain your composure and effectively advocate for yourself or speak your mind. On the other side of this moment, and remembering that there *is* an other side of this moment, is crucial, you will either resolve things, or you will move on. The feeling you are having right now is temporary, and reminding yourself of that will start to take the burn out of your lungs and the sting out of your throat, and you'll begin to feel back in charge.

Getting Specific: Was It on Purpose?

You can also turn off the amygdala when you know that you are less threatened than you initially thought. Your first conclusion, "She meant to humiliate me at that party by bringing up my husband's gambling problem," makes you see red. Is it possible that she is clumsy or she even thought she was doing something good because someone else in the group struggles with addiction? Understanding the why doesn't preclude confronting such people to let them know that what they did felt bad to you. But once you can let go of your assumptions of mal-intent, which may or may not be true, you can be on the solid ground of talking about your experience. You are the expert on that.

Who's on Clean-Up Duty?

Distinguish between your right to feel angry and the other person's obligation to make things right for you. The more you hold on to needing an apology, even when it's warranted, the less control you have, because you are waiting for something that you can't will into being. Rather than wait, if you can separate the action from the person, you can begin to forgive or let go, realizing that it's what that person did that upset you, not who the person is. You can be the moving part and say that. Often when we lower the stakes in this way, the other person is better able to come forward and apologize. Children don't like to be forced to say sorry, and neither do adults.

What are the possible ways of looking at this situation? What's the moving part? Your expectations? The other person's behavior? Take an evenhanded look at the different options. Who and what can change?

Optimize: What If There's No Bad Guy?

Looking for a culprit narrows your perspective while it blocks your creativity and flexibility. Our rigidity is contagious. Instead of itemizing the list of charges, think of your goal, the goal of your better self: understanding, moving on. In this way the questions shift. Instead of thinking: *How could he have done that to me? I refuse to ever forgive her for that!* you think instead: *I need to tell him how angry I feel. Maybe he doesn't know. We don't usually try to hurt each other, how can we figure out together what the problem is here?* If you were trying to make things work to get back to a place of wholeness and understanding, what would that look like?

Speak to the Best in Each Other

Anger can make us—even the most mature adults—behave in petty, irrational ways that we often regret later. When we let anger speak unfiltered, it speaks to the lowest common denominator. And when we speak that language, it is often returned to us in kind. What's the alternative? Round up. Hand the microphone to your best self, and imagine speaking to the best that other person can be: "I don't think this is the way either of us want things to go. I think we can both do better than this—and we'd both like to. Let's try."

Mobilize: Asking for What You Want

Make clear requests: In almost any situation we encounter, a win-win is the most desirable outcome. The dry cleaner that messes up the pleats on your pants doesn't want a miserable customer, and you don't want to look bad. When you make requests, use language that presumes the win-win and the other person's good intentions. "This is not going to look good for either of us, is it? I have a meeting tomorrow; what can we do to make this work for both of us?"

Be Willing to Do First Things, Second

When we are angry, the first thing we want to do is vent or demand an apology—and we won't budge till we get it. If you can be flexible and do things out of order, you might instead say something open-ended like, "What happened?" or "We're both upset, let's talk this out." If you can be patient a few more minutes and willing to let other people answer first, you may be rewarded by their calmness—not only might they be able to apologize in a way that they hadn't before, but they gain a sense of safety and learn a new approach to conflict from you. It's about listening to each other.

FREEING YOURSELF: IN ACTION

Jane felt stressed all the time. People at work, her friends, and most important, her boyfriend of three years added to the strain. Jane and Mike were serious about each other, but they fought a

---

REHEARSE YOUR NEW LINES

- I don't want to be doing this, do you?
- How can we fix this so that it works for both of us?
- I want to work together on this, how about you?
- I don't know how to fix this, but I know this isn't comfortable for me; are you willing to work through this together?

---

lot. Jane grew up in a highly defensive family where it was always each "man" for himself. Fights had always been about someone winning and someone else feeling foolish and angrier than before. Mike came from a family in which arguing was discouraged, even if it meant not confronting others about important things. Jane knew that her quick spark and inflammatory reaction to anger was a problem and confused Mike, who felt that he was being attacked ruthlessly. Not only was Jane not getting what she wanted, which was increasingly less about "winning" and more about being understood, but she felt childish and out of control, like a bully to Mike. Yet she was at a loss for what else she could do.

Changing the meaning of anger was crucial for Jane. The hard part for her was making the shift to the idea that she could or should be flexible even when maybe it was the other person's fault. We talked about the idea of a Pyrrhic victory, in which you push so hard to win that you actually lose, and we discussed the many more effective choices she could make about her anger. The shift for Jane was realizing that at least in close relationships, she could start to *trust* that the other person would be interested in her complaints and would want to try to fix them, out of love rather than out of fear or shame. This was very different from the model in her head, which told her she had to verbally pummel the other person until they felt terrible about what they had done. Otherwise, they wouldn't care or try to work it out. She used the optimizing step the most to look at the situation from different perspectives; so instead of walking through the anger door, she would think about the negotiation door, the increasing intimacy door, and the many other ways to look at the problem. When she realized the good that could come from working things out, she started to calm down her impulse to pounce.

ENVY AND JEALOUSY: TAKING THE POWER BACK FROM THE ONE THAT GOT AWAY

> *To cure jealousy is to see it for what it is, a dissatisfaction with self.*
>
> —JOAN DIDION

Anatomy of Jealousy, a Self-Inflicted Wound

"How come *he* got the red car? I wanted that car!" says the inconsolable child. He had his heart set on one thing and now he has nothing. Not one single thing. Well, except for everything else he has. We've all starred in that show, both as kids and in the grown-up remake. Just as we want to help little kids see that pushing the heart "reset button" will get all their *other* stuff back that was on hold, that's what we need to do for ourselves in a moment of jealousy. Amazingly, even your heart can reset when you push the right buttons. And, often when you do, you may find that your version of the "red car" is not the be-all and end-all, after all. If you decide that it is, you can figure out how to get it back for

---

BOTTLENECK BELIEFS

- Your distress is caused by the other person.
- Getting the object of your jealousy is the only thing that will relieve your distress.
- Your distress can only be relieved if the other person *doesn't* have the object of your jealousy.
- Not having the object of jealousy reflects poorly on your entire self-worth.

---

yourself. The more you get away from the arbitrary measurements and comparisons, you can get back on your own track. The less you look in the rearview mirror to see what others have, the more you can focus on what is right for you.

New Understanding: Who Is Really Standing In Your Way?

Jealousy is the ultimate in all-or-none thinking. They have all, but you have none. Those of us with a good sense of self may not be as frequent sufferers as those of us struggling with our confidence and self-esteem, but no one is immune from the occasional bite of the green monster. With jealousy you have a two-part punch. First comes the sadness, loss, and feelings of inadequacy of not having what you want, or being who you want to be. Then you feel anger toward the people you're jealous of, as if they have *caused* your distress. Not only do you begrudge them their good fortune, but you multiply your resentment by perceiving them and their success as an obstacle to your own. Here is the bottleneck of jealousy. You waste your time going at others with anger and resentment, asking, "Why do they get to have those goodies?" when, in fact, you are the only person in the way. The longer you stay in that place, convinced that your road to success has been blocked by others getting there first, the more you prolong your own misery (and waste time with this rather than pursuing what you want). This misunderstanding becomes your own roadblock. The sooner you can express frustration without aiming it at others, the sooner you get to the heart of the matter, which is how you feel about yourself.

BETTER BELIEFS

- The other person is not trying to make you feel bad.
- No one is standing in your way.
- You decide what you want to pursue or what is meaningful to you.
- You can learn from those who have what you may want.

Jealousy triggers a spiral of negative thinking about yourself. Instead of seeing *the one* thing that is missing or that you are upset about, you start tearing down everything else around it. Getting specific is the most important step with jealousy. Because jealousy tends to spread, you need to ask: What part is really about you? What is it that you need to learn? Do you really want to pursue the object of your jealousy, or do you need to move on? Or, looking at it from a different angle, perhaps you can learn something from the person who has the higher monthly sales figures, the better-behaved children, or the happier marriage? Can you look squarely at the fact that maybe those people know something that you don't know, and can you try to learn how they do it and if there's anything you can adopt in your own life? Suddenly the dead end of jealousy shifts into a gateway to learning.

STRATEGIES FOR OVERCOMING JEALOUSY

Getting Specific: What Is Really Missing?

If you feel that your life lacks something that you see in others, rather than lament it, pinpoint it. Is it an achievement, or the way they approach life. Imitation is the highest form of flattery. While staying true to who you are, see if you would like to try adopting one part of whatever it is—their work ethic, their generosity, or the daring way they do their hair that you'd like to try. There is no harm in trying.

To Thine Own Self Be True

Stop and think. Is what you are coveting in another person's life something that you really want? Or does it just seem desirable on the surface? If it really does matter to you, recommit to working on it. If not, refocus on what it is that you seek in your own life.

The More Things Change, the More They Stay the Same

Often we are convinced that if we had that thing, or did that one thing, we'd be happy. But the hedonic treadmill principle suggests

GETTING SPECIFIC:
Rehearse Your Lines

- How important is this to me? Separate out the difference between how much you want the object of the jealousy and how much you don't want the other person to have it.
- What would really be different if this happened? Ask yourself what matters most to you about getting this item or recognition, and what would happen if you did get it?
- Is there any other way to meet this goal besides through this path?
- Are there ways you have already made progress toward this goal?
- How essential is this item or recognition to your achieving your goals?
- Will this matter in the long run, or just in the short run?
- How long do you want to be feeling this way?
- What is on the other side of this feeling, or, when you let go of this, how will you be feeling?

that we adapt quickly to both positive and negative changes in our lives and return to our baseline level of happiness. In other words, things like earning more money or getting a new car, or even an accolade for your work, may have a very short satisfaction shelf life. Given this factor, think hard about how your life will really be changed by having the object of your jealousy. What are the things that you *aren't* doing now that you think you could do if this came your way? See if there is anything on that list that really doesn't depend on your circumstances changing—and commit to doing that thing now. For example, if you wish that you had lost weight like your co-worker did, because now she is putting more effort into her appearance and getting compliments, consider this—is your weight really holding you back from valuing how you look? Couldn't you start paying more attention to your appearance now if you wanted to?

Get Closer to the Source

Jealousy puts distance between ourselves and others, compounding our sense of isolation and inadequacy. Get closer by directly interacting with those you keep at arm's length. They are really just people, like you. Rather than idealizing them, or scorning them, why not compliment them, or at the very least get to know them a little bit better? You'll likely find that they share some of the same struggles and insecurities that you have.

Value What You Have and How You Got It

Life is not a zero-sum game. One person's success doesn't negate another's. Go back to Chapter 10, and to combat the feeling of coming up short, round out the picture of yourself. You've probably diminished your value *because* it's yours. If it were someone else's, would you cheer him or her on? Share that with yourself.

FREEING YOURSELF: IN ACTION

Seth spent a lot of time angry at his older brother, Joe. They had gotten along better when they were young and could wrestle things out. Seth was physically bigger than his big brother, and he would win. But now in their thirties, old feelings continued. After every family gathering, at least those that he couldn't avoid, Seth felt critical of Joe for showcasing himself, and Seth would get angry with himself for not being able to stop him. He would get even angrier when he would try to show off himself. Seth would come home enraged, *seeing meat*. He couldn't sleep and would fly off on angry spins about his brother and about himself, feeling inadequate that he wasn't defending himself.

In session, Seth realized that he wasn't truly jealous of his brother in the sense of wanting what he had. He was glad to be himself. His feelings of inadequacy were not global, and he really didn't feel inferior in other situations in his life. He was jealous only in the family context of the attention that Joe was getting from acting in a way that Seth would never attempt himself. At first this frustrated Seth, but then he realized this was good news. Opening the door of his jealousy, Seth realized that if he wouldn't get attention his brother's way, then why was he jealous? Did he really want what his brother had? Did he need to begrudge his brother his attention, or could he go about it a different way? He didn't have to bring a diminished sense of himself into those family gatherings—that was a choice he made. Seth realized that the resentment was a carryover from childhood. In fact he could even enjoy his brother's entertaining, charismatic style, which was very different from his own style. In this way he could connect to Joe rather than exclude or absent himself. Letting go of the jealousy also allowed Seth to participate more in family events. He was no longer competing or trying hard not to compete—he was just being himself.

SADNESS: FINDING OUR WAY THROUGH THE INEVITABLE LOSSES IN LIFE

What we call the beginning is often the end. And to make an end is to make a beginning. The end is where we start from.

—T. S. ELIOT

The Anatomy of Loss: It Will Never Be the Same; It Will Be Different

If you want to be truly happy—learn how to be sad. What? Often we set out on our path with sadness having our loss of direction as the only map in our hands. We are scared. We worry that the unbearable sadness may never go away. We worry that we are doing something wrong by having this feeling. That is anxiety.

Because loss is inevitable for all of us at some time, it's important to know how to navigate through these experiences. Knowing that you can survive sadness—it isn't a wrong feeling but it is an uncomfortable one, and like any feeling, it won't stay indefinitely. It will come and go. When exactly will it go away? As we saw in Chapter 9, if you could track your grief or sadness waves on a monitor, like women in labor watching the rise and fall of contractions, you could pace yourself and see that you were getting to the crest of the wave and breathe an anticipatory sigh of relief. You can't see ahead, but you can feel secure in the knowledge that the body, programmed for a steady state, rights itself on its own. If you listen to your anxiety—*This will never go away*—then certainly that will accelerate the spike and prolong the wave.

I remember learning firsthand how sadness really works when a dear friend in her early thirties died of breast cancer. The loss of my friend Gael, a vibrant, indefatigable woman, was a horrible shock to the very many people who loved her. I dreaded driving in my car for months after she died, because on those long, quiet commutes back home from work in the city, snaking along a winding road that goes through a big urban park, the feelings of grief would overtake me. Each time, I felt afraid. I couldn't see how I could survive the pain. Why was I afraid when grief was the most expected feeling to have in the situation? Eventually, I started, without any specific intention on my part, to desensitize to the fear of the grief. With time, when the wave came I felt something different happen. It was a calm, solid feeling. I no longer feared that the feelings would knock me down. I remember saying to myself, *It's a wave, it will come and it will go.* I started to understand the physics of that wave and how to soften to it rather than resist it. I came to understand that the feelings wouldn't hurt me. With the losses that have come since, I have needed to repeat that lesson, but now, rather than feel frightened by the sadness, I know to soften, let go, and let it happen.

New Understanding: Loss
Takes Us Somewhere Different

When you feel sad, usually that is because for one reason or another there is an ending, or a loss. You lose a relative after a prolonged period of illness and care giving, and a relationship that has been the center of your life ends and you are at a loss. Not only do you grieve that person, you grieve the loss of your identity. You were on one path, and now that path has changed.

In the popular essay *Welcome to Holland*, Emily Perl Kingsley writes about her experience as a mother of a child with disabilities. She describes how awaiting the arrival of a child is like planning a trip to Italy. It is exciting, fabulous, and full of familiar landmarks and points of interest. When you have a child with disabilities, it's as if suddenly you are rerouted and your ticket is changed to Holland. There is loss about not going to Italy as planned. But you also don't know the sights or language in Holland, and it is all new and confusing, and at first, unwelcome. But with time you notice the beauty of the tulips, the windmills, and the Rembrandts. In time, we adjust, and contrary to what we could ever have imagined at first, we are at home in our lives in Holland. We have all experienced loss—the relationship that fell apart, the business that failed, the health condition that changed everything, or the wholly unfamiliar world we find ourselves in when someone close to us dies. We exhaust ourselves trying to find the familiar landmarks and wonder what will make the sadness leave.

When you try to outrun sadness, you don't just find yourself out of breath, you can enter bad situations trying to distract yourself. Maybe it's only a fleeting distraction such as buying things, overeating, or being reckless with your time. But if you get used to this life on the run, it can feed destructive patterns like addictions, because whenever you fear sadness *might* come, you run for cover into something that you think will seal you securely

REHEARSE YOUR NEW LINES

- I won't have that life that I was planning, but I will have a different life.
- Just because I don't know what's next doesn't mean that nothing is next.
- Whatever I'm feeling is okay.
- The loss is a process and it keeps changing. It won't always feel the way it does now.

from letting it in. You may also dodge friends and isolate yourself. Avoidance takes up time and energy with no good results. This is another instance where opening the door a little at a time will help you identify what is difficult, and will ultimately set you free.

The Upside of Loss Is Growth

If you look back on difficult times in your life, such as an accident, the breakup of a relationship, a serious illness, or the loss of a loved one, those dark times marked a significant shift in your life path, unexpectedly toward greater depth and meaning, and even satisfaction. Researchers have coined the term *post-traumatic growth* to describe the experience of realizing a positive shift (emotional or spiritual) after enduring a highly stressful circumstance. Although you might never invite these difficult opportunities into your life, you may find opportunities for growth and meaning inside these hard packages that are transformational, bringing you far beyond a return to baseline, normal life. This may be a gradual process of becoming more appreciative of your own strengths and internal resources, and of the connections in your life. This may culminate one day in your realizing that it is hard to think of the circumstance as a loss anymore, given all that you have gained from it. If this is *not* your experience, don't think that it needs to be. But don't be surprised if one day, suddenly, this perspective finds you.

STRATEGIES FOR MANAGING
SADNESS AND LOSS

Living the Double Life

During grieving, you may feel guilty for veering from the sadness to celebrate or enjoy life. At the same time, you may also feel inadequate or have no hope that you will ever be able to feel differently than you do now. Yet you *can* simultaneously, or alternatively, live on both tracks. You will never forget what has happened, and that's normal. Yet you can go on and honor your aliveness by engaging fully in what life has to offer. There is no contradiction. We all live the double life.

Relabel Grief as True Feelings and Accept Them

When you experience a loss, you are flooded with thoughts of regret, sadness, and doubt that things will ever change or feel good again. Allow those thoughts to come, and understand that they are genuine reflections of how you feel right now. As painful as they are, accept them and be glad that you are not hiding from them. Rather than worry that they are true, simply accept them as what you are feeling now. Then, distinguish those thoughts from how you may feel later.

Usually with sadness you know what you've lost—a relationship, an aspect of your health or mobility. Sometimes it isn't clear exactly what the loss has triggered in you, or what meaning the loss has in your life. The loss may be about regret: *I wasted time fighting,* or guilt: *It was my fault,* or fear: *I'll be lonely the rest of my life, I can't live without that person.* When you can get to the root thought, the seminal idea, then you can begin to hold it up to the light and see if that is really the right caption that represents or reflects what you feel, or what is true about your situation. Claim what's yours and what you got from the struggle. Sometimes the cognitive dissonance is too great to look closer at what happened. Once the relationship is over, or the loss has happened, you can see not just what you lost, but what you may have gained.

Optimizing: Managing Moments of Sadness

It is hard to imagine being flexible in a moment of sadness. We feel frozen, unable to move. But there are many ways we can find a direction to move through a moment of sadness. We may consult our Possibility Panel from Chapter 6 and get support, ask for guidance from the wisdom of the ages, consider how many others must be feeling this same thing right now. Also, consider that others who may have experienced this before are *no longer* feeling this now. We can take the time pressure off ourselves to move through this more quickly and know that we will recover at our own pace.

The Moving Part: Finding Meaning in the Big Picture

Whether it's finding a new understanding of what happened or a new sense of yourself, there are many different possibilities that come when processing a loss. You find these by listening to your reactions and how they change over time. Often, the new meaning finds you when a new perspective snaps into place. There may be times when a loss is more of a change in expectations than a total loss. When you learn something about a loved one, for example, about that person's past, or find yourself in a situation where a loved one won't change certain behaviors that you find objectionable. It is not necessarily that you are losing that relationship, but the moving part may be that you are accepting or changing your expectations of that person—you grieve that your spouse or parent will never understand you the way you want, but that doesn't mean that you've lost them. You let go of the relationship you always wanted to more fully connect with the relationship you actually have.

FREEING YOURSELF: IN ACTION

Sometimes Margaret felt like the past ten years had been a blur. Her husband had been diagnosed with an autoimmune disorder when their children were in elementary school. The multiple consultations, the bad news, the occasional hope, the reality of decreasing health and mobility of her husband—all of it swept up the family. There was always something else—talking to a teacher for her children, doing laundry, attending to her job—so the process of grieving the life she had hoped for never happened. They were too busy living what they had. Fortunately, with the development of new, more effective medications, her husband's condition began to stabilize, but interestingly, when her second child was heading off to college and she was anticipating a lighter load in her life, she found herself crying and feeling very anxious about what was going to happen next. It was as if, finally, the coast was clear, and Margaret could start to look back at the very lonely road she had traveled for so long. Every time she would think about it—replaying key moments in her mind—she would feel panicky. There was so much sadness and loss: missed events for her kids; anxious financial times; wondering if her husband's disability insurance would keep them in their home. It was overwhelming to look back, even though, the fact was, she had already lived through it.

We started to construct a story, writing down chapters and scenes to break down the history for Margaret to integrate one scene at a time. There was so much about which she was sad; things that she hadn't been able to do for her children or for her husband. But as she was able to look at some of that loss directly, she started to feel an incredible appreciation for the family's resilience and her own fortitude and success in all the things she *had* done for her family. She was thinking about how different their lives were from what she had hoped, and as she was able to sit with those feelings, she was able to marvel and take solace in how creative and strong they all were. Maybe this was exactly the best that any family could have come through. But in the midst of grieving for her husband's struggles and for the ways that her sons didn't have a "normal" life, Margaret realized something important that may have been holding her back and keeping her locked in her grief: that this had happened to her, too. It was only when she was able to look through the door of her own wishes and losses and see how her path had been changed by her husband's illness that she was truly able to move forward from grief. She didn't have to be afraid of the feelings jumping out at her; she saw them, understood them, and with that compassion for herself, was ready to move on and re-engage fully with her good life.

SHAME: RELEASING OURSELVES FROM AN INTERMINABLE SENTENCE

The basis of shame is not some personal mistake of ours, but the ignominy, the humiliation we feel that we must be what we are without any choice in the matter, and that this humiliation is seen by everyone.

—MILAN KUNDERA

Anatomy of Shame: It's Personal

We all know shame. For some of us it looms large and painful, with a capital S. It may be the dyslexia we try to hide, the ghost of an eating disorder that still haunts us, the alcoholism we are overcoming, our impoverished childhood of cockroaches and moving just ahead of the rent, or the trauma we suffered at the hands of others that we've never revealed to a soul. For others, with lowercase shame, it looks terribly familiar. We may have said too much in a conversation, written an angry e-mail we regretted, made an advance at an office party that was rejected. What unifies these disparate experiences is that we don't just feel bad about what we did, we feel bad about who we are. And so, in a preemptive strike, rather than waiting to be shunned, rather than hanging on to see the look of disdain on others' faces, we hide.

The problem with toxic shame is that in forcing us to stay hidden, it does even more damage than whatever triggered it in the first place—it cuts us off from life. We ground ourselves by clipping our own wings. That is understandable as a short-term

BOTTLENECK BELIEFS

- All of me is bad, damaged, and unacceptable.
- I am at fault.
- There's nothing I can do about it.
- I am on hold.
- Someone else has to release me from this, and they never will.

strategy, but when hiding becomes the default, it takes on a life of its own and causes more problems. Whether it is a serious situation or a more *felt* humiliation, you've decided that you are unacceptable and that's final. Hiding cuts you off from finding, exploring, and analyzing, the very processes that could break down shame and release you from its grip. You wait frozen. Your anxiety is fueled by fear that you will be discovered, and negative thinking digs the hole of that shame deeper and wider. It feels like you can never just do your time and be released. You feel outside the lines of acceptability. It's not just this one thing, it's every single thing about you that is tainted. How do you turn that around?

New Understanding: You Can Release Yourself from Shame

Forgiveness is giving up hope of a better past.

—UNKNOWN

With shame, you are the one who puts yourself outside the lines of acceptability, and yet you wait for someone or something else to let you back in. Optimizing is the key step. Because shame contracts your perspective, you need to dare to find other perspectives, even if you just start with your compassionate self.

What characterizes shame is that in your time of greatest vulnerability, whether a victim of another or simply a victim of circumstance, you feel profoundly implicated. You are convinced that you are at fault and the problem. Sometimes people believe that they are permanently defective as a result. You are locked

BETTER BELIEFS

- The things that have happened have affected me, but they don't define me.
- This is not who I am; this is what happened.
- I can focus on how this has hurt me, and I can also acknowledge the strength I used to overcome the hurt.
- Not all of this belongs to me. Maybe none of it does.
- I am going to find what's mine and what's not.

into a very small cell that contains a secret about yourself, yet paradoxically that is the very place that you feel entirely alienated from yourself. Your shame may feel permanent and intractable because while you are looking far and wide for something to release you from these feelings, you don't realize that you have been holding the key all along.

What's Done Is Done, and What's Next Is Up to Us

Yes, what's done is done. You can't change it, whether the shaming event is from your own construction or from an indisputable violation. But why perpetuate the badness through rings and rings of growth? The present and future are wide open.

Part of this is releasing yourself from blame and forgiving yourself for being human, and for not knowing what to do. Another part may be releasing others from blame. Although that may seem hard or even wrong to do, carrying around your anger at someone makes more work for you. So forgiveness is a gift you give yourself. You aren't condoning another's behavior, but you aren't going to be the one whose anger ends up burdening you.

LETTING YOURSELF OUT OF THE SMALL BOX OF SHAME TO REWRITE THE STORY

Relabeling: Feeling Bad Doesn't Make Shame Deserved

I feel unacceptable, but this is just what happens with shame. Shame makes us feel like we are damaged. That is a feeling, not a fact. Did you feel unworthy before this situation occurred? Separate your enduring value from the specific action or insult that occurred. What is temporary, and what is permanent?

Getting Specific: Don't Take What's Not Yours

When your experience of shame comes from an interaction with another, you need to separate what belongs to you from what belongs to someone else. If someone made you feel compromised or diminished in some way, that belongs to him or her. Your integrity of living through that moment and bringing yourself to the point of feeling your shame and releasing yourself belongs to you.

Optimizing: Writing the Next Chapters

With shame, you feel frozen, waiting to be released from bad feelings and thus may feel that there can be no future for you, or at least no good future. Allow yourself to imagine the story through the voice of forgiveness. What would you do if you forgave yourself or the other person for whatever is the source of shame? What would you be doing in your life now if that forgiveness was there? What would be some small steps to act on some of those new ideas?

Question the Authority of the Shame

Don't be afraid to ask, "What does this have to do with who I am?" Left unasked, shame shrinks you, diminishes you, and colors your entire being. When you begin to ask and look, you can begin to see the shades of gray. Some parts of me are impacted, others are not. Sometimes I see myself in this diminished way, sometimes I do not.

Who Is Judging Us?

Is it necessary to test yourself against some nameless, faceless mob of harsh critics? Wouldn't a handpicked few really be more to the point? You don't need the most heartless, remote person to understand. Maybe you just need to understand yourself.

Forgiveness: A Gift to Give to Yourself

If others have hurt you, you may hold on to your rightful anger with the thought that forgiveness would signify that what happened wasn't terrible. This is not the case. Forgiveness is a gift you give to yourself, first and foremost. You allow yourself to release the heavy burden of your anger toward another person. You needn't forgive a person directly unless you choose to. The most important place where forgiveness counts is within yourself. You may also let go of blaming yourself for things that were not your fault. Forgive yourself for not knowing, for believing that you could control everything.

Mobilizing: Acting "As If" You Are Free

You can free yourself from the idea that you are hateful or less than others. Researchers on shame find that feelings of uncontrollability can be combated by believing that you have options, that don't have to cut yourself off from others. You can be part of things, whether that means going back to Facebook or the water cooler at the office, or starting to talk to a higher power. And in these moments, little by little or very quickly, you see that you can be yourself and that nothing bad happens. So these experiences can seal you off, and they can also be a deep reservoir for compassion and understanding others and yourself; and that ultimately allows for meaningful connections.

REVELING IN YOUR SURVIVAL

And so in that very shame I suddenly begin a hymn.

—FYODOR DOSTOYEVSKY,
THE BROTHERS KARAMAZOV

As you are overcoming shame and reintroducing yourself, whether you've been out for a few hours, or a few decades, you find that you've been on hold. Now you have choices that open up a whole new world of possibilities. Many of us may not be able to revel as Dmitri, in *The Brothers Karamazov*, does, seeing light in the dark, but it is helpful to see that this is an option. Listen to giants like Dr. Dan Gottlieb, a psychologist on public radio, who at age thirty-three was in a near fatal accident when a tire flew off a truck when he was driving on the highway, rendering him paralyzed from the chest down. Countless people have benefited from the courage that Dan has cultivated within himself and shared. He teaches his listeners and readers how rich life can be when you embrace the idea that we have nothing to lose.

In his book *Learning from the Heart: Lessons on Living, Loving, and Listening,* Dan tells a story of doing a bedside interview with a woman dying of cancer who wanted to share her experience of preparing to die. Recording from a cramped hospital room, Dan tells how he began to hear water dripping and was concerned that it would be heard on the audio recording. Trying to track the source of the dripping, he realized that it was coming from his own catheter, which had become inadvertently dislodged by his producer while they were closely huddled together at the head of their interviewee's bed. Sensing the possibilities in the darkest of moments, Dan took the opportunity to connect rather than re-treat. "Jane, I hate to mention this to you now at this moment, but I think I just peed all over your floor." Jane reassured Dan and told him not to be embarrassed. Taking the opening further, Dan said, "Since I'm embarrassed and you're not, can we say that you did it and I didn't?" The three of them laughed as Jane graciously agreed. When the nurse came in, Dan said, "Jane did it!" They all laughed until they cried. The antidote to shame is connecting. Intimacy redirected a potentially mortifying moment and brought with it a deep connection. Knowing that tucked into even the grimmest realities the possibility of connection exists may help you seek it out and embrace it when found.

Overcoming Shame: Reconnecting More Fully

When you see that shame is a natural reaction to taking in some-one else's mistaken view of you, then you can set about separat-

TRY THIS

The next time you feel a big feeling coming at you, try not to run from the wave. Instead, change the picture. Imagine that the feeling appeared because you need it to tell you what's really happening in your life. Narrate the picture: "I am feeling angry, sad, ashamed, right now. It's okay. I can have this feeling and move through it. It is temporary." Welcome the opportunity, knowing that the sooner you let it in, the sooner it will deliver the message and leave you more informed and better prepared to act with clarity in your life.

ing a few things. First, keep in mind that their distorted lens creates a view that probably has nothing to do with who you are. It's probably the lens through which they also see themselves, but that's for later. Once you correct that distortion, you can set about readjusting the perception you have of yourself. Shame was a knee-jerk reaction to incoming input, but it has nothing to do with who you are. You don't have to internalize it—you can hold it out in front of you and say, "I think this belongs to *you*. It's not mine."

FREEING YOURSELF: IN ACTION

The issue for Tasha wasn't her appearance. She was a striking woman in her thirties with lovely red hair and a feminine build. The problem was the idea of her appearance that she carried in her head. She had been overweight in junior high and high school, and she paid the price with jabs from classmates. But it was the hypercritical adults in her life whose harsh words and worried looks did the most damage. Feeling brainwashed by her parents to see her curvy figure as a sign of excess, as something that would never attract boys, Tasha felt she needed to hide. She dressed in "big clothes" because she believed that was what she needed. She dated only very occasionally, and she was really afraid of getting

---

YOU AND BEYOND

So much of life happens in quick interactions with others. When we ask, "How are you?" we are taken off guard on the rare occasions where we get a real answer beyond, "Fine." Understanding more about how our emotions work, you may be in a better position to be patient with others when they are struggling with a difficult feeling or situation. But beyond patience, you could be instrumental in helping others do the things they need to in order to overcome the struggle. You could be the lone voice suggesting that they go into the feeling *more* in order to move through it, rather than the one giving the common advice: "Just get over it." This isn't about encouraging wallowing, although there is a time and place for everything. It's about encouraging others to not shy away from what they are feeling, but rather to face it and ask the hard questions about the hurt or jealousy or shame, questions like, "What is there for me in that tangle of emotion that I need to understand about myself?" Pointing to this alternate route for each other is like discovering the back roads to your destination that all the locals know but that you won't find on any map.

---

rejected or disgusting others, so she kept her distance. She knew on some level that this made no sense, given the more realistic picture of herself, but the feelings still lingered.

Was there something fundamentally wrong with Tasha's appearance or her whole self? Or was this really about her parents' anxieties about her? In a subtle way, it seemed that even when Tasha was thin, her parents' comments remained the same. To whom did the shame belong at this point? Opening the door on that shame, Tasha found compassion for a young girl who hadn't had anyone she could turn to. As an adult now, Tasha could stand up for that girl. She wanted that young version of herself, as well as her current version, to know: "This is not about you. There is nothing wrong with you."

Relabeling the situation as her parents' mishandling of their anxiety, Tasha began to work her way to a different understanding of herself. Her specific issue now was not her weight, it was the messages in her head about her weight, so she set out to make those more accurate. She created a panel, including good friends, her sister, and me to consult in her mind when the old thoughts got kicked up. She asked herself what she would be doing now if she wiped out that history and started fresh, and the answer came back that she would be dating. She began to do just that.

Chapter 14

HOW TO THINK YOUR WAY OUT OF PROCRASTINATION, PERFECTIONISM, FAILURE, AND CRITICISM

Faith is taking the first step even when you don't see the whole staircase.

—MARTIN LUTHER KING JR.

HOW YOU GROW: UNDERSTANDING THE PROCESSES THAT SUPPORT GROWTH AND EXPANSION

Want to start something new? No. Yes. Well, maybe later. Anxiety and negative thinking lurch out of the uncertainty that comes from attempting anything new, be it a new relationship, a term paper, starting a family, taking on the care of an aging parent, or even a first day at the gym. Doubts rush in. *Will it work, what could go wrong, should I do it?* Things don't feel great *yet*. Wait,

257

ride it out. Even with positive things we think, *Why don't I feel happy now? Why isn't this going great yet?*"

It's perfectly normal, but we assume that the doubts and fears signal a problem with our project rather than just a problem with our time line. These doubts are part of the process, stirred into the mix of what ultimately allows us to grow. When we embark on a new project, we need to build into the bricks an understanding and acceptance of the givens—mistakes, failures, criticism, changes, and yes, procrastination, and perfectionism. In Dr. King's words, we need to get comfortable with making a first move when we can't see the rest of the staircase. There aren't false moves, there's just information, and all of that counts toward our ultimate progress.

Perfectionism, failure, procrastination, and criticism are only demons if we don't get to know them. In this chapter, we dive into these common bottlenecks of daily life and learn how to get out.

PROCRASTINATION AND AVOIDANCE: YOU CAN RUN, BUT YOU CAN'T HIDE

It takes as much energy to wish as it does to plan.

—ELEANOR ROOSEVELT

The More You Avoid Pain, the More Painful Life Becomes

Nathan sits and plays games in his cubicle, hiding from a monster: the monthly report his boss expects. Each month, it's the same. He promises his boss he's working on it, only to stay up the night before to finally put in the measly three hours of work required to finish it.

Zola wants to start dating again after a long lapse. But the more she thinks about it, the more anxious she gets, and does nothing for months. The whole picture looks too daunting, and she has no idea where to begin. From her lack of progress, she concludes that no one will want to date her anyway, so there's no point.

Guthrie has trouble packing up and leaving his office every night. He feels guilty about being home later to see his kids, but he anticipates the stress of the dinner and bedtime transition and feels glued to his chair, even though he loves being home with his kids and always wishes he had gotten home earlier.

We wish, we wish, we wish that whatever it is that we set out to do will be perfect and wonderful, and *painless*. But when you're ready to write the great American novel, minutes after sitting down with a piping hot cup of coffee, you find the blank screen utterly unforgiving and unyielding. So you abandon one ship and jump on the procrastination cruise liner. It promises all manner of diversion—finding those lost high school friends on Facebook, scrubbing between the keys of your computer keyboard with a toothbrush, and catching up on reruns of *The Office*. Yet something is missing. Diversions are not diverting when you know you are hiding from something.

Sound familiar? You're not alone. Procrastination is rampant and on the rise. Canadian business professor Piers Steel, one of the leading researchers in the field of motivation and procrastination, sees the "putting off until tomorrow" experience as so central to human nature that he dared to call it a basic impulse. The percentage of people who admit to procrastinating quadrupled between 1978 and 2002. It is, of course, a vicious cycle. The more you avoid while the clock keeps ticking, the more your catastrophic fears of terrible consequences may come closer to resembling actual possibilities.

And yet, it's not fatal. You do want to get things done. There's a certain center of the brain devoted to a sense of completion. It lights up on PET scans when we finish things and have a sense of satisfaction. You just need to get out of your own way so you can light up that center more often.

NEW UNDERSTANDING AND DIRECTIONS

Much of what fuels procrastination is having a rigid idea of how things should move along. It traps us. And we run. Like picturing

BOTTLENECK BELIEFS

- It has to be perfect.
- I have to know how to do it right away.
- It has to go well from the start.
- I don't know where to start, so I can't.
- This is a hassle; I'll do it later.

being stuck on a harrowing ride at an amusement park where you can't get off until they lift up the bar at the end, we don't want to commit to starting something from which there is no escape. But wait. If we switch the frame back to reality, we know there are exits, and there are choices; we're not trapped, except in our minds. Perfectionism and procrastination are fraternal twins. They look different, but they go hand in hand. The more the perfectionist in you thinks that things need to go off without a hitch, the more you will want to procrastinate, staying away from the daunting tasks you have set yourself. And the longer you put things off, the more perfect you'll think things need to be. After all, you've had *that* much more time to work on it, right? Wrong. The answer is to put perfectionism and procrastination aside and understand growth. The more you see the hesitations and hitches in any growth process as expected, tolerable, and wholly survivable, the less you will need to hide under the covers from them. That's true whether you're hiding from a dissertation or a sink full of dishes. Hesitation doesn't signal a problem. It signals a person.

As much as you feel like you are the only poor sloth succumbing to distraction, procrastination is rampant. In earlier years, there simply weren't enough ways to waste time, but now Facebook, Twitter, and Google provide plenty of diversion. You know procrastination impacts your life, but you don't want pressure to finish something soon to cut short the time you spend procrastinating. This all leaves us looking pretty bad as a species.

BETTER BELIEFS

- Perfect doesn't exist, and things don't start out even close to that.
- I don't have to know where I'm going right away; it's a process.
- I just need to start working; that's how I'll figure out what to do next.
- If I don't know where to begin, I can start in the middle.
- Think small; I'll feel much better if I get a little bit done, rather than none.

FINDING THE ON-RAMP AND OFF-RAMP TO YOUR PROJECT

A feng shui consultant once came to our house and commented that it wasn't immediately clear which way to enter. The driveway led directly to the side of the house and forked vaguely to the right and left to the front or back door. It was confusing and off-putting for that reason. The consultant suggested that people would not know how to reach the front door without the path clearly marked. It sounded so obvious once she pointed it out.

Often it is the ambiguity of how to embark on a project that makes us want to run the other way and not expose ourselves to that confusion. If we can't find the on-ramp to the project, we can't start. A driveway can be fixed, a pathway marked, and once you find the on-ramp to any project, that, too, helps fix the procrastination problem. Ambiguity is the poison in procrastination.

Strategy #1: Create the On-Ramp, or Welcome Mat

Bring your supplies with you *before* you sit down, open the briefcase, set out your papers, sharpen your pencils, and then walk away for a bit. When you come back, it's as if a personal assistant has set up a surprise just for you. Your workstation is waiting, and you won't get stuck at the point of, "Ugh, I can't even open my briefcase."

Strategy #2: Start in the Middle

Some projects have to be done in a certain order, but with most, there are no rules. With creative work, whether writing, drawing, composing, or brainstorming, when you insist on coming up with that brilliant opening idea, you rarely do. Instead—go for the meat—the inspiration and the ideas that are the gist that you care about most. Once you find the substance in the middle, you can then go back to the beginning, by working backwards, and create a case for where you are going—because now you actually know.

Strategy #3: Three Minutes on the Clock

Want to get past the blank page or screen, or even organize an overwhelming life into a to-do list? Give yourself three minutes on the clock to brainstorm your ideas or needs in phrases, not full sentences. This is a way of bypassing your internal critic and getting down to business. Once you have your ideas scribbled down on the page or computer file, you can highlight or circle the ones you like and put them in order, and you've gone from stumped to start in a manner of three minutes. If you need extra help to get the wheels turning, ask yourself how you would describe the project to a good friend who is always interested in what you're up to, rather than to a boss or someone who is in a position to judge.

Strategy #4: Do Something, Anything

When a construction crew is building a house and it rains, they don't sit and wait for it to stop. An aspect of the project may be blocked, but there's always *something* that you can be doing to advance the cause. So if your creative juices aren't flowing for the ad campaign, find the moving part: Do more research about the product, copyedit the material you already have, or find the graphics you're going to use. Who knows, when you finish those other tasks, you may have the ideas you need for the part that was stalled.

Strategy #5: Don't Be Shy, Take a Look

Often, we avoid because we think something will be too hard; meanwhile, we haven't even investigated enough to discover that it is much simpler than we thought. So go ahead, open that envelope or e-mail to see what that colleague wants from you, instead of imagining what it says. Call that lead, or research leads online. Before you embark on building obstacles from your imagination, take a peek first to decide if that's really needed. You're not committing yourself to anything more than looking, but chances are that once you've taken this first step, you'll find yourself already doing more. It helps to put a fifteen-minute time limit on this primary investigation so that it won't feel overwhelming. Then you can decide what's next.

Strategy #6: Designate an Exit Strategy/Earn Your Breaks

Checking e-mail and getting a snack are perfectly good activities if you plan to do them rather than allow your anxiety or avoidance to call the shots. Designate an optimal time goal or chunk of work you want to complete before your break. That will give you an incentive and a sense of accomplishment when you reach break time.

Strategy #7: Don't Finish the Project—Leave a Few Crumbs for Tomorrow

Because being greeted by the proverbial blank page or canvas can intimidate the best of us, rather than finish a whole piece at the end of your work session, end work sessions with one piece left undone. That will provide a transitional activity or on-ramp for starting right up the next day. Leaving something undone can give you some momentum and pings the brain's neural satisfaction center at the beginning of your next work session.

What I find when I'm writing is that rather than aiming to finish something in each work session, I am less likely to procrastinate when I intentionally *almost* finish something, but not quite. I start a new work session by finishing the piece that I had left to do, because I'm already clear on how to do that. Then with that sense of satisfaction as a springboard, I'm ready to move ahead with the next step. This way I'm not confronted with that ice-cold transition each time. It's as if I start the morning warmed up. Intentionally leaving a few crumbs is not "putting off to tomorrow," but rather, it's strategically creating an on-ramp to get right back in your groove. The feeling of completion early on in your work session propels you to keep making progress.

PERFECTION VERSUS
REASONABLY GOOD ENOUGH

When you aim for perfection, you discover it's a moving target.

—GEORGE FISHER

Thumbing through my mail at the end of a busy patient day, I found a postcard from an architectural firm displaying bathroom shelving with perfectly rolled towels, bottles of soaps and perfumes lined up at attention. The caption read, "Wouldn't life be better if everything had it's place?" No! Did they consult a psychologist? The pressure to keep those towels from being just stuffed in those shelves would be so stressful! But the seductiveness of "perfect" is something we all understand. Like anything seductive, you must stand firm in deciding—is this *really* good for me?

I think of my friend Anita, a forty-something mother of three who confides in me that she is afraid she is ruining her children's lives because seeing a piece of paper or a dish out of place sends her into a anxious and angry fury. She hates to put this anxiety ahead of her children's well-being, but having her life be "a mess" feels unbearable. And that's the first clue to the bottleneck belief of perfectionism—that anything short of it is completely inferior.

Tessa, a young attorney, has perfectionism about her job that is leading to a need for antacids and sleeping pills. Every aspect of her work, every single e-mail or phone call, is as stringently handled as her court argument preparation. The level of attention is simply unsustainable and beyond even what the partners in her office encourage as they see the dark circles under the eyes of a promising lawyer in their practice. Many perfectionists don't want to be perfectionists, but they fear letting it go because *not* being a perfectionist means you're mediocre, sloppy, or a failure.

On the surface, perfect sounds like the prize. But scratch a smidge below that elusive shine and what you quickly see is the trap and the impossibility of perfection. Clutching to a goal of perfection (in itself a static unimprovable, unsustainable state) is a sure way to keep yourself in a constant state of irritability and frustration, which, in most cases, doesn't stop with you. So the no-cost bonus of perfectionism is that you share its misery with the people around you. Look at what Hara Estroff Marano, editor of *Psychology Today*, says: "You could say that perfectionism is a crime against humanity. Adaptability is the characteristic that enables the species to survive—and if there's one thing perfectionism does, it rigidifies behavior. It constricts people just when the fast-moving world requires more flexibility and comfort with ambiguity than ever. It turns people into success slaves." Notice she did not say success stories.

The Perfection Paradox

People who suffer from perfectionism truly suffer. But consider that perfectionism, ironically, may interfere with their doing their best, not simply because working too hard may result in missing deadlines, but the quality of the work itself may be compromised. Psychologists have found with athletes that the more that they focus on perfection in their performance, the less they approach it.

The Anatomy of Perfectionism

Like the all-or-none binary system, when perfectionists think that something is not perfect, they hear that it is mediocre or worse. It is not the pursuit of excellence that tortures perfectionists, it is the fact that they cannot tolerate mistakes. Rather than see mistakes as an opportunity to *improve* and integrate, they translate mistakes into complete failure and loss of stature, and they doubt that anything has been accomplished. Randy Frost, a psychologist at Smith College, writes that the belief connected with these less-than-perfect experiences is one of feeling incompetent and unworthy. With the stakes so high, the perfectionist will often avoid trying altogether. Perfectionists never feel a project is finished because the moment they let go of it, the judging begins. Sometimes this is reinforced by parental expectations early on with overt, or even covert, criticism of mistakes and parents' reinforcing product, not process. Why is it that often perfectionists appear to be unproductive, miss deadlines, drop classes, and fail big? If they can't see their way to perfect, they can't bear the alternative, so they opt out. Carrying the feeling that they are only as good as their *next* accomplishment, perfectionists and their misery make for bad friends, especially to themselves.

A second aspect of perfectionism is seeing everything as of equal and of paramount importance. As I explain to my young patients, when a celebrated chef makes a peanut butter and jelly sandwich, is it a masterpiece, or is it basically just a PB&J? Not

---

BOTTLENECK BELIEFS

- Perfection exists and if I work harder or longer, perfection is absolutely attainable.
- Anything less than perfect is not only unacceptable, it means a person is lazy or incompetent.
- People who succeed never have failures.
- Everything is of equal importance. Everything I do must be perfect.

everything that we do, and actually very little that we do, is going to hang in a museum. Switching to a pursuit of excellence instead is the first step. The second step is being able to prioritize projects, or parts of projects.

SHORTCUTS TO A NEW UNDERSTANDING: LIVING WITH IMPERFECTION

Strategy #1: Increase Your Tolerance for Process and Growth

One exit from the perfectionism and procrastination tendency is to appreciate development and make friends with the idea of "process." In nature, whether babies or great oaks, things start small. They are headed for more complexity, but each imperfect step along the way to that complexity is a stage. As imperfect, or simply unfinished, as they are, you would never judge these steps as failures. Projects of a simpler scale are no different. In their piles of ingredients or supplies, a cake and a house don't look like much at first, beyond a lot of potential. In Japanese, the term *wabi-sabi* describes the beauty of something that is imperfect or transient. In Japanese culture, imperfections are viewed in the same aesthetic light as the Western ideal of beauty in perfection. In Japan, imperfection reveals the personal touch, and the natural process, and it offers a way to connect. In the traditional Japanese tea ceremony, tea is often served in a cracked cup with the crack facing the guest because the flaws and the imperfections mark its

---

BETTER BELIEFS

- When I'm thinking about being perfect, I'm not focusing on what I'm doing.
- If I am judging myself while I am going along, it's going to slow me down.
- I need to strive for excellence, not perfection.
- I can enjoy myself more and do better work when I allow for some give in my expectations for myself.

---

beauty and moment of creation and distinguish it from all other cups. You don't have to focus on the flaw, but nor should you see the cup as unusable or not beautiful. Rather than judging the slightly misshapen handmade cookies, the slightly frayed beautiful pillow as needing to be fixed, try to take a second look and see these imperfections as distinct signs of life.

Strategy #2: Create Scale and Prioritize

The problem with perfectionism is that every little detail, from the dust on the baseboards to the way you sign your checks, from the crease on your pants to the presentation you give at work, weighs equally heavily on your mind. Decide what is most deserving of your best attention today. Rethink the idea that it's the little things in life that matter, if by that you mean whether your dishes are done and counters clear each day. Instead of feeling a loss or disdain looking at those unfinished (and insignificant) details, feel good knowing that you were able to let those things go to make way for more important things, like going to your son's soccer game, visiting your mother, or even taking a much-needed, sanity-preserving bike ride.

Strategy #3: Relabel; the Critic Doesn't Know Best

It will take a while before the critic takes a backseat in your mind, but you can turn down the microphone. When you think, *It's not perfect, it could be better, it's not good enough,* imagine that those messages are like a broken record coming from a machine, automatically replayed regardless of the situation. Imagine that you put that record on pause or turn it off. Relabel and rethink, and rather than listening to the critic scrutinize the work, simply describe it without judgment.

Strategy #4: Invite the Possibility Panel

When perfectionism is your default setting, you will benefit from consulting other resources regularly. Have a list of trusted people, real or imagined, from whom you will ask advice. Perhaps one of the members of the panel can be your compassionate self, the one who knows that striving for perfection is an unkind act to yourself because it fails to recognize your accomplishments. Another panel member could be you one month from now; when looking back on this day, you are clear that it isn't significant in and of itself and has been long forgotten.

Strategy #5: Is This a Difference That Makes a Difference?

Rather than keeping your nose to the grindstone, working and polishing right up until your deadline, look up from what you are doing and consider whether this is a good use of your time. Will the efforts that you put in yield an appreciable difference in the quality or outcome to anyone besides yourself? If the answer is no, that no one but you will notice, then do the daring thing and say—"It's done." Compare the true consequences to the catastrophic ones that you imagine.

Strategy #6: Dare to Walk Away

Challenge yourself to walk away and leave something that feels "unfinished" but expect discomfort. With time, you will desensitize to the inevitable uncomfortable feeling that will hit. Your brain will learn to deliver the "all clear" message, but until it does, know that when something doesn't feel good when you leave it, you are doing a great job of breaking the perfectionism habit.

Strategy #7: Highlight the Good Parts and the Progress

Look at your project, life, children, or whatever the object of scrutiny and find the things that are good or even great about them. Use the "Some Shaker" from Chapter 2 to see past the flaws or frustrations to see how *some* parts (and maybe even many parts) are working or progressing. Say them out loud or write them down. You need to double click or put extra effort into noticing the good, because otherwise it won't stick.

Strategy #8: Rethink What It Means to "Waste Time"

Perfectionism flows seamlessly into workaholism. Every square inch of space could be well used to be fixing, doing, improving.

Remember, sustainable living means appreciating the need for balance. Dose yourself with increasingly longer periods of time where you are unscheduled, unproductive, and perhaps even relaxed. Start small and build up to truly appreciate *il dolce far niente*, as they say in Italy—the sweetness of doing nothing.

Given how unpredictable life is, a worldview that requires everything to go exactly right is a recipe for disaster. You can free yourself from perfectionism *without* lowering your standards, but rather by lowering the stakes of and changing the meaning of making mistakes.

EMBRACE MISTAKES AND FAILURE FOR NOW TO FIND SUCCESS LATER

Success is the ability to go from one failure to another with no loss of enthusiasm.

—WINSTON CHURCHILL

Quick, name the rock group that back in the 1960s was turned down by a recording company because guitar music was thought to be "on the way out." Yep, those poor British boys otherwise known as The Beatles.

The book that was rejected a total of 140 times with the explanation that anthologies don't sell? Bestseller *Chicken Soup for the Soul*.

Who developed an electric rice cooker—his first product—that sold only 100 units because it burned the rice? Akio Morita, owner of the $66-billion-a-year business known as Sony electronics.

Which scientist didn't speak until age four and was told that he would never amount to much? Albert Einstein.

Who was cut from his high school basketball team because he lacked skill? Michael Jordan, the greatest basketball player of all time.

The world is full of these "famous failures," and yet despite these stories, we continue to cling to an idea of success that would have all of these giants out of the running at their first fumble.

What is our understanding of success? Most of us ignore the ups and downs and instead see simply the meteoric rise. Kids do it: "He's a star because he's lucky." Adults do, too: "He's gotten all the breaks, he knew someone, he's just a natural talent, he's had a charmed life." With all due respect to the people out there whom we consider to have a charmed life, read their memoirs and learn all the ways they didn't have it easy.

Success is built on hard work, opportunities, and being able to learn from and persevere through failures. But we take our own failures harder than we might, because doing the side-by-side comparison, we think, unrealistically, that failures and disappointments shouldn't happen. When they do happen to you, you think something must be wrong with you or with what you are doing. Instead of seeing those moments as signaling the end of the road, we need to see them as a detour or simply a jog in the road that may ultimately lead us to a better place than we would have gotten to without it.

ANATOMY OF FAILURE: LOSING TAKES ALL

Winston Churchill's epigraph, given above, tells us that success means being able "to go from one failure to another with no loss of enthusiasm." Successful people know that the way to *not* lose enthusiasm is to expect that failure is part of the process. Normally, we view our goal for success very narrowly, like balancing on the head of a pin. If you miss the spot, you miss everything, and the narrower the bull's-eye, the greater the chance that you'll

---

BOTTLENECK BELIEFS

- Failure means you should have known.
- Failure means you shouldn't have tried.
- Failure means *you're* a failure.
- Successful people never fail.
- Nothing can be salvaged from a failure.

BETTER BELIEFS

- Mistakes are made by the most capable, successful people every single day.
- We learn most from places where things don't go as planned.
- If I'm so afraid of making mistakes or failing, it will hold me back from pursuing something new.
- Mistakes are part of life; I'm not going to read more meaning into this than it deserves.
- I may not know how to handle this yet, but that doesn't mean it's a bad thing.

---

miss it. What happens next is that people who think this way feel they've put all their chips on the table, and if it doesn't work out, they've lost it all. The failure envelops and negates who they are and any successes or integrity they previously had. What's the way out? Just as we learned: It's not the thought, it's what you do next. We need to adopt the mind-set: It's not the failure, it's what you do next.

DON'T CRUMPLE UP THE TEST

When you fall down, don't get up empty-handed.

—ANONYMOUS

Last year, my eight-year-old daughter was preparing for her first cello recital. Like most people, she worried, "What if I make a mistake?" I suggested that mistakes aren't a big deal and that she just needs to keep going when she makes a mistake. Her reply captures the problem for all of us: "But Mom, how can I learn to keep going if every time I make a mistake, my teacher tells me to stop?" We don't take kindly to mistakes, at any age.

Ben Zanders, music director and conductor of the Boston Philharmonic, boldly insists that his students make a special occasion out of mistakes. As a teacher, coach, and conductor, Zanders is not trying to spotlight mistakes with, "There it is—see, you messed up!" Instead, as he relates in his book *The Art of Possibility*: "I actively train my students that when they make a mistake, they are to lift their arms in the air, smile, and say, 'How fascinating!'" He recommends that everyone try this.

Something happens in a mistake. Something can be learned. Maybe even something fascinating. Leaders of successful corporations know that if they are going to be on the cutting edge of innovation, there must be room for trying new things, and that means creating a culture of reasonable risk-taking without penalty. Bottom line: Mistakes and failures must be de-stigmatized with an image makeover that is more in line with reality.

NEW UNDERSTANDING: MISTAKES ALLOW FOR GROWTH AND IMPROVEMENT

Often with my young perfectionist patients, when they don't perform perfectly on a test or paper, I'll ask to look at the paper with them to find out what happened. At that point, they give me a confused look. "Oh, I threw that away." When life is all or none, there is no gray area. Perfectionists want to remove the evidence as soon as possible. Evidence of what? That they are human? That they are on their way to great things and this is one step on that route? Do you ever lose faith in people when they admit what they did wrong or that something didn't work? Often, those are the very moments that bring us closer.

Failure saves you from wasting time. If you fail, make use of it sooner rather than later. Like a rattle in your car, consider it a sign that you need to reassess before it shuts you down.

FAILING ACCURATELY

What is failure? At first glance it seems like a very bad thing, and it feels like getting the wind knocked out of us with a precise blow directly to our core. Whether it was not getting the job, tenure, the audition, the mortgage, or the book deal; having your marriage or business fail; or your grandchild not getting into the college of his dreams, failure looms large. As we've seen in our discussion of disappointment in Chapter 11, failure *feels* like it changes everything. The momentum of dreams crashing seems unstoppable. That is an amygdala hijack of another sort. Once we can slow down and come back to our senses, we can do the sorting out to see how all is not lost, but yes, some things are lost. Looking further, however, we discover that some things are found, too.

A second challenge to failing accurately is our sense that the world is a stage and we've just fallen unceremoniously on our seats. Failure is public, at least in our minds. We may or may not be compassionate about others' struggles, but when it comes to our own, we assume that we are on the world's stage and the spotlight is following us. In real life, the stage is an illusion. People are not really watching because, surprisingly, they are busy living their own lives.

If there is a spotlight, it's temporary and generated by the power in our own minds. Although it may highlight the thing that *didn't* work, the work of finding the benefits within the failure is crucial. We need time to absorb disappointment and shock. Then we can begin to sort through what feels like wreckage and find the key to proceeding with greater intelligence. Life is an ongoing process with transformation at its core.

REHEARSE YOUR NEW LINES

Strategy #1: Be Proactive: Go into a Venture with Safer Expectations

Restate your needs in the language of preferences. Distinguish between the real and imagined consequences of things not working out.

Strategy #2: Find Your Place on the Learning Curve

Chart the course of this experience. What allowed you to even try what you attempted here? Look at all of the lessons that brought you to that moment. You probably wouldn't have been able to do that a year ago. Now, look at the next points on the curve. Where do you want to go next, and how will this experience help you to navigate toward that goal?

Strategy #3: All Is Not Lost, Find the Partial Successes

Usually our endeavors are built of complex intertwining parts; they're not like a one-shot losing lottery ticket. Look for the parts that worked. For example, look for the parts of the presentation that went well. You mastered the new technology you were using, but that distracted you from the content. So next time, the technology will be familiar and you can redouble your efforts on your message.

Strategy #4: Mine the Mistake for All It Is Worth

Don't crumple up the test that you failed. Once you've recovered, look bravely right at what happened and learn as much as you can about yourself and the situation, so you can benefit from your new wisdom.

Strategy #5: Contain the Spill: Separate Yourself from the Failure

Although it feels like the mistake spills over into every aspect of who you are, do your pie charts. How much of you *feels* like this now defines every part of you doesn't necessarily believe that it is every part of you. Get back in touch with the hero who is going to help you move on.

Strategy #6: Fail Early, if Not Often

We innovate and grow by trying. Rather than hanging on to something that's just not working and sinking slowly with the ship, be willing to jump to dry land and say, "That didn't work." The earlier you do this, the sooner you can take what you've learned and try again to see how it could work *better.*

Strategy #7: Consult the Possibility Panel

As you relabel this from a failure to a noble attempt, invite others for real advice. Invite people who have been through this before, people who believe in you, including the wisecracker who can get you unstuck by reminding you kindly of how much worse this could have been.

DEALING WITH NEGATIVE FEEDBACK AND CRITICISM

In criticizing, the teacher is hoping to teach.
That's all.

—BANKEI

The Gift of Criticism: Someone Does the Job for Us

When I was writing my dissertation, the final hurdle in my graduate school career, my advisor returned a draft of my 150-page paper. This paper had consumed my mind, my house, and my marriage for the better part of a year. My adviser had written extensive comments *in red* on every page about things that needed to be changed or fixed. The paper lit up like lights on a Christmas tree, except edits aren't lights, and well, this wasn't a happy occasion. Approximately three comments per page, times 150 pages, created roughly one graduate student–size meltdown.

My first reaction after all the hard work I had put into that paper was, "Forget it! I'll become a shoe salesperson instead." But then I realized how much work my adviser had done for me. He had pointed out exactly where things needed to be fixed to improve the paper, which ultimately I would submit for publication under even more scrutiny. And P.S., he really liked the paper. So, all I had to do was put my ego aside and sit down at the computer and make all those darn changes. This paradigm shift from "disaster" to "to-do list" has come in handy on many occasions when, supervisors, editors, and even friends have "done the job for me" of pointing out the parts of the boat that need shoring up so that it won't sink. Criticism at its best is not about poking holes in our work. It's pointing out where the holes are so that we can seal them and stay afloat.

Of course, it doesn't feel like help. When you receive criticism, even if it is constructive, it still hurts, *at first.* But what happens next will determine whether you can benefit from the temporary blow. If your expectation is perfection—that whatever you do, say, or create *should* be flawless—and your worth is contingent on that condition, then the criticism will be a deal breaker for your self-esteem. If, on the other hand, you can appreciate the criticism with the knowledge that the feedback enhances or benefits you, then it will provide an incredible source of information for how to improve. In the section that follows, you will identify the beliefs and expectations that get in your way of welcoming other points of view, and you will learn how to construct a new sense of self.

SHORTCUT TO A NEW UNDERSTANDING: WELCOME THE EXPECTED

Expecting the expected means that when we do our job of marching our work in front of a teacher, boss, or others, they will respond in kind, doing their job of helping us improve. Although your first thought may be *Ouch!* the second thought, even if it comes hours, days, or even years later, can be *Thank you.* Imagine. Whether you agree with every word, or just a few, these teachers, bosses, colleagues, and friends are necessary for helping us improve and grow. We couldn't do it without them.

There are some caveats. First, just because someone gives you feedback doesn't mean you need to agree with it. But it will behoove you to listen and then decide what to do with it. The people on your Possibility Panel may not always tell you what you want to hear, but they may be telling you what you need to know.

A second caveat is that we are not on this planet to just be stoic heroes improving ourselves constantly and bearing the pain. If you have a boss who doesn't mince words and is *always* doing her criticism job but is not so good on the appreciation front, find other people to appreciate you. Maybe that is even you yourself. Remember what we said at the beginning of the chapter—this is about growth. It can be good for a plant to be pruned hard in the fall, but it also needs good nutrients to help it grow. We need both.

REHEARSE YOUR NEW LINES
They Can't Take That Away from You
Even the mightiest leader may feel affronted and cut down to a very small size in the face of criticism. That's a temporary first reaction. Realize that even if the criticism is warranted (and if so—great, see what you can learn from it), it is about what you've done, not who you are. No one can take away who you are without your permission. You simply won't allow it.

What's the Gift of This Information?
Although it might temporarily be better for our egos to not have to deal with criticism, you wouldn't want to discover some feedback late in the game that could have drastically improved the trajectory of the last five years. So, after licking your wounds, come around to see if there is something useful for you in the feedback you received.

Sometimes the Messenger Should Be Shot (Down)
Well, not exactly. Just because someone gives feedback doesn't mean that it is worthwhile even after the wounds have healed. It's just one person's opinion, and that person may be having a really bad day, and may have chosen you as the recipient of their venom. You may disagree with their point of view, which is fine, as long as you truly consider it and don't immediately dismiss it simply because it differs from yours.

Let's say you're watching a friend play tennis and his serve is off. You see that if he followed through more on his stroke, his game would improve. What do you do? Do you avoid telling him because you don't want things to be awkward? Or do you risk it, understanding that we are mirrors for each other and we can let each other know gently what we see? We are not talking about snarky criticisms like the compliment with a knife in it—"Oh, where'd you get that dress? It looks, um, cute." (Translation: "How could you leave your house looking like *that*?") Those comments are not about you, they are about someone else's issues, so send them along their merry way. When you destigmatize criticism and let go of perfection, then transformation, progress, and improvement can take place.

To recap all of this:

Relabel: This feels bad, all bad. It's just the sting. How bad I feel is not a reflection of how bad things are. This will pass.

Get Specific: What upsets me most about this feedback? Do I think I should have known it myself? What do I think it says about me? How realistic is that? Is it everything or just one thing—is it fixable? Is it about all of me or just one small part of what I have done?

Optimize: Ten years from now, will I be grateful for this feedback? I was worthy of getting the feedback. I don't have to pick this up with my ego. I can pick it up in the spirit of learning valuable information from others.

Mobilize: How do I want to make the best use of this information? What part of this am I ready to put into action? Do I need to take a walk to shake off the shock, or am I ready to go?

FREEING YOURSELF: IN ACTION

Jenny generally enjoyed her work as an architect. Now at her second job since graduating from college, she was feeling more confident about her designs and concepts. Every weekend she would work overtime, creating designs that were "perfect" in her mind. But every Monday at the staff meeting, Jenny would suffer a blow as she was summarily chopped down (at least it felt like this to her) by the lead designer. *But they were perfect!* she thought. Week after week, month after month, she would build herself up at home, thinking this was the week her work

---

TRY THIS:
Enjoy the Ride and the
Temporary Gift of Being Stumped

Know what ride you are on. We want things to be perfect, we want everyone to love what we do and we don't want to fail. Yes. But when that doesn't happen, know that you're not taking a nosedive, you're simply on the learning curve. What it feels like now won't be how it always feels. What you know now won't be what you know tomorrow or a week or a month from now. Trust the process. Remember that things will change, and they'll change more quickly and better if you don't get in their way with your fears. We need to destigmatize learning; it's nothing to be ashamed of.

It wasn't until college that I realized that saying, "I don't understand this," was perfectly respectable. We have a success-minded culture, but you create the subcultures in which you live. So, in families, workplaces, among friends, at schools, we can decide that not knowing is safe, and learning and trying are good. Start today. Find the good in the package that doesn't look like a shiny gift box with a bow. Encourage growth!

You may ask yourself, "Why am I going so slowly? What's wrong with me? What's wrong with this project? Why am I not enjoying it?" The gift of being stumped for a while gives us a front-row seat for the great rush of the *Aha!* moment when things click.

would be perfect in her boss's eyes. Yet each week she left the staff meeting crestfallen. What's wrong with this picture? Is it Jenny's work, or her expectations?

"Was his feedback helpful?" I asked Jenny. She really hadn't thought about it that way. The simple fact that she was getting critiqued felt like a failure. We considered relabeling the criticism as not a rejection or lack of confidence in her work, but as collaboration or a mentoring process that would not only help the project improve for the client but would also quite directly help Jenny's work improve. Looking at it from another angle, I asked Jenny to consider how she would handle the situation if she were in the position of authority. Would she hold back, or would she see it as her role to chime in to possibly make things better? Realizing that she would do the same, although less clumsily than her boss, helped Jenny to see this as an opportunity to build her skills and her toughness to feedback. Her new approach was to guess what her boss would object to when she marched into the Monday-morning meeting. It made it lighter for her and less personal, and

---

YOU AND BEYOND

Note how you offer criticism. Some people take umbrage at the need to muss themselves up by criticizing another, as if people should already know the assessment. The secret to good criticism is to characterize it not as a *mistake* but just something someone hasn't yet learned. Let's help each other out compassionately and share knowledge rather than judge the lack of knowledge as a weakness. What's the best way to share feedback? Think of how you would say it to someone from another culture who you wouldn't assume *should* or would know how things are done around here. The reinforcement sandwich helps: Start with something positive; next, insert the "meat" of what you want to convey; and finally, top it off with another positive statement.

she could think of it a bit more as "the" work rather than "her" work.

Rebecca had been very risk-averse throughout her life. But having been shot down by a number of insensitive and overly critical teachers in high school, she had found it difficult to get work done in college because she always anticipated the crushing rejection. A turning point for Rebecca was sitting in her first group critique in a painting class. Painting was a new interest and felt like a reprieve from her traditional academic classes. As the professor went around and talked about each student's work, Rebecca had a revelation—this was what was *supposed* to happen. That was the point. She had her role; the teacher had his.

FREEING YOURSELF FOR (EVERYONE'S) GOOD

Nothing in life is to be feared. It is only to be understood.

—MARIE CURIE

STAYING ON YOUR PATH

What does it really mean to free yourself from anxiety, that live-in agitator that brings us sleepless nights, cold sweats, and a knotted stomach, all in the name of self-protection? What we've seen in these pages is that worry and fear are natural first reactions to moments of uncertainty and that freeing ourselves means expecting and accepting them. And it goes beyond that. Freeing yourself is not about trying to stop on a dime the thoughts that are coming at you at eighty miles an hour. It's about changing your relationship with those thoughts—and understanding that you are not beholden to them. They are but one idea coming down the pike, and you can get out of the way. We have choices besides jumping in and being rerouted by them. We can let them go by.

When you realize that you are in charge of how you think and feel, there's no limit to where you can go with that. You start to see that life isn't the obstacle, it's the opportunity. And you get to narrate experiences in ways that are true and best for you. By being more discriminating in what you listen to and take to heart, you can learn to invest more time and focus on the thoughts that come from the best of what you can imagine, instead of the worst of what you fear.

You can choose to keep following the path deeper into worry and distress, or to relabel your first reactions as the first take on a story. Then you can turn around as soon as possible to pursue a different path. As Madam Curie suggests, we have a choice between fear and understanding. Truly understanding yourself is how you create a life in which you are not limited by fear. It's how you can imagine thriving.

Those moments where you are caught feeling unprepared about what's happening and what you should do are really bridges to growth. And therein lies the most compelling reason to free yourself from anxiety. It's not just about saving yourself from the round-trip catastrophizing tour. It's that by sidestepping those excursions into unnecessary anguish, you are lifted up to higher ground. From that vantage point, you see all the possibilities of where your thinking could take you. Maybe even taking you somewhere extraordinary.

WAIT FOR IT

Listen to what Mati, a college student who has been a worrier since he was a child, recently described. "I still worry about how things are going to go, but something different happens with those worries now. I think to myself, *That's interesting,* about the catastrophic thought and then I think, *Other things are interesting, too.* I don't feel required to stay with my worry anymore. I know that accepting the worry doesn't mean agreeing with it. I can just let it be. Before, I always thought I had to take my worries seriously and figure out a way that whatever I was worrying about could be okay. I realize that if I don't have a good answer to something now, that's okay. Eventually I might. Just knowing that I have that choice changes how I feel every time. I don't feel as trapped because of the bad luck of being born a worrier—I can break my-self out."

Previously, Mati's anxiety just kept spinning. If he had doubts about things, he would need to think and think until he completely wore himself out with worry and then got disgusted with himself for all the time he had spent resolving nothing.

A big step for Mati was grasping the concept of "not yet." Thinking he had to fill in all the blanks and figure everything out about the future roped him into worry. He learned to say, in his words: "I'm not sure what's going to happen, *yet,* or, I haven't figured it out *yet,* but I will sometime." Instead of worrying until the issue gets resolved, he no longer feels the need to stick with ideas that aren't worth his time. Not only is Mati not worrying as much, his mind is free to pay attention to and enjoy the full richness of what's actually happening in his life. "Even if things aren't perfect or great—they are so good. For the first time in a long time, I see what it's like to live just like anyone else—without all the extra work."

From Mati's story, we might add a few words to Madam Curie's good thought. We could say that nothing in life is to be feared, *for long.* The problem isn't the fear, because we quite naturally feel it *at first.* The problem is when we decide that first impressions are final bids, and instead of using curiosity to open the door to our fears and understand the situation, we clutch at the unpleasant-ness of our uncertainty. When we avoid learning what we truly fear, we stay afraid indefinitely and rob ourselves of the opportunity to see, even in the most difficult of situations, that we can survive. There is so much that we can do to come to our own aid. We can take exactly what is worth learning from the fear and be only as afraid as we need to, and not one ounce more.

TUNING YOUR EARS
TO THE SOUNDS OF WORRY

As you learn to name your demons, you realize that you are not beholden to them. You may even befriend them, and you find that you have a different reaction to them. It is harder for worry or discouragement to take root because in the instant that the words "I'll never," "it's always," or "what if" leave your lips, they strike a different chord. These "words" are no longer the starting gun telling your imagination to go off to the races. You greet them with a familiar, "Oh, it's you again." You may take them as a signal to pause and ask the question, "Do I *really* feel this way, and, do I need to? Or is my mind just looking for trouble?" Rather than setting off a worry session or a magnifying-glass critique of your self-worth, after which you are left feeling that you need to clutch at something for safety, you emerge victorious, deciding where you want to go next. You become more patient and less critical of yourself, and because of that, more adventurous and open to exploring.

There are other beneficial side effects that you may have noticed as you've worked through the ideas in this book. The ripple effect means that this new way of thinking is not just better for you.

THE CONTAGION OF HEALTH

You may notice that as you spend less time with your own worry, you are free to spend more time with others. As your perspective broadens out from the narrow search for problems and dangers, life opens up to you. It's been there all along, but you might not have noticed the good things. Worry is an isolating, lonely endeavor. There's barely room for you to breathe in the tunnel of worry, so it's hard to imagine inviting others down there with you. But learning about anxiety offers us an opportunity to help each other out. As we are less critical and more compassionate with ourselves, we can have more empathy for each other. We can hold the mirror of reality out to help us get a truer view of our situation. As we tune our ears to the sounds of worry and pessimism in ourselves, we can help others recognize them, too.

Freeing ourselves from anxiety liberates our precious resources, allowing us to pay attention to each other. As you step off the worry wheel and into life, you enrich your life and the lives of others. Taking care of yourself in this way spills over to the common good. You are available to help, to create, to expand, and to preserve. This is how managing anxiety becomes a collective endeavor, a group effort. We do it for ourselves and for each other. It's an upward spiral.

Not only are we the stewards of our own mental health and well-being, we are stewards for each other. When you need perspective someday, there's a great chance that someone around you will help you find it. This is the great community cleanup effort. With everyone on board, we create less work for ourselves and each other. This is how we thrive. Together.

Together, we are all looking for the good things—happiness, joy, meaning, connection, and the many moments of the day that make up the path to those destinations. The amygdala has one version of those moments. Thankfully, you have learned to make your version look very different. Expect anxiety, and don't be afraid when it weighs in first on the moments that make up our lives, but don't stop there. Remember, you are the protagonist in your life story, and you get to decide who narrates.

ACKNOWLEDGMENTS

On a hot and humid Philadelphia afternoon in early September 2008, friends, family, and colleagues gathered at our neighborhood bookstore, for the launch of my third book, *Freeing Your Child from Negative Thinking.* As I listened to the questions and feedback from the audience, relishing the amazing support from a great community, I noticed something interesting. No one was asking questions about their children as they normally would at such an event, even though this was a book for parents. Instead, they were reacting to the material for themselves. They were asking questions about their own worry and their own lives. Although my not-so-secret mission over the last decade or so in writing books for parents of kids with OCD, anxiety, and negative thinking has been for parents to free themselves of their own fears and doubts so they will be better able to help free their kids, it hadn't occurred to me until that day that adults needed a book of their own. Later, when a friend came up to me and said: "I didn't realize that this is what you did. These ideas were really helpful—to *me*." That was the tipping point and the true beginning of this book.

For urging and inspiring me to spend lots of time thinking about these ideas, first and foremost, I thank my patients. It takes great courage to decide to improve your life, and I have had the great privilege to work with thousands of very courageous people. From the youngest ones who look for simplicity—not because they aren't capable of complexity, but because they know simplicity is better—to the adults who decide that enough is enough and they want relief from worry in their lives, each of my patients has helped me understand these challenges a little better. Special thanks to those patients and others who have shared their stories and ideas here to further our understanding and provide relief to their fellow sufferers.

Working on this book has been a new experience. Although I did what I always do in preparing to write a book, reading voraciously what colleagues have written on these subjects, scouring research, and culling my experiences as a therapist with adults with anxiety and depression, I also did something different this time. I talked to people about what I was writing, and often. Sensing that this book could be for all of us—from the clinically anxious patients whom I treat to the worried well travelers whom most of us are at one point or another—I have shared my questions with people in many different contexts. So, a big thank you to those of you I talked to: at dinner parties, bed and breakfasts, on walks and park benches, in e-mails, parking lots, coffee shops, at Bar Mitzvahs, during a couple of memorably intense and inspiring conversations at holiday parties in 2010, and these days, of course, thanks to the great community of friends on Facebook: my think-tank and potluck dinner rolled into one. Anxiety and what to do about it is very much on our minds. As much as the challenges of anxiety are ubiquitous in our lives, I found that the eagerness to solve these problems together, for each other as much as for each of us alone, is ubiquitous as well. I am truly moved by and grateful for this generosity and genuine common interest.

I am fortunate to work in a great community of fellow mental-health professionals. Thank you to the psychologists, pediatricians, psychiatrists, school personnel, and especially my colleagues at The Children's and Adult Center for OCD and Anxiety, who make the work so rewarding. I am grateful for the work of the many colleagues who have committed themselves to improving the quality of life for others. My shelves are overflowing with their inspiring books. Some I've never met, and others have been directly instrumental in encouraging me or generously giving permission to share their work here. I am grateful for all, and I want to give special mention to: Aaron Beck, Judy Beck, Phil Kendall, Rick Hanson, and Daniel Pink. And special thanks to the inimitable Therese Borchard for getting me working on the article that turned into this book. And to my dear friend Dan Gottlieb, for everything, always.

It has been a great pleasure to work with my editor, Katie McHugh at Da Capo Press. I am grateful for the collaboration from our first conversation in shaping the vision for this book to all the conversations in between that have brought it to fruition. I'm delighted to have the opportunity to work with the wonderful Da Capo team once again. Thank you to my agents, Gareth Esersky and Carol Mann, for making the connections.

It does take a village to make things happen in life, and I am very grateful to the wonderful friends in our village, from the essential coordination around carpooling and child care to the deep support and meaningful conversation around life passages as we grow. It makes all the difference. Special appreciation to Joanne Buzaglo, Sonia Voynow, and Sandy Kosmin, and the rest of the crew, Georges, David, and Jonathan Buzaglo, and Bret, Julia, and Noah Boyer for being our other extended family.

There are many ways that I feel I've hit the lottery in my life, and meeting my fellow Wordspace writers is one of them. I could not possibly find more incredible friends and inspiring colleagues: Hilary Beard, Meredith Broussard, Eileen Flanagan, Miriam Peskowitz, Jude Ray, Andrea Ross, Eleanor Stanford, and our ever spirited and visionary leader, Lori Tharps. I will always be grateful to you for being the holding environment for my creative self.

Thank you to Paul Mychaluk for always bringing me back to my path, and to my assistant, Amanda Schlitzer, part of the home team, who has been invaluable in keeping all the pieces together for me and our family.

I appreciate so much the steadfast support of my family. Special thanks to my parents, Norman and Elissa Chansky, for always supporting my family through all the projects we take on. A special nod and grin to my brother, James Chansky, for jump-starting this project and just in general for never laughing at my ideas or questions—except, of course, when it really helped to laugh. To Allison Chansky, who has always been wise beyond her years, for once again sharing her insight from long ago. To my late father-in-law, Melvin Stern, and to my mother-in-law, Astrid Stern, for teaching me so much, and for always encouraging me with my writing.

My deepest gratitude goes to my husband, Phil Stern, who once again generously and willingly made room for this project when creative space in our family was at a premium. You have been encouraging me, kindly and compellingly, for over half my life; this couldn't have happened without you. And how fortunate am I to not only have your writing and editing help, but your gift for taking my fuzzy ideas for illustrations and coming up with such clear representations of the metaphors. Everyone knows these drawings help make the book what it is. My daughters, Meredith and Raia, have shared their mother with another "book sibling." Mer, you have grown up so well and independently that I would never have thought to take on this project during such a big transitional time for you. What an inspiration you are. And Raia, not only have you cooked for us, and kept us laughing, but you were not afraid to ask the tough questions like—"Mom, if this is so hard, why are you writing this book?" It was always just enough to get me back to the answers I needed.

With each book I write, I find two potentially opposing strong currents gathering speed—an increasing press to find solutions to our complex and uncertain world, and a shift in how we are defining those solutions to prioritize sustainable well-being for all. There isn't a contradiction. I hope that these ideas may inspire you to find the points that intersect on the path.

INDEX